A CANADIAN
WRITER'S
WORKBOOK

An Interactive Writing Text for ESL Students

Trudy Smoke
Hunter College

Sheila Maidstone
Camosun College

Mission Statement
*Nelson Canada—Your partner in TESL. We aim
to be the leading publisher and distributor of quality ESL material.*

Nelson Canada

I(T)P An International Thomson Publishing Company

Toronto • Albany • Bonn • Boston • Cincinnati • Detroit • London • Madrid • Melbourne
Mexico City • New York • Pacific Grove • Paris • San Francisco • Singapore • Tokyo • Washington

I(T)P™
International Thomson Publishing
The ITP logo is a trademark under licence

© Nelson Canada
A division of Thomson Canada Limited, 1995

Published in 1995 by
Nelson Canada
A division of Thomson Canada Limited
1120 Birchmount Road
Scarborough, Ontario M1K 5G4

Canadian Cataloguing in Publication Data
Smoke, Trudy
  A Canadian writer's workbook : an interactive
writing text for ESL students

Includes index.
ISBN 0–17–604823–5

1. English language – Textbooks for second language
learners.* 2. English language – Rhetoric.
I. Maidstone, Sheila, date. II. Title.

PE1128.S56 1995   808'.042   C95–930011–2

Adapted from *A Writer's Workbook: An Interactive
Writing Text for ESL Students,* 2nd edition. Copyright
© 1992 by St. Martin's Press.

Acquisitions Editor: Andrew Livingston
Developmental Editor: Joanne Scattolon
Senior Production Editor: Deborah Lonergan
Production Editor: Bob Kohlmeier
Senior Production Coordinator: Sheryl Emery
Composition Supervisor: Zenaida Diores
Art Director: Liz Harasymczuk
Cover Design: Julia Hall
Managing Editor, College: Margot Hanis
Input Operators: Elaine Andrews and Michelle Volk
Cover Illustration: Linda Bleck

Printed and bound in Canada
1 2 3 4 5 6 7 8 9 0 / BG / 4 3 2 1 0 9 8 7 6 5

Copyright Acknowledgments

Marty Chan, "Fall from University Grace," in *Contest Essays by Canadian Students,* second edition, edited by Robert
    Hookey, Murray McArthur, and Joan Pilz (Toronto: Harcourt Brace & Company Canada, 1994), pp. 133–35.
    © 1994 Harcourt Brace & Company Canada, Inc. All rights reserved.
Sung Hoon Kim, "Too Much Pressure," in *New Canadian Voices,* edited by Jessie Porter (Toronto: Wall & Emerson,
    1991), p. 60. Reprinted by permission of the publisher.

Copyright acknowledgments are continued at the back of the book, on page 331, which constitutes an extension of
the copyright page.

Chapter Two Observing the Family   22

Eugen Lupri: "Family Types"   22

Chapter Three Growing Apart   42

Morley Callaghan: "The Snob"   42

CONTENTS

Mission Statement

Nelson Canada—Your Partner in TESL.
We aim to be the leading publisher and distributor of
quality ESL material.

To Alan and to all my students

—*Trudy Smoke*

To my family and students
and in memory of Diana Louise Hirt

—*Sheila Maidstone*

UNIT TWO
Language and Communicating   67

Chapter Four **Encountering a Different Culture   69**

Carolyn Parrish: "Between Two Worlds"   69

Chapter Six Communicating and Caring   115

Ernest Buckler: "Penny in the Dust"   115

UNIT THREE
Society and Playing Roles   133

Chapter Seven Dating Practices   135

Barbara MacKay: "Who Pays the Cheque When You're Dating?"   135

UNIT FOUR
Finding a Job and Working   197

UNIT FIVE
Home and Finding One's Place   259

Chapter Fifteen Responding to Change   294

Nahid Rachlin: "Foreigner"   294

ALTERNATE CONTENTS

Reading and Thinking Strategies

Includes: Discussion Activities • Journal Writing

Writing Strategies

Includes: Essay Strategies • Essay Form • Suggestions for Writing • Getting
Started • Student Essay • Revising

Editing Strategies

Includes: Vocabulary Development • Commonly Confused Words • Mechanics • Editing Practice

Preface

A Canadian Writer's Workbook is written for academically oriented, intermediate–advanced-level ESL students who are studying or planning to study in Canada. A variety of unadapted Canadian expository and literary selections have been woven into the original fabric of the text *A Writer's Workbook*, in order to provide a Canadian cultural context for reading and writing activities. The content promotes cross-cultural understanding while fulfilling the academic needs of college or university-bound ESL students.

Because writing improves only with practice, the focus of the exercises in this text is on written expression. Using this book, students will write and learn to give and receive feedback. In addition, research and common sense tell us that students write, read, and think better when teachers and texts make the connections between writing and reading clear. *A Canadian Writer's Workbook* is organized to increase student awareness of the reading/writing connections; as a result, students read about and discuss new concepts, ideas, and problems before they begin to write.

The book is organized into five units, each dealing with a different aspect of life—Family and Growing Up, Language and Communication, Society and Playing Roles, Finding a Job and Working, and Home and Finding One's Place. Each unit contains three chapters, each organized around a specific type of reading selection. The first chapter in each unit begins with a selection of journalistic writing—taken from a newspaper or a magazine, and chosen because students have found it interesting, informative, and filled with ideas about Canadian culture. The second chapter in each unit contains an excerpt from a textbook or educational source. These selections are from required and/or commonly paired courses for ESL students in colleges and universities across Canada; they also introduce to students some aspect of Canadian culture and include articles on the family, intercultural communication, sociology, and psychology. The third chapter in each unit features a short story or an excerpt from a novel or autobiography. Chosen because of their themes, these literary selections exemplify high-quality writing. Moreover, the authors represented either have written about feeling like an outsider in a society or are themselves users of English as a second language. The selections are by Morley Callaghan, Ernest Buckler, Pablo Casals, Han Suyin, and Nahid Rachlin.

The book also contains short excerpts by such authors as Emily Carr and Alice Munro that also relate to the overall themes. This edition also contains more than fifteen essays written by ESL students from countries all over the world, thereby exposing students to a wide variety of writing styles and approaches.

Every chapter begins with "Prereading Activities." These are designed to help students make predictions and think about the reading topic before they read that chapter's selection.

Following each reading, "Reading and Thinking Strategies" gets students thinking about what they have read and discussing the responses and ideas it generated. This edition also features the dialogue journal, in which students and teachers develop a written dialogue through an exchange of letters kept in student journals. Although many students rely on the journal suggestions in each chapter, the letters can be written about various subjects. Teachers respond in brief to the content, rather than to the grammar or surface errors, of each letter. Some teachers have found that modelling correct responses through the journals helps students deal with specific problems. Responding to the journals should take no more time than reading a set of student essays and, in many ways, it is more enjoyable for teacher and student. Dialogue journals are valuable for enabling students and teachers to get to know one another in a way not usually provided in the classroom.

The section that follows, "Writing Strategies," gives students the opportunity to write letters, short responses, and essays after reading and discussing each chapter selection. Although each chapter includes "Suggestions for Writing," encompassing a variety of rhetorical modes, the emphasis in the book is on description, narration, comparison, and persuasion—the most commonly taught modes in ESL writing courses. Each chapter also includes a section on revising, and teachers should encourage their students to experiment with different revision techniques to discover which ones work best for them. Each writer is unique, and each writer's process is unique as well. Students can revise their own writing or use the student essays provided in each chapter to practice particular revision strategies.

To assist students in understanding the differences between revising and editing, each chapter also contains "Editing Strategies" and related practice exercises. However, like most teacher-researchers, I am convinced that the best editing assignments involve students working on their own writing. After focusing on highlighted editing strategies, students can work alone or in pairs and apply what they have learned to their own writing. In this way, students become better editors and, as a result, more self-sufficient writers. The book also offers supplementary exercises that teachers can assign to students based on individual needs.

Editing strategies are followed by "Grammar Strategies," some designed to be presented to the entire class, and others recommended for small group or individual work. Many teachers and tutors find it useful to assign material from the editing or grammar strategies sections to students while they are working with others in writing conferences. No one student will need to do every exercise in the book. However, the wide variety of types and levels of activities should fulfil the student's individual needs.

TRUDY SMOKE

Acknowledgments

I would like to thank Andrew Livingston and Joanne Scattolon, editors at Nelson Canada, for facilitating my work on this project. I am also indebted to reviewers across the country for their helpful suggestions, among them Merrilee Brand, Toronto Board of Education; Bruce Jackson, Collège André-Grasset; Donna Kelly, Sheridan College; and Louise Lemieux, University of British Columbia. Many thanks go as well to Hemi Gunasinghe and Elizabeth West, my colleagues at Camosun College, who provided insights that influenced my thinking and writing. For their love and support, I thank my family: Norman and Hanna Hirt, Karla, Peter, Ezra, and Ira Maidstone.

SHEILA MAIDSTONE

U N I T

1

FAMILY AND GROWING UP

UNDERSTANDING EXPECTATIONS

PREREADING ACTIVITIES

1. In a small group, discuss the following question: Should parents pressure their children to do well in school? Why or why not?

2. Make two columns on a sheet of paper. Write "What I expect of myself" at the top of the left-hand column, and "What others expect of me" at the top of the right-hand column. Then discuss the various academic, social, personal, and physical expectations that you have had or have been subject to, and fill in the two columns. Think about the differences in the expectations your family, classmates, teachers, and friends have had for you as well as your own expectations of yourself. What have you learned about expectations from this exercise?

3. When you read the title "Fall from University Grace," what do you expect the selection to be about?

Fall from University Grace

This essay first appeared in a published collection of award-winning student writing. Marty Chan, who was a student at the University of Alberta when he wrote this essay, regards discipline as the key to writing. "I found that forcing myself to sit and write, rather than waiting for inspiration, allowed me to write with more precision. The key is to read and rewrite your work over and over until you are sure it says what you mean."

Just as Adam was cast out of Eden, I was kicked out of university; but while his transgression was eating the fruit from the tree of knowledge, my sin was ignoring the tree. After my dismal performance in my first year of university, I contemplated the reasons for my failure. Now, I understand the two factors that contributed to my downfall: the lack of a career goal and premature independence. 5

Without a career goal, I lacked direction and motivation. About halfway through my final year of high school, I was hounded by my parents to enrol in university, but until that time I had not given any thought to what career I wanted to pursue. Two of my friends were already in the engineering program at university, so to silence my parents' nagging, I told them that I wanted to be an engineer. In retrospect, I realize that this was a big mistake. Though I got high marks in math, physics, and chemistry — core courses of the engineering program — I was bored with them, and my dislike of the sciences became apparent in the first four months of university. I failed all of my science courses.

Had I been more motivated, I might have passed those courses, but I just wasn't ready for university. In fact, I wasn't ready for any career. I assumed that the amount of studying I did in high school — an hour per day — would be sufficient to attain respectable marks in university. I was wrong. After the first two weeks, I realized I had to study more, but I couldn't confine myself to a desk for longer than an hour. Because I could not see myself as an engineer, I could not motivate myself to study harder; then I began looking for excuses to avoid studying.

Before study sessions, I often wandered around the library for half an hour, looking for just the right carrel in which to study. When I finally found my niche, I left my backpack, unopened, on the chair and I went to the arcade in a nearby mall. My excuse for doing this was that I needed inspiration to study dull formulas; I believed playing *Space Invaders* would help. It didn't. Two hours later, I returned to the carrel, took my backpack, left the library, and went home.

Even when I was reading my textbooks, I wasn't studying. Daydreams of sleeping on a patch of cool grass on a breezy summer day intruded upon my concentration, chasing away calculus and physics theories. By the time the daydreams ended, I had forgotten most of what I had studied in the previous hour. As the midterm week drew closer, the daydreams grew longer while the study sessions grew shorter. Studying was avoidable as long as daydreaming was possible. I escaped often and as a result I failed my math, chemistry, and physics exams.

Why didn't I transfer to another program? Why didn't I just drop out? First, my parents had paid for my tuition and I feared they would pull out their financial support and leave me destitute. Second, my aspirations were still cloudy, so if I transferred out of the engineering faculty I would still lack direction. Without a definite goal, afraid of disappointing my strict parents, I remained in the program until Christmas, hopeful that my marks would improve as well as my disposition towards engineering.

However, passing grades eluded me, as did maturity. Coming from a small town and being unaccustomed to the fast-paced routine of campus life, I inhabited the residence hall, believing that it would shelter me from competitive courses and merciless engineering professors. After the first month of adjustment, I learned that the place 55 offered the niceties of home without the watchful eye of parents. Also, I found other students who felt just as unhappy as I did, and we complained for hours in the local pub about the emotional wounds university professors inflicted on below-average students.

Snow fell in mid-December — final exam time — but I didn't 60 notice either event, because I had become a creature of the night, preying on full beer mugs in smoke-filled bars. A week later, snow covered every building on campus, which promised a white Christmas for everyone but me: my exams had been returned and the test scores were so low that if I added all four marks together, 65 they amounted to one grade of any average student. I didn't care; neither did my friends, who received similar marks. We bragged of our freedom from our parents, not realizing that their influence was more beneficial than the influence we had on each other.

When my friends and I were not in the bar, we were playing 70 cards in somebody's room or inviting ourselves to private parties held by other students in the residence hall. It never failed that, at least twice a night, someone would knock on my door in an attempt to lure me into a card game or to cajole me into accompanying him to the bar. Every Thursday, a game of hockey took place in my hall- 75 way and, feeling obligated, I left my studies and played in goal. On weekends, we became warriors determined to prove our stamina by consuming dozens of bottles of beer — I had lost every battle — followed by marathon vomiting contests, of which I had won too many.

At the time, my independence was exhilarating; freedom, 80 denied me for eighteen years, was mine to experience and abuse. I got drunk with impunity. No angry mother awaited my return home at five in the morning. No enraged father tongue-lashed me for lousy grades. I was self-reliant. But freedom had its price: nobody told me to study harder; no one said that if I didn't get an eighty on 85 my next three exams, I would fail; no one told me to take responsibility for my actions. I answered to no one but myself. I was self-reliant; I was an ass.

When Christmas day arrived, I found a "withdraw from university" notice in my stocking. My refusal to claim responsibility for my 90 actions and my abuse of newly gained independence and freedom from parental rule had combined to ensure my marks were below the passing grade and to make my Christmas black.

Unearned independence was the fruit from the tree of knowledge that tempted me and caused my downfall. Because I was not 95 mature enough to accept the responsibility for my own future and because I abused my privileges of independence, I failed my first year of university. The causes of my downfall have taught me maturity and responsibility, and in the future, I will not ignore the tree of knowledge again. Falling from Eden was enough to teach Adam; the same is true for me. 100

READING AND THINKING STRATEGIES

DISCUSSION ACTIVITIES

Analysis and Conclusions

1. When writers write, they usually think about the people or audience for whom they are writing. Is Marty Chan writing mainly for his peers (other students) or is he trying to reach a broader audience?

2. Based on what you have learned from reading this essay, describe Marty Chan.

3. Describe Chan's friends. Why did he choose these particular friends? How did they influence him?

Writing and Point of View

1. In small groups in your class, discuss Chan's essay. What two factors led to his academic failure? Give examples of how each contributed to his "downfall."

2. In what ways has your position on this issue been influenced by the essay you have just read?

3. If you were to write an essay on the same topic from the parents' point of view, how would the details differ from Chan's essay?

Personal Response and Evaluation

1. Do you sympathize with Marty's procrastination? What do you do to avoid getting your work done? Give suggestions for overcoming this common problem.

2. Do you believe that Chan has learned his lesson? Does he finally live up to his own expectations? Why? Why not?

3. How do your own expectations for yourself differ from the expectations of your parents towards you? In what ways are they the same?

DEBATE

Divide the class into two groups, one in favour of external pressure (from parents, teachers) to help students succeed at their studies, and the other in favour of self-motivated learning. Debate the issues, using personal experiences and observations to support points of view. You might want to videotape or tape-record this debate and then review it and discuss what occurred.

JOURNAL WRITING

Keeping a journal will be a major part of your writing experience while you use this book. Your journal will be a place where ideas count much more than spelling or grammar. You may be able to use some of these ideas in other writing assignments; even more important, you will use them to get to know yourself better and to get to know your teacher. We will use dialogue journals in which you write to your teacher and he or she writes back to you. However, many students also keep private journals in which they write their private thoughts. Each chapter includes questions and suggestions about things to write about in your journal, but you may also decide to write about something else that is important to you. Sometimes the topics will simply point you in a direction, and you can explore as many or as few as you choose.

EXTRA READING

Sung Hoon Kim, a high school student from Korea who is studying in Canada, expresses the pressure resulting from the expectations of self and others in the following way:

Too Much Pressure

In the last year of high school we suffer under much pressure. We must pass our exams and try to get into the university of our choice so that we can get a good job and have a secure future.

Where does this pressure come from? First, we hear stories from students who have graduated from school and who are now studying in universities. They keep telling us how difficult it was for them while they were studying at high school and how it is even more difficult at university. This makes us totally depressed.

Also teachers pressure us. They give us piles and piles of homework, expecting the Great Wall of China to be built in a day. In addition, they give us too many tests. I have had a test almost every day and essays to hand in within a short period of time. As a result, because of studying for these tests, I have had to give up my study for exams. Since I cannot catch up with the work, I have begun to worry about getting good marks on the exams.

Lastly, our parents push us too hard to get good marks. They want us to obtain the finest education. This means getting into university. Since parents pressure us at home and teachers pressure us at school simultaneously, we have no time to relax.

Perhaps this pressure keeps us studying hard and is good for us because it helps to shape our characters. On the other hand, it might lead us to a nervous breakdown.

Sung Hoon Kim

After reading about Marty Chan and Sung Hoon Kim, think about your own experiences as a student. Close your eyes and think about the word *school*. Think about the word *pressure*. What thoughts come to your mind? When you are ready, write down your thoughts. Do not worry about writing complete, grammatically correct sentences. Write, and the writing itself will help you become a better writer.

WRITING STRATEGIES

THE WRITING BIOGRAPHY

"Know thyself" is one of the foundations of writing. The more you know and understand yourself as a writer, the better you will feel about expressing yourself in writing. The purpose of the following assignment is for you to think about yourself as a writer and to write your own "writing biography."

> *Because there is no neat, gradual way to learn to write and because progress seems so unpredictable and just plain slow, a major part of learning to write is learning to put up with this frustrating process itself.*

> PETER ELBOW

In essay form, write a "writing biography" about yourself in which you describe some of the experiences and people who have influenced your writing. Try to answer some of the following questions in your biography.

1. What is your earliest memory about learning to write in your first language? How old were you?

2. What is your earliest memory about learning to write in English? How old were you?

3. What types of writing did you do in elementary school? How did you feel about writing when you were in elementary school? What did your teachers do in elementary school that helped or did not help you to learn to write?

4. What types of writing did you do in high school or in other schools you have attended? How did you feel about writing in those classes? What did your teachers do that helped or did not help you to learn to write?

5. Do you write for any college classes other than this one? If so, which classes? What do you write for those classes?

6. Do you write letters, poems, stories, or do other kinds of writing for pleasure? What kind of writing do you prefer to do?

7. How do you feel about writing today?

8. What is the easiest part of writing for you?

9. What is the hardest part of writing for you?

10. What one aspect would you like to change about your writing?

ESSAY STRATEGIES

The Paragraph

Part of learning to write in a new language is learning how readers of that language expect ideas to be organized. Most native speakers of English expect essay, text, and story writing to be divided into paragraphs. Each paragraph serves as a guide for the reader. It shows what the writer thinks is important, what belongs together, and where a new idea begins. Paragraphs help the reader digest writing, just as breaking up a meal into courses such as soup, salad, main dish, and dessert helps in the digestion of a meal. If all the food from a meal were piled on the table in front of you at once, you might not know where to begin to eat. When writers do not use paragraphs, readers often cannot understand the big blocks of sentences piled up in front of them. So a clear, considerate writer breaks up ideas into paragraphs.

A paragraph begins with an indented line. This makes it stand out from the rest of the text. A paragraph is not too long, usually not more than 250 words, but you do not have to count the number of words. You can use your judgment. When your ideas are changing or when you want to divide a general concept into smaller parts, you should begin a new paragraph. A paragraph is a group of sentences related to a single subject.

A paragraph usually has a topic sentence or main idea that tells the reader what the paragraph is about. This topic sentence can appear anywhere in the paragraph. Sometimes it is implied, which means that it is not actually stated, but the reader can find it by inferring or reading into what the author has written.

A paragraph may have different purposes in a piece of writing. It may explain a concept introduced in a topic sentence. It may illustrate a point or give support to an argument. Each paragraph works together with the rest of the paragraphs in a letter, essay, story, or book to help the reader understand the writer's point of view.

Fill in the following blanks with the seven characteristics of a paragraph discussed so far.

_____

_____

_____

_____

_____

_____

_____

EXERCISE

Paragraphs make writing easier to read. They help the reader know how the writer thinks. The following piece of writing would be easier to read if it were divided into paragraphs. Read it with a classmate and decide where new paragraphs should begin. Remember that each time you begin a totally new thought, you should indent for a new paragraph.

Marty Chan's essay made me think about my family and what they expect of me. I am the first child in my family to go to college in Canada, so they think I should set a good example for my younger brothers and sisters. I have tried very hard to study and to do well in my courses, although it was not easy at first. When I started col-   5 lege, I was nervous about English. I still made a lot of mistakes and did not understand everything my teachers said in class. Since I felt nervous about raising my hand, I usually did not ask questions, and I missed some important information. The best thing that happened to me in college happened when my biology teacher required each of us to join a study group. I found that I could ask my questions to the other students in my class, and some of them even knew the answers. We all share our notes, and that helps me, too. It also helps me to say the new words from biology out loud to the whole group. After I do that, I remember them better. Joining a study group has helped me become a successful student in college. As a result, I suggested to a few of the students in my anthropology class that we meet to discuss the class lectures and the reading. It seems to be helping them as much as me.

ESSAY FORM
Paragraph Development

Learning to write in English involves more than just learning new vocabulary and grammatical structures. Part of learning to write is finding out the order in which readers expect ideas to be arranged.

Some researchers have stated that readers of English expect a straight line of development. In this kind of writing, the paragraph often begins with a statement of its main or most important idea; this is called the topic sentence. This main idea is divided into connected ideas that are developed further in the paragraphs that follow the first one. Although this is the traditional approach for most English speakers, it may be different from what you learned in your first language.

For example, Fan Shen, who was born in the People's Republic of China, and is now living in the United States, wrote an article in 1989 about this difference. The article states:

> In English composition, an essential rule for the logical organization of a piece of writing is the use of a "topic sentence." In Chinese composition "from surface to core" is an essential rule, a rule which means that one ought to reach a topic gradually and "systematically" instead of "abruptly."

Robert B. Kaplan, like many other linguists, has studied the ways in which writers arrange their ideas. This field of study is called contrastive rhetoric. In 1966 Kaplan created a diagram to illustrate the arrangements of ideas in different language systems. Examine the following diagram carefully.

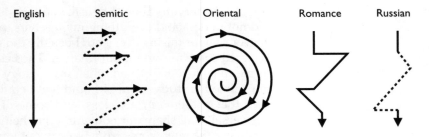

Diagram from Robert B. Kaplan, "Cultural Thought Patterns in Inter-Cultural Education," *Language Learning* 16 (1966): 1–20.

In the space provided, draw a diagram of the way you think ideas are arranged in your first language.

How does your drawing compare with Kaplan's illustration? Write a paragraph in which you explain whether such diagrams are helpful or not in your understanding of the differences in the arrangement of ideas in your first language and in English. Write about the differences you have noticed in the way your first language is organized and in the way that English is organized.

EXERCISES

1. In some cultures, writing is organized differently from English. Discuss the answers to the following questions based on your first language or any other that you have studied other than English.

   a. In writing in your first language or any other language you have studied, do you divide your writing into paragraphs?

   b. If you do, how do you know when to begin a new paragraph?

   c. If you do not, how do you indicate to the reader that you are beginning a new thought?

   d. Is the idea of a topic sentence new to you? How are the ideas about a subject grouped in your language? What usually comes first, second, or last?

2. As part of focusing on paragraph structure, the class should divide into small groups. Each group should look at paragraph 2 in Chan's essay. Copy the topic sentence of that paragraph here:

_____

List the supporting details that tell more about the topic sentence or main idea:

_____

_____

_____

_____

_____

_____

3. To help readers understand what they have written, writers connect their ideas from paragraph to paragraph. Answer the following questions about how Chan's essay is connected from sentence to sentence and paragraph to paragraph.

   a. What subject is introduced in the first paragraph and dealt with in more detail in the second?
   b. In sentence 4 in paragraph 2, to what does *this* refer?
   c. In sentence 5 in paragraph 2, to what does *them* refer?
   d. How does the subject of paragraph 3 relate to paragraph 2?
   e. Which of Kaplan's diagrams seems to fit Chan's style of writing in this essay? If none is appropriate, draw your own diagram of the way Chan seems to organize his writing.

SUGGESTIONS FOR WRITING

Give yourself time to think before you write. If you have any difficulty beginning your writing, look in your journal or at the "Getting Started" suggestion below. When you do begin to write, keep your audience in mind. Try to make your writing interesting to your readers as well as to yourself.

1. In an essay, describe the most important ideas that you learned about yourself when you wrote your writing biography. Try to organize your writing so that it moves from your specific experiences to general concepts about how students learn to write.

2. Some people think of success as the attainment of high grades, educational degrees, and good jobs. Write an essay in which you define the qualities that mean success to you. Illustrate the qualities you choose with your experiences, observations, and readings.

3. Many ambitious parents push their children to succeed in school. Do you agree or disagree with the idea that pushing children helps them to succeed? Support your point of view with your experiences, observations, and readings.

4. Write an essay in which you describe the differences between your own educational, social, and personal expectations and those that your family has for you. Review the prereading activities on page 3 for ideas.

5. "Work hard, play hard." Use this statement as the thesis of an essay on the necessity for a balance of activities in student life.

6. In many families, the oldest child is treated differently from the younger children in terms of educational expectations. Write an essay in which you give examples of this and explain why you think this happens.

GETTING STARTED

Talking to Get Ideas

If you have any difficulty getting started, talk to a classmate about what you are planning to write. Begin by discussing each topic and the ideas on which a writer could focus. Take turns explaining to one another why you would choose or not choose a particular topic; this will help you narrow down your choices.

When you have narrowed down your choices to two or three possible topics, discuss your ideas for each topic. Then, together choose the topic that interests you the most. Before you begin to write, together make a list of ideas that you will refer to as you write your essay. When you finish your first draft, share it with the same classmate.

A Student's Writing Biography

The following writing biography is a draft written in 15 minutes in an ESL writing class. The student, Lendsa Guillaume, is from Haiti. As you read her essay, determine which of the suggested questions she focused on.

Writing is a very difficult course, mostly for the foreign students. You have to think critically and think in English. You have to know your punctuation and be careful about your grammar, plurals, and more and more. But in my case, it is not the same because I love writing.

The first time I had to write was when I was seven years old. I had to write a little letter for my mother for Mother's Day. I was so happy to write it, but I was writing in my first language.

When I had to write in English I was happy too. I remember when I was in high school, the teacher asked the students to write one sentence and I wrote "I love you" and he was laughing. He said, "That's nice." All the other students did not want to show their sentences; they were ashamed, but that was nice anyway. When I first entered college, I did not like to write about anything because I thought my writing was too poor, but I tried hard anyway.

The first thing I like about writing is, for instance, if one is upset with his or her friends and cannot communicate verbally, then he or she can write about what caused the upset. In other words, I like writing because it is another way to communicate.

In summary, I personally think everybody, once you are in college, must like writing because that's mostly what college is about. If you do not know how to write, you'll never make it in college.

Lendsa Guillaume

REVISING

Reread this student's writing biography and answer the following questions about what she has written. You can do this on your own or with another student in your class.

1. What in her essay reveals Guillaume's attitude about writing?
2. What part of her writing biography did you like the most?
3. What would you like to know about her that she did not include in her writing biography?
4. Whom do you think she expected to read her essay, to be her audience?
5. How could she revise the essay to make it communicate better? Here is a suggested revised version of Guillaume's first paragraph:

> *Writing is a very difficult course, particularly for foreign students. All students have to think critically when they write, but foreign students also have to learn to do this in English. They also have to be aware of punctuation and grammar, plurals, and many other things. In my case, I am aware of the problems, but I am willing to try to do my best because I love writing. Whether I am writing in my first language or in English, my goal is the same: to communicate my ideas and feelings.*

Apply the five questions just listed to your own writing biography. Then exchange papers with a classmate and discuss them. Writing is a very personal experience, but it is a communicative activity. One way to judge how well your writing is communicating is to share it with a peer. When you and a classmate exchange papers, it is important to show respect for each other's writing. Read slowly and carefully. Do not mark the other person's paper. After reading, ask each other questions and listen carefully to the answers. These answers can help you when you actually rewrite your paper. Here are some suggestions for questions:

1. What do you think I am trying to say?

2. What did you like best about my essay?

3. Did any part of it make you stop and read it over in order to understand what I meant?

4. What do you remember most about my essay without looking at it again?

You will certainly think of more questions, but keep in mind that the purpose is the sharing of writing. Do not evaluate or judge each other's writing, but offer support and suggestions. After discussing your essay in this way, keep your peer's comments and suggestions in mind as you rewrite. Then share your revised essay with the same classmate.

EDITING STRATEGIES

LEARNING NEW VOCABULARY
Classifying

One way to learn new vocabulary is to classify words, terminology, or concepts according to their meaning or attributes.

1. Make a list of all the words in the Chan essay that are used to describe people (for example, *parents, friends*).

2. Make a list of leisure activities referred to in this essay (for example, *playing, Space Invaders*).

3. Make a list of all the expressions that refer to time (for example, *two weeks*).

4. Make a list of all the words that refer to school (for example, *university, engineering program*).

COMMONLY CONFUSED WORDS

to/two/too

> *A number of people in Canada speak two languages: English and French. Also, because Canada is a country with a large immigrant population, many people speak a third language. However, too many Canadians refuse to learn more than one language. Throughout the world, being able to speak at least two languages, and sometimes three or four, is necessary to function in society.*

Examine how *to*, *two*, and *too* are used in the preceding paragraph, then review their usage in the writing of Marty Chan and Sung Hoon Kim. On the basis of what you observe, complete the following definitions.

_____ refers to the number 2.

_____ means "also" or "overly."

_____ means "toward" or is part of the infinitive verb form.

Fill in the blanks in the following sentences with *to*, *two*, or *too*.

1. Knowledge of _____ or more languages makes travel _____ different countries more interesting and rewarding _____.

2. Scientists are beginning _____ believe that people who know _____ or more languages make more use of their brains than monolinguals.

3. Therefore, when it comes _____ languages, there is no such thing as _____ much knowledge.

Now write your own sentences using *to*, *two*, and *too*.

MECHANICS
Paper Format

When you hand in a paper to a teacher or to another student to read, make sure that your paper is neat and readable. To do this, you should follow these ten steps:

1. Use $8\frac{1}{2}$-by-11-inch paper whether you are printing from a word processor or writing by hand. Smaller pieces of paper get lost and are harder to read. Tear off the holes on the sides of continuous computer paper before handing it in.

2. Use dark blue or black ink if you write by hand. Pencil smudges easily, and other colours can distract your readers.

3. If you use a word processor, double-space. If you write by hand and have large handwriting or if your paper has narrow spaces, write on every other line.

4. Use one-inch margins on all sides of your paper — top, bottom, left, and right. This is easy to do when you are writing by hand; margins are also easy to set on most word processing systems.

5. Put your name, date, and course number on the top of the page unless your instructor requires that they be somewhere else on the page.

6. Use a title, and centre the title above the rest of the writing. Capitalize the first word and all major words in your title. Skip a line between the title and the first line of your writing.

7. Indent each paragraph about one inch, or five spaces on a word processor. Do not indent the first paragraph.

8. Make sure that your capital letters are distinct from your lower-case letters. Also make sure your *e*'s and *i*'s are distinguishable.

9. Make all your punctuation marks clear and distinct. Leave a space after each period.

10. If you break a word at the end of the line, break it between syllables. Use the dictionary if you do not know where a syllable ends.

EDITING PRACTICE

After revising their writing for content (see page 15) writers often edit their writing for errors. The following is a draft of a response to the Chan essay. Some of the errors the author has made are one formatting error, one paragraphing error, and five *to/two/too* errors. Find as many errors as you can and correct them. Answers are on page 325.

my poor study habits

I have been a college student in Canada for two years. Last semester,

I failed to courses, and, as a result, realized I was spending to much time on social activities. My friends and I watch videos together five times a week and we go too the local mall every day. When we want two chat, we go to our favourite restaurant, where we stay until late at night. I rarely get to bed before two. I know I should study more, but I am having to much fun to really care.

GRAMMAR STRATEGIES

THE SIMPLE PRESENT TENSE

The simple present tense is used for several purposes:

1. *To describe habitual or routine activities.* Adverbs of frequency such as *often, usually, each day,* and *always* (see page 21 for a more complete list) sometimes are used with the simple present tense.

   Often I *wander* around the library for hours trying to find the best carrel.
   I usually *daydream* when I *sit* at my desk.

2. *To describe states of being.* Verbs that refer to sensory perceptions, emotional states conditions, judgments, and states of being are called *stative* verbs and are almost always in the simple present tense unless they are describing the past.

   I *like* my courses this term.
   My parents *want* me to be an engineer.
   I often *feel* like daydreaming.

3. *To describe future actions.* Verbs that are used this way usually describe acts of arriving and leaving, and beginning and ending.

   My English class *begins* at eight o'clock.
   The bus *leaves* at ten minutes past each hour.

4. *To describe what is going on* in scientific experiments and other types of research, on television or radio, and in newspaper headlines.

   She *puts* the chemical in the tube and *heats* it slowly.
   The pitcher *throws* a curve ball at the batter.
   "Fires *rage* in California; they *threaten* many homes."

EXERCISES

1. With a partner or in a small group, reread Sung Hoon Kim's essay, underlining each use of the simple present tense. Then together decide for each example you find which of the listed uses it illustrates.

2. Many people have problems with the subject-verb agreement involved in the simple present tense. Using Sung Hoon Kim's essay, list the subjects and verbs in each sentence in separate columns. Write the pronoun (he, she, it, they) that can be used to replace the various subjects:

Subject	*Verb*
teachers (*they*)	give
our parents (*they*)	push

Circle a final *s* when it occurs in the verb form.

Notice that when using the irregular verb *be*, the following pattern applies:

I	am
you	are
he, she, it	is
we, you, they	are

Also notice the simple present tense for other verbs:

I, you, we, they	suffer
her, she, it	suffers

Decide whether to use the final *s* on the verbs in the following sentences:

a. Many ambitious parents _____ their children to succeed in
     (want/wants)

   school.

b. Marty _____ as he _____ that he _____ with
     (yawn/yawns)   *(explain/explains)*   *(talk/talks)*

   his friends until after midnight every night.

c. Sung Hoon Kim's classmates _____ her that she _____
                                    (tell/tells)   *(study/studies)*

   too much and _____ too little.
                  (sleep/sleeps)

d. Marty _____ that he _____ to work harder in school;
   (feel/feels)   *(need/needs)*

   his sister always _____ straight A's in her classes.
                        (receive/receives)

e. The problem faced by this student _____ to be related to
                                        (seem/seems)

   to motivation.

ADVERBS OF FREQUENCY

Adverbs of frequency are used to tell how often something happens or someone does something. On a continuum from the most often to the least, adverbs might be arranged this way:

always → generally → usually → frequently → often →
occasionally → sometimes → seldom → rarely → never

Another adverb of frequency, *ever*, which means "at any time," is often used in questions.

EXERCISES

1. Interview a member of your class, asking the following questions. Write down the answers so that you will be able to use them later.

   a. What subjects do your teachers generally ask you to write about in your classes?
   b. What subjects do you usually prefer to write about in your classes?
   c. Do your teachers generally give you a choice of several subjects to write about or only one?
   d. Do you ever find it difficult to get ideas when you start to write? If you do, what do you usually do to help you get going?
   e. Do you ever talk to your classmates before you start to write?
   f. When you write, what do you usually concentrate on?
   g. Outside of school, when do you usually write in English?
   h. Do you usually do your homework at home or in school?
   j. Do you sometimes find it difficult to understand your teachers in your classes? If you do, what do you generally do to help you understand what is going on in class?

2. Reread your answers to the questions in Exercise 1 and discuss with the student you have interviewed any areas about which you are confused. Write a paragraph describing the student you interviewed, using his or her answers from Exercise 1.

2

OBSERVING THE FAMILY

Bonnie
Stephanie

PREREADING ACTIVITIES

1. In a small group, discuss the differences that you have observed in family life in your country and in Canada.

2. Think about the ways in which your daily life has changed or responded to living in a different country. If you are here with your family, how has your home life changed?

3. Do/would you raise your children differently from the way your parents raised you? In what ways? Why are such changes beneficial?

Family Types

terminology = technology

Sociology =
An introduction

Eugen Lupri is Professor of Sociology at the University of Calgary. This selection is an excerpt from his chapter on the family which is part of an introductory textbook entitled Sociology: An Introduction, *which analyzes large-scale institutions in relation to the everyday experience of individuals in society.*

polygamous
outlaw – against
the law.

thesis statement

Comparative family research has identified three main types of families: (1) nuclear, or elementary, family; (2) extended family; and (3) the polygamous, or composite, family.

The nuclear family in its complete form consists of a husband, a wife, and their offspring, natural or adopted. It can also consist of one parent and a child, a brother and a sister, or a childless couple. The nuclear family lives in its own residential unit, separate from other relatives. It is identical to the Canadian census definition of economic family in that it refers to any two persons who are related by blood, marriage, or adoption, and who share a common residence. The conjugal family is a nuclear family based on the husband-wife relationship.   *transition*

Cross-cultural evidence suggests that nuclear families are combined into larger units in one of two ways. When they are combined through the parent-child relationship, through blood ties, they are

5

10

15

New Vocab.   22, 23, 32, 56
polygamous   adj
conjugal   adj
dispelled   -verb
prevalent   adj
monogamy.   noun

called extended families; when combined through plural marriage they are called polygamous families. The extended family comprises two or more nuclear families related by blood and sharing a common residence. Murdock (1949) notes that nearly half of his 250 societies had some form of extended family. Recent historical research, however, has dispelled the belief that the extended-family system was the most prevalent family organization of pre-industrial Europe. Even in those times, nuclear households predominated. Emily Nett (1981) has reached similar conclusions about the Canadian family of the past.

The extended family has a number of advantages over the nuclear family: continuity through time; maintenance of family tradition; keeping the family property intact; assured care of the sick and the elderly; and finally, a sense of belonging, stability, and permanence (Leslie, 1979: 35–38).

The second way of combining the nuclear family into composite families is through plural marriage. Polygamy involves plural spouses, whereas monogamy involves one spouse. The most common form of polygamy is called polygyny, an arrangement consisting of one husband with two or more wives. If the arrangement consists of one wife with two or more husbands, it is called polyandry. The third form is group marriage, the marriage of several men to several women.

Group marriage is quite rare. When it does occur, it is usually found along with polyandry. The Todas of southern India, for example, practised fraternal polyandry (in which the wife's husbands are brothers), which occasionally slips into group marriage.

Monogamy is the marriage form preferred by most individuals, including Canadians. High divorce rates and high remarriage rates produce serial monogamy — one after another — more than one partner over a period of time, but only one partner at one time.

READING AND THINKING STRATEGIES

DISCUSSION ACTIVITIES

Analysis and Conclusions

1. Explain, using your own words, each of the three main types of families. What is the difference between a nuclear family and a conjugal family? What is serial monogamy?

2. Do you agree with Lupri that "the extended family has a number of advantages over the nuclear family"? What advantages might

the nuclear family have over the extended family? Think about your own family and about other families you have observed. Describe the ways, if any, in which family structure has changed in the past few generations of your own family.

3. How do you think family problems are dealt with in each of the three main types of families? Who makes the decisions?

Writing and Point of View

1. Reread the excerpt and notice the way in which Lupri uses definitions to help readers understand unfamiliar terms. What words does he define? How does he define these words?

2. Write an outline of the excerpt, giving the main idea of each paragraph in point form.

3. Does the author emphasize one family type over the others, or is each given equal weight? Look up the terms "objective" and "subjective" in your dictionary. Is the author's point of view objective or subjective?

Personal Response and Evaluation

1. Some sociologists think that family structures are too complicated for researchers to be able to classify families as simply nuclear, extended or polygamous. Do you think Lupri would classify a family comprised of a mother, her two children, and their grandmother as extended or nuclear? Using your observations and experiences, describe other types of nontraditional families you have seen. Would you classify them as nuclear, extended, or polygamous? How do you think decisions are made in families such as these?

2. Sociologists have observed that people usually choose marriage partners from the same ethnic, religious, geographic, and class background. According to what you have observed, what happens when people from different backgrounds fall in love? Which books, movies, or plays can you name that are about such people? What happens to those people?

3. Would you rather live in a nuclear or an extended family? Share the reasons for your choice with your group.

INTERVIEW

Write down questions about your family or that of a friend that you would like to find out more about. Then interview a member of the family — an older relative if possible, a grandfather, grandmother,

[handwritten margin notes: you ~~were~~ are the only one that whom I know ~~better~~ beneficial connection with ~~olderest~~ elder. older people like to look back, except my parents]

aunt, or uncle — asking your questions and any others that occur to you as you conduct the interview. Tape your interview or take careful notes. Some of the questions should be these: Where did the person grow up? What was the person's school life like? Did he or she have brothers and sisters? Did they get along? Did the extended family live together? What are the biggest changes in life that the person recalls? Write out your interview, both questions and answers. Then write an essay describing the person you have interviewed, which you will share with your class.

JOURNAL WRITING

[handwritten: 1½ pages. My Ideal family.]

In the past, a large family consisting of parents, children, grandparents, aunts, uncles, cousins, and even more distant relatives often lived together or very near each other. In today's world, this is changing. In your journal, write about your ideal family, the family you imagine for yourself in the future. You may prefer to describe your own family of today and your feelings about that family.

WRITING STRATEGIES

ESSAY STRATEGIES

The Formal Essay

Although you will learn about many types of essays and styles of writing as you write in your college classes, it is important to know what is meant by the traditional or formal essay. Readers have particular expectations when they read an essay. To meet these expectations, writers begin by learning the structure of the traditional essay.

Simply put, an essay is a series of paragraphs written on one theme. Traditionally, the main idea for the essay is found in the first paragraph, which is called the introduction. The main idea for an essay is called the thesis statement. The supporting points and details of the essay are found in the body paragraphs that follow the introduction.

Each of the developmental or body paragraphs contains a topic sentence that tells the main idea for that paragraph. The rest of the paragraph is made up of ideas or details that tell more about the main idea. These paragraphs may have different purposes, depending on the topic of the essay. A particular paragraph may describe, define, tell a relevant story, provide evidence to argue a point, compare and contrast, or analyze an issue. A writer often begins a new paragraph with a transition that connects the paragraph to the one that preceded it in order to help the reader follow the writer's train of thought.

The traditional essay ends with a concluding paragraph. In this paragraph, the writer ties together the important points that have been made in the essay. The conclusion lets the reader know that the writer has thought the topic through and believes that the ideas presented in the essay are complete.

Conclusions are usually short and may include a brief summary of the main points of the essay. Most writers agree that new ideas should not be presented in the conclusion, although a related story or idea might pull the theme of the essay together effectively.

Keep this standard structure in mind when you write your next essay.

In the preceding paragraphs, circle the words *introduction, main idea, thesis statement, body paragraphs, topic sentence,* and *conclusion.* Then answer the following questions on the basis of the information in those paragraphs.

1. What is the first paragraph of an essay called? *Introduction*

_____

2. What is the main idea for the whole essay called? *thesis*

_____

3. What do the body paragraphs contain? *explaination,*
Example and Definition

4. What is the main idea for each body paragraph called? *Topic*
sentences

5. What is the final paragraph in the essay called? *Conclusion*

_____

6. What is the purpose of the final paragraph? *Summarize*
extend.

A diagram of a formal essay follows. (Remember that this is a sample essay form; not all formal essays contain five paragraphs.)

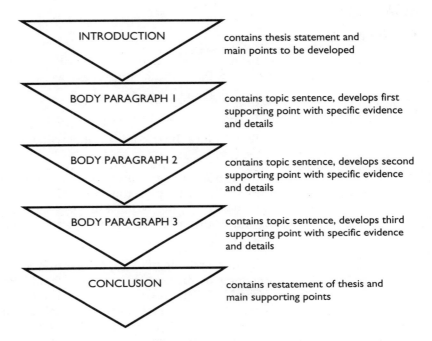

INTRODUCTION — contains thesis statement and main points to be developed

BODY PARAGRAPH 1 — contains topic sentence, develops first supporting point with specific evidence and details

BODY PARAGRAPH 2 — contains topic sentence, develops second supporting point with specific evidence and details

BODY PARAGRAPH 3 — contains topic sentence, develops third supporting point with specific evidence and details

CONCLUSION — contains restatement of thesis and main supporting points

Although this approach to writing is quite formal and traditional, it is the type of writing required in many college first-year writing courses. It is useful to know these terms, and it is also good discipline for the writer to organize his or her ideas to fit this model. However, remember that this is just one model of writing.

EXERCISES

1. Reread the Lupri article with a classmate. With that classmate or in a small group, underline the main idea or thesis statement for the entire selection. Next underline the topic sentence or main idea for each paragraph. Then decide together which are the supporting details and what their purposes are (to describe, define, tell a story, and so on). Discuss your choices with your partner or group.

2. Reread one of your own essays with a classmate. Underline the main idea or thesis statement for the entire paper. Then underline the topic sentence or main idea for each paragraph. Discuss the supporting details and decide the purpose for each. After discussing your writing, you may decide to rewrite parts of your essay to clarify your main idea or supporting details.

ESSAY FORM
The Introduction

A formal essay usually begins with an introductory paragraph. Generally, the introduction serves several purposes:

1. To capture the reader's interest.
2. To state the thesis of the essay.
3. To introduce the major ideas that will be developed in the body of the essay.

The introduction is useful to the writer as well as to the reader. It helps the writer plan the rest of the essay. If the introduction is well structured, the writer knows what the rest of the essay will contain. There are several ways to write an introduction in a formal essay.

1. **General statement.** One type of introduction starts with a general statement: "In recent years a new family structure is occurring in Canada." The essay then becomes more specific. "The two-parent, one income family, the common arrangement thirty years ago, now stands at less than 10 per cent." In this type of introduction, the writer takes the reader from the general (family structure) to the specific (the demise of the traditional conjugal nuclear family).

2. **Anecdote.** Another way to begin an essay is with an anecdote or a brief story. This is a very good way to capture readers' interest. This technique is often used by newspaper and magazine writers.

3. **Question.** The introduction might ask a question that will be answered in the body of the essay. "Are we a thoroughly modern family? A work in progress? A failed experiment?" This technique creates a great deal of reader interest.

4. **Quotation.** An introduction can contain a quotation. Be sure to use quotation marks if you are using the exact words spoken or written by someone. "The extended family has a number of advantages over the nuclear family," writes Eugen Lupri.

5. **Definition.** Some writers define a word or phrase in their introduction that they will use throughout their writing to help readers grasp their ideas.

When you write, you can use one of these types of introductions or a combination of several of them. You may create your own method of introduction, but your overall goal is to make your reader want to continue reading what you have written.

EXERCISES

1. What are five ways of writing an introduction? What is the overall goal of the introduction?

2. Read introductions from other selections in this book. What kinds of introductions have the various writers used? Is textbook material introduced differently from journalistic writing?

3. Independently or in a small group, look at the latest issue of a newsmagazine. What types of introductions do you find? Why? Discuss this with your group.

4. Using one of the techniques described in this chapter, rewrite the introduction to an essay you have written. Then read the original and the rewritten essay. Which do you prefer? Why?

SUGGESTIONS FOR WRITING

Give yourself some time to think before you begin to write. Some people close their eyes when they think, and some stare at the wall or at the person in front of them. Do whatever feels right for you. Then choose one of the following topics to write about. If you have difficulty beginning to write, try the "Getting Started" suggestions on page 30.

You may find it useful to look at your journal or at the Lupri selection before you begin to write. As you write this essay, try using the structure of the traditional essay. Think about the ways in which this structure is helpful in organizing your ideas and the ways in which this structure causes specific problems for you as a writer.

1. With the help of family members, construct a family tree in which you trace your great-grandparents, grandparents, aunts, uncles, cousins, and other relatives as far back as you are able. After studying your family tree, write an essay describing your family through the generations. As part of your essay, explain how the concepts of the conjugal nuclear family and extended family relate to your family.

2. Learning to live in a new society and culture can create problems in the relationships between parents and children. Do you agree or disagree? Write an essay in which you support your point of view with your observations and experiences.

3. Some people believe that teenagers in North America have too much freedom. They think that if teenagers were required to have more responsibilities in their family, they would grow up to be better adults. Do you agree or disagree? Write an essay in which you support your point of view with your observations and experiences.

4. In your essay, define and contrast the extended family and the nuclear family. Using your observations and experiences, explain how these two family structures might deal with child rearing, school problems, and social problems such as drugs or premarital sex.

5. Write an essay in which you compare your life at your present age with that of one of your parents at the same age. In what ways are your lives different? In what ways are they similar? Explain the differences and similarities. As part of your conclusion, include what you have learned from writing about this.

GETTING STARTED
Freewriting

If I'm to write about the present, I have to write in the language of the present, even if it's not the language of the self. ... I learn English through writing, and in turn, writing gives me a written self.

EVA HOFFMAN, *LOST IN TRANSLATION*

It might take me ten pages of nothing, of terrible writing, and then I'll get a line, and I'll think, "That's what I mean!" What you're doing is hunting for what you mean, and what you're trying to say. You don't know when you start.

ANNE SEXTON

This will be one of the simplest yet probably most productive exercises in this book. Freewriting is a way of getting yourself to write. The technique is easy. Take out a pen or pencil and a blank piece of paper. Note the time and start writing. Write for ten minutes. Do not think about spelling, grammar, punctuation, or organization. Just keep writing. Do not stop even if the only thing you can write is "I have nothing to write about." You will not have to hand this paper in. Freewriting is simply for you; it is a way for you to loosen up your hand and your mind.

Many people say that freewriting helps them get over writing blocks, times when they feel they just cannot write. You can use this technique at any time. All you need is paper, pen, and ten minutes. So anytime you want to practice your writing, freewrite.

Eventually, you may find that freewriting will help you produce ideas that you can use in your formal writing.

EXERCISES

1. Before you begin to freewrite, reread some of your earlier journal entries. These may give you ideas. You may also find it enjoyable

to see how much progress you are making in your writing.

2. Choose a reading selection from this book and then freewrite. The reading may stimulate your thinking and give you some interesting ideas.

REVISING

As practice in learning to revise an essay, it may be helpful to work with someone else's writing first. Working with a classmate, read the student essay that follows.

A Student Essay

Today, many teenagers enjoy their teenage years very much because they have a lot of wonderful times for themselves. They have more of the freedom and power to do whatever they want than teenagers of the past. Many of these teenagers do not have to carry the responsibility of supporting their families or of thinking seriously about making a living.   5

In today's world, many young teenagers still depend on their parents. Their parents support them in everything such as their schooling and housing. For example, when I was a teenager, my parents earned money to raise me. They provided for me to go to school   10 and they paid for my food. My parents also gave money to me to buy books, records, and movies. Thus I didn't have to worry about financial problems.

Many teenagers also have a lot of opportunities for themselves. They can find jobs and make money to spend on themselves. Some   15 teenagers work in supermarkets as cashiers for a few hours to earn some money. Others work in stores as helpers to get a small amount of money for themselves to buy such luxuries as new clothes, albums, and trips. This money helps take away some of the pressure from the teenager's families.   20

Also, teenagers enjoy many types of entertainment during these years. Many young teenagers spend their time going to parties, movies, and other activities. They can also spend some times gathering with their friends. For example, many teenagers enjoy their time with their friends in the parks playing various kinds of sports,   25 like basketball and soccer. These are all advantages that the teenagers can have during their teenage years.

Lastly, as a teenager, many young people don't have the responsibility of supporting their own families yet because they still depend on their parents. Some of the teenagers are not ready to have   30 their own families. They need more time to explore more about themselves. They want to go out to learn and to participate more in

the outside world. So this is the time for the teenagers to enjoy themselves more than when they are older and have to work and have
family responsibilities.   35

   Therefore, we can see that many teenagers have a lot of fun in
their teenage years. They have more of the freedom and power to
enjoy themselves. I think that many teenagers should enjoy themselves more before they become adults because the teenage years can
be the happiest time of a person's life.   40

                                   Ping Ruan, People's Republic of China

With your partner, answer the following questions about this student's writing. (It is useful to write out your answers.)

1. What is this student trying to say — that is, what is her main idea?

2. What details did she include to support her point of view? Did
   she use a sufficient number of details to convince you?

3. What did you like best about the essay?

4. What part of the essay confused you?

5. If you could make two suggestions to help this student revise her
   essays, what would they be?

   Next exchange a draft of an essay you are working on with that
of a partner. After reading your classmate's essay, write the answers
to the same five questions, and discuss them with your classmate.

   Keeping your classmate's comments in mind, revise your own
essay. Then share your revised essay with the same classmate.

EDITING STRATEGIES

LEARNING NEW VOCABULARY

Key Words and Concepts

One way to develop new vocabulary is to focus on the key words
and concepts used by the author in the selection you have read.

1. List six key vocabulary words that a student needs to know to
   understand the meaning of the Lupri selection (pages 22 to 23).

   nuclear family   conjugal

   polyandry   composite (n, adj)

   polygamous   fraternal (adj) brotherly

How did you choose these words?

2. List four major concepts that a student has to understand to comprehend the meaning of the Lupri selection. ~~The first one is done for you~~.

~~extended~~ *family (siological relationship)*
nuclear family.   serial monogamous
cross - culture   divorce rate

How did you choose these concepts? *they represent*
a new abstract general idea

What is the difference between a <u>word</u> and a concept? *common can do many many thing in a* *underlying*
(abstract) general idea   sentence!

3. Draw a line from each word in column A to the word or words in column B that are opposite in meaning. The first one has been done for you.

A	**B**
1. nuclear family	a. polygamy
2. marriage *c.*	b. different
3. separate *e*	c. divorce
4. fraternal *g*	d. extended family
5. identical *b*	e. common
6. offspring *h*	f. single
7. monogamy *a*	g. maternal *(paternal)*
8. plural *f*	h. parents

~~With a classmate, write a paragraph using as many of these words as possible.~~

COMMONLY CONFUSED WORDS

than/then

Hélène called Thomas when she saw that the movie star he liked better than any other was starring in a new movie in their neighbourhood. Then they went to see it together. When it ended, they talked in front of the movie theatre more than usual. They thought the movie was better than the star's last one. Then they went to get something to drink and then they continued talking. Then it was almost midnight and they both had to rush home.

Examining the use of *than* and *then* in this paragraph should help you complete the following definitions.

_____ means "at that time."

_____ is used to show comparisons.

Fill in the blanks in the following sentences with *than* and *then*.

She lived in Ecuador until she was 5; _____ she moved to

Canada. _____ she started school, where she found it was easier

for her to understand English _____ to speak it. Her teachers

thought she knew less _____ she really did because they

did not know how to communicate with her _____.

Reread the last essay you wrote, and notice how you use these two words in your writing. Correct any errors you made.

MECHANICS
Final Sentence Punctuation

Every sentence ending is signalled with a mark. A *period* is the most common indicator to the reader that a sentence has ended. A period is used to end a sentence that makes a statement or gives a command.

When is a *question mark* used? It is used at the end of a direct question. It is not used after an indirect question.

An *exclamation point* is used to express strong feeling. It can be placed after a word or a phrase or at the end of a sentence. However, writers should be careful not to overuse the exclamation point and not to use more than one at a time!

The word that follows the period, question mark, or exclamation point begins with a capital letter. Make sure that your reader always knows where your sentences begin and end.

EDITING PRACTICE

After revising their writing for content, writers often edit their writing for errors. The following paragraph is a draft summary of the Lupri article that has not been edited. Some of the errors that the author has made are two punctuation errors, five tense choice errors, one pronoun error, two *than/then* errors, and two *to/too/two* errors. Find as many errors as you can and correct them. Answers are on page 325.

Eugen Lupri is writing [writes] about the family from a sociological point of view. He mentions three types of families: nuclear, extended and polygamous. Nuclear families will be [are] the most common family type in Canada. The term can refer to any too [two] related persons, and their offspring sharing a common household. If the couple were [are] married, they form a conjugal nuclear family. Extended families, composed of to [two] or more nuclear families related by blood and sharing a residence, will be [are] less common in Canada then [than] nuclear families. Although it is [they are] advantageous for many reasons. Polygamy was [is] less common then [than] either of the above-mentioned family structures, but it does still exist.

GRAMMAR STRATEGIES

THE PRESENT CONTINUOUS TENSE

Draw rectangles around the subjects in the following sentences. Then draw circles around the verbs. The first one has been done for you.

1. People are living in a changing world right now.
2. Many families are experiencing changes in their relationships.
3. Like the extended family, the conjugal nuclear family is becoming less common in today's world.
4. Divorce and remarriages are creating new and different kinds of family structures.
5. At present, more children are growing up in single-parent families than in traditional two-parent families.
6. Many children are living with stepparents, grandparents, and aunts and uncles for some time in their lives.

Let's use these sentences to examine the present continuous tense.

In this tense, the verb *be (am* ____, or *are)* is followed by the

_____ form of the verb. Some expressions that are used with the

present continuous tense are *now, right now, at this moment,* and *at*

present.

As a class or in small groups, answer the following questions using the present continuous tense.

The present continuous tense is used to describe actions that are happening right now or at the moment of speaking.

1. What are you doing right now?
2. What are two things that you are not doing right now that you would like to be doing?

The present continuous tense is used to describe things that are happening around us or in the world right now.

3. What do you think is the most interesting thing that is happening in the world right now?
4. Is your family changing in relation to the things we have read about in this chapter?

The present continuous tense is used to describe things that are happening in the near future.

5. When you watch the news, what are you waiting to find out about?
6. Are you doing anything special this weekend?

Certain verbs are not usually used in the continuous tenses (present continuous, past continuous, future continuous, present perfect continuous, and so on). Here is a list of these verbs:

appear	have	own	smell
appreciate	hear	possess	sound
be	know	prefer	taste
believe	like	recognize	understand
cost	love	remember	want
dislike	mean	see	
hate	need	seem	

These verbs can be divided into three basic categories:

1. *Words that relate to feelings.* For example, "I hate you" or "I love you" is treated as a permanent state of being, not just a present-moment feeling, whereas "I am feeling sick today" is correct because the verb is expressing a temporary state of being.

2. *Words that relate to ownership or possession.* For example, "I own a green convertible" or "I have a house in the country" is regarded as permanent, whereas "I am having some people over to dinner tonight" is correct because the verb does not express a permanent state of being.

3. *Words that relate to perception.* For example, "I see the blue sky above me" or "I smell the potatoes burning" is not treated as a continuous action, whereas "I am hearing Bach for the first time" is correct, since it expresses a perception that takes place at the moment the sentence is spoken and refers to an event that takes place over a period of time.

EXERCISES

1. In the following paragraph, choose the simple present or the present progressive tense. If either tense is possible, discuss the difference in meaning created by the tense you choose.

   Some verbs you might use are *study, try, rely, find, want, depend, support, change,* and *receive.* You may also choose other verbs; there are many correct possibilities. Experiment and see how changing the verb or its tense can change the meaning of a sentence.

   Sociologists such as Lupri _study_ the family all the time. They _are trying_ to find out about the family structure in different parts of the world and during different periods of history. Family structure _is changing / changes_ all over the world. In many places, families _find / receive_ help outside of the nuclear family. The help _is received / comes_ from the extended family, the community, or the tribe but not usually from outside institutions. However, in Canada, families _depend / rely_ on institutions such as schools and religious groups to help them while they _are supporting_ their children. Newcomers from other societies

wants their children to be successful in their new society. At the
same time, they want to _teach_ their children _about_ their traditional culture. The attempt to hold on to traditional values and to
find success in the new culture _causes_ stress for many.

2. The writing in Exercise 1 would be easier to read if it were divided
   into paragraphs. Read it with a classmate and decide where new
   paragraphs should begin. Mark each new paragraph with the
   symbol.

   If you have any difficulty with this, review "The Paragraph"
   on pages 9 and 10.

TRANSITIONS AND TENSES

The following paragraph is adopted from a magazine article on the
current state of the family. For easy reference, the sentences have
been numbered. Underline all the transitions used in the paragraph.
In the spaces provided after the excerpt, give the transition words in
each sentence, the verb, and its tense. Then answer the questions.
The first one has been done for you.

[1]In recent years, new family structures have been appearing in
Canada. [2]Until a generation after the Second World War, Canadians
experienced an unusual period of family stability. [3]By the 1970s the
situation had radically changed: "There is no such thing as a uni-
dimensional family anymore," stated the experts. [4]In the 1980s,
about forty percent of all marriages ended in divorce; at the same
time, a growing variety of living arrangements were occurring. [5]In
more recent reports, even further changes to the traditional family
structure have been noted. [6]It is estimated that there will be continued growth in non-traditional families throughout the 1990s, including blended families, single-parent families, homosexual unions,
unmarried couples with children, and married couples without children. [7]Thus, before reaching adulthood, the average child can expect
to experience more than one family environment.

Sentence 1

Transition: _In recent years_

Verb: _have been appearing_

Tense: ~~past continuous~~ present perfect continuous

Why did the author use this tense in this sentence?

This tense describes actions that began in the past and are still happening now.

Sentence 2

Transition: After the second World War

Verb: _____

Tense: _____

Why did the author use this tense in this sentence?

_____

_____

Sentence 3

Transition: _____

Verb: _____

Tense: _____

Why did the author use this tense in this sentence?

_____

_____

Sentence 4

Transition: In 1980s

Verb: ended, were occurring

Tense: _____

Why did the author use this tense in this sentence?

_____

_____

Sentence 5

Transition: _____

Verb: _____

Tense: _____

Why did the author use this tense in this sentence?

_____

_____

Sentence 6

Transition: _____

Verb: _____

Tense: _____

Why did the author use this tense in this sentence?

_____

_____

Sentence 7

Transition: _____

Verb: _____

Tense: _____

Why did the author use this tense in this sentence?

_____

_____

We have analyzed the structure of this paragraph so that you as writers can understand how and why writers change tense within a paragraph. What are some of the reasons?

_____

_____

_____

As readers, we are also interested in the content of the paragraph.

1. What is the main idea of this paragraph?
2. How did the writer develop the paragraph?
3. Would you be interested in reading more about this subject? In other words, did the introduction engage you?
4. Were you able to understand the main idea of the paragraph even if you did not know every word? Did you use context clues to help you with unfamiliar words, instead of interrupting your reading to look up each unfamiliar word in the dictionary?

The technique that we used with this paragraph is one that you can use with other reading materials — newspapers, newsmagazines, textbooks, and so on. It can help you to understand how a piece was written and why the author made certain decisions. Moreover, it can help you with your own writing.

GROWING APART

PREREADING ACTIVITIES

1. "The Snob" is about disappointments children and their parents often feel in one another. With other students in your class, make a list of the qualities you think make for a good family life.

2. After reviewing your list of positive family qualities, discuss the expectations that children have for their parents and that parents have for their children.

3. Discuss in what ways children may disappoint their parents, and in what ways parents may disappoint their children. What do you think can or should be done by parents and children about these disappointments? How can the quality of family life be improved?

The Snob   *who look down on other people.*

Morley Callaghan (1903–1990) was a Canadian novelist and short story writer who had an international reputation. He often wrote about noble but troubled characters, faced with moral dilemmas. This story is a good example of his writing; it is a psychological study.

It was at the book counter in the department store that John Harcourt, the student, caught a glimpse of his father. At first he could not be sure in the crowd that pushed along the aisle, but there was something about the colour of the back of the elderly man's neck, something about the faded felt hat, that he knew very well. 5 Harcourt was standing with the girl he loved, buying a book for her. All afternoon he had been talking to her, eagerly, but with an anxious diffidence, as if there still remained in him an innocent wonder that she should be delighted to be with him. From underneath her wide-brimmed straw hat, her face, so fair and beautifully strong with its 10 expression of cool independence, kept turning up to him and sometimes smiled at what he said. That was the way they always talked, never daring to show much full, strong feeling. Harcourt had just bought the book, and had reached into his pocket for the money with a free, ready gesture to make it appear that he was accustomed to buying books for young ladies, when the white-haired man in the faded felt hat, at the other end of the counter, turned half toward him, and Harcourt knew he was standing only a few feet away from his father.

The young man's easy words trailed away and his voice became little more than a whisper, as if he were afraid that everyone in the store might recognize it. There was rising in him a dreadful uneasiness; something very precious that he wanted to hold seemed close to destruction. His father, standing at the end of the bargain counter, was planted squarely on his two feet, turning a book over thoughtfully in his hands. Then he took out his glasses from an old, worn leather case and adjusted them on the end of his nose, looking down over them at the book. His coat was thrown open, two buttons on his vest were undone, his grey hair was too long, and in his rather shabby clothes he looked very much like a working-man, a carpenter perhaps. Such a resentment rose in young Harcourt that he wanted to cry out bitterly, "Why does he dress as if he never owned a decent suit in his life? He doesn't care what the whole world thinks of him. He never did. I've told him a hundred times he ought to wear his good clothes when he goes out. Mother's told him the same thing. He just laughs. And now Grace may see him. Grace will meet him."

So young Harcourt stood still, with his head down, feeling that something very painful was impending. Once he looked anxiously at Grace, who had turned to the bargain counter. Among those people drifting aimlessly by with hot red faces, getting in each other's way, using their elbows but keeping their faces detached and wooden, she looked tall and splendidly alone. She was so sure of herself, her relation to the people in the aisles, the clerks behind the counter, the books on the shelves, and everything around her. Still keeping his head down and moving close, he whispered uneasily, "Let's go and have tea somewhere, Grace."

"In a minute, dear," she said.

"Let's go now."

"In just a minute, dear," she said absently.

"There's not a breath of air in here. Let's go now."

"What makes you so impatient?"

"There nothing but old books on that counter."

"There may be something here I've wanted all my life," she said, smiling at him brightly and not noticing the uneasiness in his face.

So Harcourt had to move slowly behind her, getting closer to his father all the time. He could feel the space that separated them narrowing. Once he looked up with a vague, sidelong glance. But his father, red-faced and happy, was still reading the book, only now there was a meditative expression on his face, as if something in the book had stirred him and he intended to stay there reading for some time.   60

Old Harcourt had lots of time to amuse himself, because he was on a pension after working hard all his life. He had sent John to the university and he was eager to have him distinguish himself. Every   65
night when John came home, whether it was early or late, he used to go into his father's and mother's bedroom and turn on the light and talk to them about the interesting things that had happened to him during the day. They listened and shared this new world with him. They both sat up in their night-clothes and, while his mother asked   70
all the questions, his father listened attentively with his head cocked on one side, a smile or a frown on his face. The memory of all this was in John now, and there was also a desperate longing and a pain within him growing harder to bear as he glanced fearfully at his father, but he thought stubbornly, "I can't introduce him. It'll be eas-   75
ier for everybody if he doesn't see us. I'm not ashamed. But it will be easier. It'll be more sensible. It'll only embarrass him to see Grace." By this time he knew he was ashamed, but he felt that his shame was justified, for Grace's father had the smooth, confident manner of a man who had lived all his life among people who were rich and sure   80
of themselves. Often when he had been in Grace's home talking politely to her mother, John had kept on thinking of the plainness of his own home and of his parents' laughing, good-natured untidiness, and he resolved desperately that he must make Grace's people admire him.   85

He looked up cautiously, for they were about eight feet away from his father, but at that moment his father, too, looked up and John's glance shifted swiftly far over the aisle, over the counters, seeing nothing. As his father's blue, calm eyes stared steadily over the glasses, there was an instant when their glances might have met.   90
Neither one could have been certain, yet John, as he turned away and began to talk to Grace hurriedly, knew surely that his father had seen him. He knew it by the steady calmness in his father's blue eyes. John's shame grew, and then humiliation sickened him as he waited and did nothing.   95

His father turned away, going down the aisle, walking erectly in his shabby clothes, his shoulders very straight, never once looking back. His father would walk slowly along the street, he knew, with that meditative expression deepening and becoming grave.

Theme – parents + children in conflict
 – son ashame of a father for all the wrong reason.
    judge people by external appearance

abstract the idea
from the character.

Young Harcourt stood beside Grace, brushing against her soft shoulder, and made faintly aware again of the delicate scent she used. There, so close beside him, she was holding within her everything he wanted to reach out for, only now he felt a sharp hostility that made him sullen and silent.

"You were right, John," she was drawling in her soft voice. "It does get unbearable in here on a hot day. Do let's go now. Have you ever noticed that department stores after a time can make you really hate people?" But she smiled when she spoke, so he might see that she really hated no one.

"You don't like people, do you?" he said sharply.

"People? What people? What do you mean?"

"I mean," he went on irritably, "you don't like the kind of people you bump into here, for example."

"Not especially. Who does? What are you talking about?"

"Anybody could see you don't," he said recklessly, full of a savage eagerness to hurt her. "I say you don't like simple, honest people, the kind of people you meet all over the city." He blurted the words out as if he wanted to shake her, but he was longing to say, "You wouldn't like my family. Why couldn't I take you home to have dinner with them? You'd turn up your nose at them, because they've no pretensions. As soon as my father saw you, he knew you wouldn't want to meet him. I could tell by the way he turned."

His father was on his way home now, he knew, and that evening at dinner they would meet. His mother and sister would talk rapidly, but his father would say nothing to him, or to anyone. There would only be Harcourt's memory of the level look in the blue eyes, and the knowledge of his father's pain as he walked away.

Grace watched John's gloomy face as they walked through the store, and she knew he was nursing some private rage, and so her own resentment and exasperation kept growing, and she said crisply, "You're entitled to your moods on a hot afternoon, I suppose, but if I feel I don't like it here, then I don't like it. You wanted to go yourself. Who likes to spend very much time in a department store on a hot afternoon? I begin to hate every stupid person that bangs into me, everybody near me. What does that make me?"

"It makes you a snob."

"So I'm a snob now?" she said angrily.

"Certainly you're a snob," he said. They were at the door and going out to the street. As they walked in the sunlight, in the crowd moving slowly down the street, he was groping for words to describe the secret thoughts he had always had about her. "I've always known how you'd feel about people I like who didn't fit into your private world," he said.

"You're a very stupid person," she said. Her face was flushed now, and it was hard for her to express her indignation, so she stared straight ahead as she walked along.   145

They had never talked in this way, and now they were both quickly eager to hurt each other. With a flow of words, she started to argue with him, then she checked herself and said calmly, "Listen, John, I imagine you're tired of my company. There's no sense in having tea together. I think I'd better leave you right here."   150

"That's fine," he said. "Good afternoon."

"Good-bye."

"Good-bye."

She started to go, she had gone two paces, but he reached out desperately and held her arm, and he was frightened, and pleading, "Please don't go, Grace."   155

All the anger and irritation had left him; there was just a desperate anxiety in his voice as he pleaded, "Please forgive me. I've got no right to talk to you like that. I don't know why I'm so rude or what's the matter. I'm ridiculous. I'm very, very ridiculous. Please, you must forgive me. Don't leave me."   160

He had never talked to her so brokenly, and his sincerity, the depth of his feeling, began to stir her. While she listened, feeling all the yearning in him, they seemed to have been brought closer together, by opposing each other, than ever before, and she began to feel almost shy. "I don't know what's the matter. I suppose we're both irritable. It must be the weather," she said. "But I'm not angry, John."   165

He nodded his head miserably. He longed to tell her that he was sure she would have been charming to his father, but he had never felt so wretched in his life. He held her arm tight, as if he must hold it or what he wanted most in the world would slip away from him, yet he kept thinking, as he would ever think, of his father walking away quietly with his head never turning.   170

   175

Conflict is not resolved

READING AND THINKING STRATEGIES

DISCUSSION ACTIVITIES

Analysis and Conclusions

1. Why was John upset by the sight of his father in the department store? Why did he not want Grace to meet his father? Was his "shame" justified? *look untimely/old clothes*

[handwritten top margin:] characters
①John Harcourt   John is always graceful to be the
② Grace   Grace company with
③ old (Harcourt)

[handwritten:] is not being himself, he don't have much value, insecure,

2. Examine the relationship between John and Grace. Would you say it was built on mutual trust and understanding? *No.*

3. Would you say that the relationship between John and his parents is one of total alienation between the generations? Support your answer with examples from the story. *the higher level, he is in conflict with feelings of shame & love*

[handwritten:] he tries to impress Grace (position money) he wants to climb up

Writing and Point of View

[handwritten left margin:]
① conflict - struggle : interior, exterior (man vs himself)
② Plot, setting (bookstore summer)
③ characters
④ Point of view - third limited (omniscient)
⑤ climax (peak moment in conflict)
⑥ imagery & symbolism

1. How does Callaghan signal a change in the relationship between John and Grace near the end of the story? How does the tone of their conversation change?

2. Trace the range of emotions each character experiences throughout the course of the story. How does the author convey these feelings to the reader?

3. Fiction creates a mood or a feeling. What is the mood of this story? What elements or parts of the story create the mood? Here are some things to think about: Where does the story take place? Does it take place in the city or in the country? How does that setting affect the mood of the story? Describe each character in detail.

Personal Response and Evaluation

[handwritten:] John's father has seen John.

1. What does the title "The Snob" mean? Why is it significant in this story?

2. What do you think will happen when John returns home?

3. Did John express his true feelings during the argument with Grace? Do you think his making up with Grace will resolve John's inner conflict? *No.*

ROLE PLAYING

[handwritten:] John sees his father, pretend he does not know his
" avoid " " father was there.
starts a fight with Grace.

Act out the short story with one student playing the narrator and other students playing the characters. One more student can read the background information. You might want to record this and play it back for the class, or individual students may want to listen to review the story. *turns his back*

[handwritten:] John's father/walks out the store
Grace and John make up.

JOURNAL WRITING

Nothing is real, nothing is true, nothing happens, until it has been observed and noted and put down in words like bells, ringing the changes of love and hate, beauty and happiness, and misery. Without words, how much of us really does exist?

HAN SUYIN, *THE MOUNTAIN IS YOUNG*

Writing in a journal, whether it is shared or kept for yourself, is powerful. It is a means of touching on feelings and experiences hidden inside ourselves. Allowing your journal to express your deepest self will have a positive effect on all your writing.

"The Snob" is about family members growing apart. It is also about family expectations and family love. How can family members remain close when children become adults? Must children grow apart from their parents as part of the maturation process? Is there a proper time for parents to "let go" of their children? Write your thoughts about these issues in your journal.

WRITING STRATEGIES

ESSAY STRATEGIES
Writing Dialogue

When you read or write stories, plays, or film scripts, you should be aware of the way people talk to each other. Writers try to make the conversation or spoken interchanges between people as realistic as possible for their particular characters.

Look at the following interchanges from various pieces of writing and notice the differences in the ways in which the characters communicate. What do these interchanges tell you about the characters and about their relationships?

Still keeping his head down and moving close, he whispered uneasily, "Let's go and have tea somewhere, Grace."

"In a minute, dear," she said.

"Let's go now."

"In just a minute, dear," she repeated absently.

"There's not a breath of air in here. Let's go now."

"What makes you so impatient?"

"There's nothing but old books on that counter."

"There may be something here I've wanted all my life," she said, smiling at him brightly and not noticing the uneasiness in his face.

After reading this excerpt from "The Snob" by Morley Callaghan, discuss the following questions:

1. Who is talking, and how do you, as a reader, know this?

2. How would you describe the relationship of these people?

3. What pictures of these people did you form as you read this? What do they look like and sound like to you as a reader?

> And then he said abruptly: *"Ain't you got no idea where you lost your penny?"*
>
> *"Yes," I said, "I know just about."*
>
> *"Let's see if we can't find it," he said.*
>
> *We walked down the road together, stiff with awareness. He didn't hold my hand.*
>
> *"It's right here somewhere," I said. "I was playin' with it, in the dust."*

After reading this excerpt from "Penny in the Dust" by Ernest Buckler, discuss the following questions.

1. Who is talking, and how do you, as a reader, know this?

2. How would you describe the relationship of these people?

3. What pictures of these people did you form as you read this? What do they look like and sound like to you as a reader?

> *"I want to get my citizenship," she says as she slaps down the* Dai Pao, *"before they come and take away my house."*
>
> *"Nobody's going to do that. This is Canada."*
>
> *"So everyone says," she retorts, "but did you read what the* Dai Pao *said? Ah, you can't read Chinese. The government is cutting back on old-age pensions. Anybody who hasn't got citizenship will lose everything. Or worse."*
>
> *"The* Dai Pao *can't even typeset accurately," I tell her. Sometimes I worry about the information Mother receives from that biweekly community newspaper. "Don't worry — the Ministry of Immigration won't send you back to China."*

"Little you know," she snaps back. "I am old, helpless, and without citizenship. Reasons enough. Now, get me citizenship. Hurry!"

"Mother, getting citizenship papers is not like going to the bank to cash in your pension cheque. First, you have to —"

"Excuses, my son, excuses. When your father was alive —"

"Oh, Mother, not again! You throw that at me every —"

"— made excuses, too." Her jaw tightens. "If you can't do this little thing for your own mother, well, I will just have to go and beg your cousin to ..."

Every time I try to explain about the ways of the fan gwei, *she thinks I do not want to help her.*

"I'll do it, I'll do it, okay? Just give me some time."

After reading this excerpt from "Why My Mother Can't Speak English" by Garry Engkent, which appeared in the anthology of Chinese-Canadian writing *Many Mouthed Birds*, discuss the following questions.

1. Who is talking, and how do you, as a reader, know this?
2. How would you describe the relationship of these people?
3. What pictures of these people did you form as you read this? What do they look like and sound like to you as a reader?
4. What differences do you find in the ways in which people talk in the four excerpts? What does the dialogue tell you about the people and their familial relationships?
5. Why do you think that writers use dialogue rather than just describing characters and discussing what they have said?

ESSAY FORM

Narration: Telling a Story

Every day in our lives all of us tell stories. For example, we come home from school and tell our families what happened in class. We might discuss a bus trip and describe one of the people on the bus. We fill our stories with details that will capture the imagination of the listener. We tell stories to give ourselves pleasure and to give our listeners pleasure. The famous literary critic, literary philosopher, and educator Northrop Frye said, "There's only one story, the story of your life." Stories are a way of making sense of the world.

When we tell stories, we are aware of beginnings and endings. We usually tell a story in the order in which it happened. When we listen to stories, we also like to hear them in the correct order. Have you ever been telling a child an old, familiar story and, in trying to rush through it, left out a part? The child will usually stop you and beg you to tell the story "right," with all its parts in the right order. The rules we follow when we tell stories to friends and family are similar to the rules we follow when we write stories that will be shared with teachers and classmates.

"The Snob" is an example of narration that uses chronological order, which means that events are told in the order in which they occurred. Reread the story, noticing each time that Callaghan uses time phrases and changes in verb tense or transitions throughout the story. How do these help you follow the story?

In addition, Callaghan includes many details that describe the characters and their life. When you write a narration, you can make your writing more interesting and richer by adding details that help the reader feel and almost see the experience. Writers do this by adding sensory details, details that help a reader see, hear, smell, feel, and taste the experiences that are being described. Reread the Callaghan story, noticing the specific details he provides. Decide whether the details help the reader to see, hear, smell, feel, or taste the particular experiences he is describing.

When you do your own writing of a narrative or a story, keep in mind chronological order and the inclusion of sensory details to help your reader understand and enjoy your story.

EXERCISES

1. Compare the writing in the selection in Chapter 1 with the writing in the selection in this chapter. Which selection do you prefer and why? Is the vocabulary similar? Which selection did you find easier to read?

2. What kinds of reading do you do for your own enjoyment? Share with a classmate the best article, book, or story that you have read in the past few months. What makes a piece of writing appeal to you?

SUGGESTIONS FOR WRITING

You may want to look at your journal or try brainstorming or freewriting before you begin to write on these topics. Always spend some time thinking before you begin to write. Try the suggestion in "Getting Started" on page 52 if you need help in beginning your writing.

The first four suggestions are narratives or stories. When you write a narrative, keep in mind the three topics focused on in this chapter: chronological order, sensory details, and the use of dialogue.

1. Write a narrative about an experience between a child and a parent. Use dialogue. Refer to page 7 to see how your journal can help you with this writing.

2. Have you ever had an experience like John's in which you were upset or confused? Write about your experience and tell what you learned from it.

3. Imagine that the father is telling the story "The Snob." Rewrite the story from his point of view.

4. Imagine that Grace is telling the story. Rewrite the story and make whatever changes should occur. You may imagine that either she is unaware of John's father or aware of his presence.

5. In a group or on your own, write a play based on this story. Use some of the dialogue from the story and some of your own. Use the following format.

JOHN: Let's go and have tea somewhere, Grace.

GRACE: In a minute, dear.

Read your dialogue aloud in a group to see if it sounds like people talking. You may decide to act out your play for the entire class.

6. Children often take for granted their parents' sacrifices made on their behalf. Do you agree or disagree? Write an essay in which you support or dispute this point of view, based on your own experiences or observations.

7. Parents can be insensitive to their children's problems. Do you agree or disagree? Write an essay in which you support your point of view with your experiences or observations.

GETTING STARTED
Brainstorming

Whenever possible, you should write about something that interests you. You will then have ideas on the subject and will probably be able to come up with something to say. Even if you are writing about a topic that interests you, however, you may have problems writing an essay. Brainstorming is a good technique to use to help you come up with ideas that will develop into your essay.

When you brainstorm, you develop ideas and supporting details by asking questions. The basic questions are Who? What? Where? When? How? and Why? The questions vary, based on the topic. For example, the following sample questions were used to brainstorm for an essay about a special relationship. Remember, brainstorming is used to help you get started writing. Don't worry about writing complete sentences. Just write down your ideas.

Who has the relationship?	My parents, who have been married for 35 years, have a special relationship.
What makes them special?	They are best friends. Even in difficult situations.
Where do they live?	In an old house that they have rebuilt themselves.
When did you realize that their relationship was special?	I came to visit them as they were refinishing a floor. They were working on the same area. They bumped heads and kissed. They were in their sixties.
How do they make you feel?	They have always made me feel like they loved me. Made me believe that I could succeed. Made me believe that relationships can last and grow.
Why do you want to write about them?	I want to show that people can be married for a long time and still be best friends, still be in love.

The next step is reading through the questions and answers and deciding what to emphasize in the writing. As you read through what you have written, this may become obvious. Although brainstorming is a good technique for getting started, you can use it at any time during the writing process. If you are stuck in the middle and need more support or more details, brainstorming can be helpful. It is a useful tool to help a writer create a rich, fully developed essay.

EXERCISES

1. Brainstorm about one or more of the following: a special relation-ship, arranged marriage, romantic love, teenage marriages, the high divorce rate, living together before marriage. Write down your questions and answers. They will be helpful when you begin writing.

2. Brainstorm with a classmate. One of you will ask the questions; the other will write down the answers. Then repeat the activity but reverse roles. At the end of the two sessions, you should have material for two essays.

REVISING

Many writers are not quite sure what to do when they are told to revise their writing. They simply look for misspellings, grammatical errors, and other surface problems, then copy the essay over and hand it in. This is not really revising, however; this is editing. Revising means rethinking and restructuring your writing.

One way to become more comfortable with revising is just to go ahead and do it. Here we suggest a simple and concrete method for getting the feel of revising. Although it is not something you would do all the time, it will give you some experience in making decisions about your writing. Use it first on the following student essay. Follow the steps in the order in which they are listed.

1. Choose an essay that you would like to revise.

2. Reread the essay slowly and carefully. Make a copy of the essay. (Save the original essay.)

3. Cross out and remove one sentence from any part of the essay.

4. Move one sentence from one place in a paragraph to a new place.

5. Add one new sentence to any paragraph in your essay.

6. Change one word in the essay to a synonym for that word.

7. Add one transition word or phrase (*therefore, however, but, more-over,* etc.) somewhere in your essay.

8. Rewrite the essay with all the changes you have made.

A Student Essay

I remember when my mother used to tell me that she would not die until she made of us independent young people. My brothers and sisters, all of us, grew up with that thought in mind. To me, that was a good statement from my mother which I will follow for my future children. I am an independent person and I feel I am the most free man to make decisions in my life without being afraid of them. And I feel free to take action on my decisions. Because of being free to decide for myself and being self-sufficient in my entire life, I am very proud of my mother. She helped me become an independent person.

I know a lot of people that at my age are afraid of what to do in their future lives. These people that I am talking about are people who are living with their parents. It has nothing to do with whether it is good or bad to live with their parents. The point is that these people are often handicapped in making decisions. I remember that one of these people that I am talking about asked me if I was afraid to live by myself or if I feel like a woman because I have to cook my own dinner when I get home.

I could not answer these silly questions because I saw that this man's hands were tied about what to do with his future life. I believe that these dependent people will not have any choice when their parents pass away. They are going to feel that it will be impossible for them to do anything without their parents to help them. They will regret the fact that they did not become independent before their parents passed away. Unfortunately, they are left handicapped to take action on their own decisions.

In conclusion, I think that all young people must become independent and not let their parents decide their lives for them. When people are no longer teenagers, they should leave their parents' homes and start their own homes. At this time, they should start their own independent lives.

Reynaldo Rivera, Puerto Rico

Look at Rivera's original essay and at your revised version of his essay. Which do you prefer? Which of the suggested changes was most difficult to make? Which of the suggested changes improved the essay the most? After you have discussed this essay, do the same revising exercise with your own writing. You may work alone or with a partner. Work through the exercise step by step.

After you have completed all the work involved, compare your original essay with the revised version. Which do you prefer? Why? Was it difficult to make the suggested changes? Think about how you decided which sentence to remove. Think about how you made the other decisions as well. These are the types of decisions that all writers make when revising their writing.

EDITING STRATEGIES

VOCABULARY DEVELOPMENT

1. List ten words that describe emotions.

_____   _____

_____   _____

_____   _____

_____   _____

_____   _____

2. Draw a line from each word in column A to the word in column B that is opposite in meaning. The first one has been done for you.

1. glimpse   a. purposefully
2. eager   b. carefully
3. ashamed   c. friendliness
4. aimlessly   d. stare
5. calmness   e. proud
6. hostility   f. reticent
7. recklessly   g. relaxed
8. uneasy   h. agitation

prepositions (in/at)

Many students of English have difficulty learning how to use prepositions correctly. One problem is that English has more prepositions than many other languages. In Spanish, for example, the preposition _en_ is equivalent to three prepositions in English: _in, on,_ and _at._ When you study prepositions, think about how they are used in your first language. Some students find it useful to create a personal association with what they already know about their own language and the new information they are learning about English.

The eight most frequently used prepositions in English (in alphabetical order) are _at, by, for, from, in, on, to,_ and _with._

In this chapter, we will look at some of the most common uses for the preposition _at_ by comparing this preposition with _in_ and _on._ _At_ is used in the following ways.

1. To locate something in a specific location:

I live _in_ Vancouver, British Columbia, _at_ the corner of Hudson and Balfour streets.
I live _in_ Ottawa, Ontario, _at_ 123 Main Street.
I worked _in_ an office and usually got home from my job _at_ night.
My sister was working _in_ the house _at_ the computer.
Grace was _at_ home when I called her.

2. To locate something in a specific time:

> I was born *in* May *on* Sunday *at* 8:35 a.m.
> He said he would meet me *on* Saturday at the library *at* noon.
> I got paid *at* the end of every eight-hour day except *on* the weekend.
> She met him *at* the opening of the Emily Carr art exhibit *in* 1990.

3. To indicate a state, condition, or involvement in a particular activity:

> I felt *at* a loss when John wanted to leave so suddenly. Soon after our argument, I was *in* tears.
> The girl was *at* ease with her hands *in* her lap until the music started playing.
> His father was *in* the living room when John left home.
> John was *at* the top of his university English class because he got A's *in* all his essays and examinations.

4. To indicate direction toward a goal or objective:

> I tried to look *at* him again, but it made me feel uncomfortable to look him *in* the eye.
> When he looked *at* me, I turned away.
> He stared *at* the back of his father still browsing *in* the store before he left with Grace.

EXERCISE

In the following paragraph, fill in the blanks with *at* or *in*, using the examples as a guide.

Callaghan writes a story that takes place _____ the book department of a large store _____ the 1950s. John and Grace are looking _____ a display of sale books when suddenly John notices his father who is also interested _____ the same display. John doesn't want his father to look _____ him, so he tries to leave, but Grace wants to stay _____ the store. John's father looks _____ John, then slowly moves away, seemingly interested _____ another department. John tells Grace he'd rather be _____ a restaurant. He thinks to himself, "When I see Dad _____ home, what will I say?"

COMMONLY CONFUSED WORDS

live/leave

> *John tells Grace that he cannot* live *at home anymore; he wants to* leave *his family and* live *on his own.*

Notice how the verb forms of *live* and *leave* are used in the preceding sentence. Now complete the following definitions:

_____ is a verb that means "to reside in a particular place."

_____ is a verb that means "to go away from a particular place, job, or situation."

Fill in the blanks in the following sentences with the correct form of *live* or *leave.*

1. John wants to _____ home and _____ alone.

2. Grace does not want to _____ the department store.

3. John's parents want him to _____ with them. They are upset that he wants to _____.

4. Grace _____ in an apartment building on May Street; she _____ for work every morning at 7:30 a.m.

MECHANICS
Quotation Marks

Read the following excerpt from "The Snob," and underline all the words that are enclosed by quotation marks, including words in this sentence.

> *"Let's go now."*

> *"In a minute, dear," she repeated absently.*

> *"There's not a breath of air in here. Let's go now."*

> *"What makes you so impatient?"*

Look closely at what you have underlined; then answer the following questions.

1. Do periods and question marks belong inside or outside the quotation marks?

2. If you end a quotation and then identify who said it, does the quotation end with a period or with a comma? _____

3. In what tense are the quotations in the excerpt written? _____

4. In what tense is the story written? _____

5. Why are the story and the quotations written in different tenses?

   _____

6. In the directions to this exercise, there are quotation marks around "The Snob."

   What do these quotation marks indicate to the reader? _____

   Why do the words begin with capital letters? _____

7. One use for quotation marks is for the names of short stories. What is another use for quotation marks?

EXERCISES

1. Imagine that a new student in your college is lost. Write a dialogue in which the student asks you for directions to the bursar's office. Write your response using quotation marks and expressions such as *I said, she said,* and *he said.*

2. Imagine that you have just received a letter telling you that there is a problem with your school registration. Write a dialogue in which you go to the registrar's office to try to solve your problem. You may want to write this dialogue with a classmate and act it out for the class.

EDITING PRACTICE

The following paragraph is a first draft that contains many surface errors: one formatting error, one quotation mark error, two *live/leave* errors, three end punctuation errors, three *to/too/two* errors, and three present tense errors. Find and correct all the errors. Check your answers on page 325.

The Snob is describing the mixed emotions of a young man, John

Harcourt. When he sees his father in the department store, he is

deciding to live and go to a restaurant! He feels disappointed with the way his father leaves. His girlfriend, Grace, is wanting too know why John wants to leave so suddenly? She doesn't seem too understand John's sudden anger. Although the father and son seem two love each other, they have some problems to resolve!

GRAMMAR STRATEGIES

FORMS OF THE PAST TENSE

"The Snob" was written in the past tense, which is the tense most commonly used to tell a story. The various forms of the past tense are shown below.

Simple Past Tense

An excerpt from the story is reproduced here. Underline all the past tense verbs. The first one has been done for you.

So young Harcourt <u>stood</u> still, with his head down, feeling that something very painful was impending. Once he looked anxiously at Grace, who had turned to the bargain counter. Among those people drifting aimlessly by with hot red faces, getting in each other's way, using their elbows but keeping their faces detached and wooden, she looked tall and splendidly alone. She was so sure of herself, her relation to the people in the aisles, the clerks behind the counter, the books on the shelves, and everything around her. Still keeping his head down and moving close, he whispered uneasily, "Let's go and have tea somewhere, Grace."

Now change all the past tense verbs to the present and rewrite the excerpt in the lines below.

_____

_____

_____

_____

_____

_____

_____

_____

_____

_____

_____

_____

Read both versions. Does the meaning seem changed? Which do you prefer? Which would you use to tell a story? Why?

Past Continuous Tense

The past continuous or progressive tense is formed with _was_ or _were_ and the _-ing_ form of the verb. It is used to convey continuous action that took place in the past.

When John looked around, his father was looking _at books._

_He_ was arguing _with her as they left the store._

The couple were walking _down Main Street._

John was apologizing _and Grace started to apologize, too._

In the following paragraph, choose the simple present tense or the past progressive tense of the indicated verbs.

Grace _was looking_ at the sale books when John _asked_ her to
    (look)   **(ask)**

leave the store with him. She _seemed_ to be reluctant to go.
                                      (seem)

She _was handed_ him a book and John _brought_ it for her. She _was looking_
    (hand)   **(buy)**   **(look)**

at more books as John _was, glancing / glanced_ at his father. He again _said_ he
                (glance)   **(say)**

wanted her to accompany him to a nearby restaurant. She _put_
(want) *(put)*

down a large, beautifully illustrated book, and they _left_
(leave)

the store, while John's father _was going_ in the opposite
(go)

direction. They _were arguing_ as they _were walking_ _walked_ down the street.
(argue) *(walk)*

Past Perfect Tense

The past perfect tense is used to express something that occurred in the past, before something else that happened in the past. If we are writing about two things that happened in the past and we want to show that one came before the other, we use the past perfect tense for the thing that happened first.

The past perfect tense is formed with *had* plus the past participle of the verb. (See Appendix A for a list of irregular past participles.)

He was buying Grace the book, which she had chosen *from among the sale items.*

He worried about his relationship with Grace even though they had worked *out their differences.*

They settled their quarrel and decided to go to the restaurant where they had planned *to have lunch.*

In each of these examples, which action came first?

The past perfect progressive tense is formed with *had* plus *been* and the *-ing* form of the verb.

The father had been looking *at the books for a long time before John noticed him.*

Among the pile of books was the one Grace had been wanting *for a long time.*

EXERCISES

1. In the following paragraph, choose the simple past, the past progressive, or the past perfect tense of the indicated verbs.

After John _had met_ Grace outside the department store, they
(meet)

decided to look at the books on sale. They _had been looking_ for about five
(decide)   (look)

minutes when John suddenly ___saw___ his father. John ___felt___
                          (see)   (feel)

embarrassed and immediately __suggested__ to Grace that they leave, but
                            (suggest)

Grace __refused__, as she __had decided__ not to go until she __had examined__ all the
      (refuse)   (decide)   (examine)

books on display.

2. The following excerpt is taken from "The Snob." Fill in the verbs
   as you remember them from the story. Decide which verb tense
   you need. Then go back to the story and compare your answer
   with the original. Decide which you prefer and why.

   Old Harcourt ___had___ lots of time to amuse himself, because he

   ___was___ on a pension after working hard all his life. He __had sent__

   John to the university and he ___was___ eager to have him distinguish

   himself. Every night when John __came / returned / arrived__ home, whether it was

   early or late, he ___went___ into his father's and mother's bedroom

   would turn (habitual) / used to turn

   and __turned__ on the light and talk to them about the interesting

   things that __had happened__ to him during the day. They __listened__ and

   __shared__ this new world with him.

SENTENCE VARIETY

Writers use a variety of sentences to keep their writing interesting
and lively. Too many short sentences can sound choppy and immature, just as too many long sentences can be dull and difficult to read.
Writers maintain a balance of different length and different types of
sentences.

Sentences are made up of different types and numbers of
clauses. A clause is the part of the sentence that contains the subject
and the predicate.

An independent clause can stand alone as a sentence.

A dependent clause cannot stand alone. It needs an independent clause to make it a complete sentence.

When students do homework, they should focus on their work.
    (dependent clause)   *(independent clause)*

Clauses determine four major sentence types:

1. The *simple sentence* has one independent clause:

   She studied hard for all of her classes.

2. The *compound sentence* has two or more independent clauses:

   I tried to speak Vietnamese, and my friend tried to speak English.

3. The *complex sentence* has one independent clause joined to one or more dependent clauses. A complex sentence contains either a subordinating word such as *although, when,* or *because* or a relative pronoun such as *that, who,* or *which:*

   When she handed in her homework, she forgot to give the teacher the last page.
   I admired him so much that I wanted to run away with him.

4. The *compound-complex sentence* has two or more independent clauses and one or more dependent clauses.
   Although she always did her homework, she often handed it in late because she copied it over until it was perfect.

EXERCISES

1. With a partner, reread the Callaghan story to find examples of the four sentence types.

2. Reread the Chan essay to find examples of each of the four sentence types.

3. Reread the Lupri selection to find examples of the four sentence types.

4. What differences did you find in the types of sentences used in these pieces of writing? What was the predominant type in each story? How does the use of a sentence type affect you as a reader? Is one type of sentence easier to read than another for you?

5. Working with a partner, read one essay each of you has written to find examples of each of the four sentence types.

The Compound Sentence

To form compound sentences, join two related independent clauses with a semicolon (;) or use a coordinating word. Some commonly used coordinators are *and, but, or, yet, for, so,* and *nor.* Use a comma before the coordinator.

> *John and Grace went to a department store, and they went to a restaurant as well.*

> *The couple ordered tea, but they did not eat anything.*

Each of the following sentences uses some type of coordination. Analyze these sentences very carefully by performing three operations on each one. (The first sentence has been done for you.)

Put a rectangle around each subject.

Put a circle around each verb.

Put a triangle around each coordinator and the comma that precedes it.

1. John's mother cleaned the house, and his father did the grocery shopping.
2. Grace was John's favourite companion, for they enjoyed many of the same activities.
3. Old Harcourt came home at 7:30, so his wife had to reheat the supper.
4. There were no tears in his eyes, but he just shuffled away.
5. I will move out of my parents' home, or I will lose my mind.
6. John seemed to want to leave, yet he couldn't explain why.
7. John didn't talk to his father about it, nor did he discuss the situation with Grace.

COMPLEX SENTENCES

Commas with Subordinate Clauses

There are several types of sentences that we can use when we write. Most writers vary sentence types to make their writing more interesting to the reader. If you examine professional writing, you will usually find a combination of short sentences and long sentences. In this chapter, we will examine the use of subordination to create longer sentences.

In each of the following sentences, draw a rectangle around the subject and a circle around the verb. The first one has been done for you.

1. I came to Canada with my parents.
2. I was almost sixteen years old.

3. I have lived in Canada for three years.

4. I am still unable to think about my home country without detach-ment.

Notice in each sentence there is one subject and one verb. If you were to read an entire essay made up of sentences such as these, you might find it choppy and immature. To vary the sentences, it is pos-sible to combine some of these sentences using subordinators. Subordinators are special words that are used to make connections. Some commonly used subordinators are *after, as, because, before, if, since, until, when, where,* and *while.*

Each of the following sentences uses some type of subordina-tion. Analyze these sentences very carefully by performing four operations on each one. (The first sentence has been done for you.)
Put a rectangle around each subject.
Put a circle around each verb.
Put a triangle around each subordinator.
If there is a comma in the sentence, underline it.

1. I came to Canada with my parents, when I was almost 16 years old.

2. Although I have lived in Canada for three years, I am still unable to think about my home country with detachment.

3. As I practised more, my English began to improve.

4. I have to return to my home country one day because I want to know myself better.

5. When I try to review my life, I feel both happy and sad.

On the basis of what you have observed in this exercise, complete the following sentences.

When two complete sentences are connected by a subordinator and the subordinating word is the first word in the sentence, a comma

_____ needed. If the subordinating word occurs in the middle of
(is/is not)

the sentence, a comma _____ needed.
(is/is not)

PAIRED EXERCISE

With a classmate, reread the Lupri article on pages 22 and 23 — and decide together what types of sentences the author used. Do this activity with your own writing. Do you need to improve your sen-tence variety?

2

LANGUAGE AND COMMUNICATING

ENCOUNTERING A DIFFERENT CULTURE

British.
Précis = condense material to ⅓
maintain author's point of view
No copying allowed - only key words

PREREADING ACTIVITIES

1. In groups, recount your first experience in another country. What was the first day like? The first week? How did you feel after a month?

2. What are some of the major differences between Canadian culture and that of your native country?

3. Discuss specific methods that have helped you adapt to life in Canada. Which aspects of life here are still problematic for you?

Chapter = family types

Between Two Worlds

the interior or central part of point
Middle (position)

Summary → more North American
Condense material to 50%, Be objective
Analyze author's main idea
No copying allowed - only key words

> *Leaving your own culture behind to come and live in the midst of a new one causes stress in many immigrant families. Carolyn Parrish looks at how these strains can cause trouble in the best of families.*

destroyed

Families, our most basic social unit, can be devastated by the immigration process — sometimes beyond repair. Although Canada needs immigrants, the social services required to help them adjust to the painful uprooting from one culture to the next, are in short supply.

5

Practically all immigrants suffer from the shock of new customs, language difficulties, economic concerns and even the weather. This shock is usually more severe among immigrant women; they are often left isolated, ignored, and neglected.

Some of the problems of these women were highlighted at a conference on immigrant women in 1981. Several problems emerged:

10

explode
exploded (adj): showing the parts / separated but incorrect to each other
the relationship
to make productive use of

- Immigrant women are exploited as cheap, unskilled or semi-skilled labour;

- Immigrant women have inadequate access to language training;

- Immigrant women have poor opportunities for education and employment training that would release them from poorly paid jobs in the garment and service industries.

At the conference, then Minister of State for Multiculturalism, James Fleming, called immigrant women, "Canada's silent heroines." He went on to say, "Surely it's as important for the Greek woman to learn English so that she can escape a low-paying, dead-end job and communicate with her children, as it is for her husband."

Little has changed since 1981. How does it feel to be isolated by language in a foreign culture? One woman answers for many: "When I first came here eight years ago, I knew 'yes' and 'no.' Whenever I'd go into a store, there would be a tight knot inside me in case I could not handle the exchange with the person serving me. I remember once having to fill in a government form — 'yes,' 'no,' 'fill in the box,' 'leave this blank' — I didn't understand even the simplest thing. I became so confused I tore up the form and ran out crying.

"I think that big knot inside me dominated my whole life. And to make it worse, people here tend to shout at you to get you to understand English."

It's hard to break out of the isolation caused by language. Unless a woman is "destined for the labour market" she can't get free language instruction in English or French. A job counsellor who sees she is headed for work in textile or plastics factories isn't required to direct her into language training — or encourage it.

In many of the cultures that our immigrant women come from, females stay home to take care of the family. Many have very little formal education even in their own language, which compounds their problems.

Immigrant women who continue the stay-at-home role become more isolated as their husbands and children become involved in the new culture. One young boy talks about this isolation: "My mother used to cry a lot back then. Every time, when I'd come home from school, she'd be putting my lunch on the table and she'd be crying and crying."

It may not be a lot better for the immigrant women who do go outside the home to work. Exhausting factory or cleaning jobs are then added to housework and child care. In many immigrant families, the males would never dream of helping with household chores. Some women cope with the strain through relationships with other female relatives. Others are considered high risks for emotional problems, illnesses, and depression.

One production-line worker expresses her frustration through an interpreter: "I'm angry. Sometimes I think I am angry all the time. And this anger goes into my bones and my muscles and my hair and my teeth. Sometimes, I don't feel like anything more than one big ball of anger." 60

In the past five years, women have gone a long way in setting up volunteer groups to help one another. One human rights worker described a woman to whom she was trying to teach 'survival English' for medical needs, shopping, transportation, and banking. 65

"She was extremely isolated — very close to a nervous breakdown. When she found out I understood Spanish she talked without stopping. Talking and talking, just to be able to say things she had never said before. I'll never forget her. I was just like a mirror for her own soul. And there are so many like her." 70

Immigrant women also suffer through their children. "I had a will to make something of our lives here when I came from Holland. But when I used to see my eldest son sitting on the corner without any friends or anything to do, his eyes just dead, that hurt me very much and made me want to return home." 75

Another mother sums up the problems children face in immigrant families: "You're neither here nor there. You want the very best for your children. But the culture and the values seem different here. Sometimes you feel you must resist. And your children are caught between two worlds." 80

Then there's prejudice. One black girl recalls the agony of casting for the school Christmas pageant. "I wanted so badly to be picked. And then this teacher came by and she nearly picked me and this nun who was with her said, 'Can you imagine an angel that colour?' " Felicia was ten years old but she already understood what being an immigrant, and part of a visible minority, was all about. 85

Children of immigrants are caught between a natural faithfulness to parents and their original culture, and peer pressure and a desire to be part of the new culture. No child wants to be different. To stand out is torture. Often, children try to hide the fact that their parents are immigrants, because in fights and disagreements this information can be used to insult them. Name-calling has long been a weapon of the young and immature. 90

Although many ethnic groups encourage the retention of language and custom, attending hours of heritage language classes after school and on weekends often builds resentment in children. "Now, since I was about eleven, I get a bit embarrassed sometimes. It's hard always to be so different from other kids." 95

An allegiance to two cultures becomes even more difficult as children enter the normal struggles of adolescence. All teens need to 100 be accepted by their peers and long to be one of the crowd. As one immigrant teen points out, it isn't always easy.

equal esp. one belonging to the same social group (age, grade, or status)

"I'm eighteen years old and I can't do anything. I can't go out. If I do I have to lie about it. I have to be home by 7:00 or 7:30. I'm not enjoying life and my friends think I'm weird. My parents don't understand — just because you're out late doesn't mean you're doing anything wrong." 105

Lilia, a seventeen-year-old Portuguese girl, sums up the situation well. "The big problem for my parents is that they are neither there nor here. The country they remember must have changed since they left, but they don't understand this. They have never really gotten used to being in Canada either. They don't belong anywhere any more." 110

Many immigrant parents see the Canadian culture as working to erode time-honoured family values — values that may even be outdated in their country of origin. In Greece and Portugal, some girls aren't allowed to date, or even speak to, men before they marry. Father is the unquestioned authority, and there is a strong double standard of morality for daughters, which has been carried into these families here today. A skirt one centimetre above the knee can cause a family war: 115 120

"In the summer here lots of kids wear halters and culottes and sensible, cool clothes like that to school. But my father has a fit and tells me 'nice girls don't go to school dressed like that. Girls back home don't dress like that.' " 125

*flagrant (conspicuously offensive.
flagrantly: so obviously inconsistent with what is right or proper as to appear to be a flouting of law or morality*

In a society that flagrantly advertises sexuality, the "good times" with alcohol and the freedom to do as you please, the children of immigrants are involved in a struggle that not only spans two generations, but is further divided by two cultures. Even when immigrant parents give in, other problems remain. 130

One woman remembers being one of only two or three Chinese youngsters in her school. She recalls being treated as "something rare and special." Although she was outgoing and was accepted into a lot of social groups, none of the boys could bring themselves to take her to the prom. What would their parents have said? 135

Canada has become a lot more progressive and accepting in recent years. However, there's still a long way to go before all immigrants settle in without being subjected to culture shock. We have to aim for what four-year-old Mark has found. "I'm the best hockey player in the neighbourhood," he says. "So, I must be Canadian now." 140

READING AND THINKING STRATEGIES

DISCUSSION ACTIVITIES
Analysis and Conclusions

1. Why do immigrant women often have a harder time adapting to a new country than men or children? Why have they been called "Canada's silent heroines"? In what ways do they cope with these problems?
2. What role does language acquisition play in cultural adaptation? Is it important? Why/why not?
3. List some examples of stressful situations undergone by immigrant children, both within and outside the family.

Writing and Point of View

1. Carolyn Parrish reports on the stresses involved in cultural adaptation. She does not give her opinions or make suggestions. Why not? For whom was this article originally written?
2. Parrish uses many quotes from immigrant women and children. Find them in the article. How do quotes affect you as a reader? Why do you think she has included so many?
3. Why do you think Parrish chose to end the essay with a quote from four-year-old Mark? What is the intended effect of his statement?

Personal Response and Evaluation

1. Do you know any families who have had to completely change their lifestyles when they moved to Canada? How has the change affected them?
2. What can women do to create better lives for themselves and their families in Canada?
3. Carolyn Parrish chose to focus mainly on immigrant women and their children. Why do you think she focused on these two groups? What do you think she hoped would happen after people read this article?

RESPONSE PARAGRAPH

After you have read the article, write a paragraph telling how the information affected you. Think about the ways in which your experiences are similar or different from those of the women and children quoted. What particular ideas from the article will you remember?

Share your paragraph with your classmates. As a group, what do you think you can learn from the article?

JOURNAL WRITING

After reading about immigrants' experiences, think about your own experiences in adapting to Canadian culture and learning English. Close your eyes and think about the word *English*. What thoughts come to your mind? Think about the word *future*. When you are ready, write down your thoughts. Do not worry about writing complete, grammatically correct sentences. Write, and the writing itself will help you become a better writer.

WRITING STRATEGIES

ESSAY STRATEGIES

The Journalistic Approach to Writing

Carolyn Parrish wrote the article about stresses involved in immigration for a newsmagazine for teenagers. She uses techniques that have been used by journalists for many years to get information about their subject and to write effective, communicative stories. Most journalists use the *who, what, where, when, why, how* method. They ask themselves these questions:

Who is involved?

What is happening or has happened?

Where is the event occurring?

When did it happen?

Why did it happen?

How will it affect the people or things involved?

Some journalists try to answer in short form as many of these questions as possible in their first paragraph, which they call the *lead paragraph*. The next paragraphs add details and support for the lead. Other journalists answer in the lead paragraph only as many questions as they think will make the reader interested in reading further. They answer the rest of the questions during the course of the article. Of course, journalists cannot always find all the answers, but they give as much support and detail as possible to keep their writing interesting, lively, and informative.

EXERCISES

1. Reread the Parrish article to find the answers to Who? What? Where? When? Why? and How? How did she add details and support?

2. Reread the Chan essay on pages 3 to 6 to find the answers to the same questions. How did he add details and support throughout the essay?

3. Reread one of your own essays, noticing which of these questions you answered and which you did not. Try adding answers to some of the questions you did not write about in your earlier draft. Decide whether answering these questions improves your essay or makes it less effective.

ESSAY FORM
Understanding the Essay Question

When you read an essay question, first ask yourself: *What is the subject of the question?* Then reread the question several times, thinking about what the question is asking. Make sure you understand all the vocabulary. Focus on the subject, and decide if you have enough ideas about it to write an essay.

What is the essay asking you to do? Usually the essay question itself suggests a particular way for you to develop your ideas. The words in the essay questions may ask you to *narrate, describe, compare,* or *classify.* Each of these is a slightly different job or method of development for you as a writer.

To *narrate* is to tell a story, to re-create a story with characters, setting or place, and plot. Narration usually includes some description and some dialogue or conversation between people.

To *describe* means to tell in a word picture how something or someone appeared. As a writer, you should keep in mind all the senses in your description — sight, sound, smell, touch, and taste.

To *compare* means to look at two or more ideas, things, or events to point out what is similar and what is different about them. To *contrast* means to look only for the differences.

To *analyze* means to break down an idea, a thing, or an event into its separate parts.

To *explain* means to discuss and analyze the step-by-step sequence in which something occurred. This sequence is also called a cause-and-effect relationship because it traces a succession of events (the cause) that led to a particular situation (the effect).

To *argue* means to use reasons to support or prove that something is true or false, has value or not, or ought to be done or not. As part of your argument, you may include comparison, description, narration, and analysis.

To *classify* means to divide a large set of items into smaller groups and to identify the qualities of each group. For example, you can divide the large set of *trees* into smaller groups: *deciduous* (trees that lose their leaves) and *evergreen* (trees that are green throughout the year).

EXERCISES

1. Look at the "Suggestions for Writing" that follow. With a partner, discuss what the subject of each question is and what the essay question is asking you to do.

2. Share an essay that you have written this semester with a partner. Together, discuss the subject of the essay and the way you have chosen to write about it.

3. As a group, reread the Parrish selection and other selections in the book. Keep in mind that many writers use a combination of methods of development in their writing. Decide which method or combination of methods the authors used.

SUGGESTIONS FOR WRITING

One of the most important parts of writing comes before you even put your pen to paper. It occurs when you are thinking about what you are going to write. Be sure to allow yourself some time to think before you write. Try "Brainstorming with a Partner" below to help you get started.

Choose one of the following topics to write about. You may find it useful to look at your journal or to brainstorm before you start writing.

1. Tell a story about someone who has had problems learning English or getting used to living in a new country. What has this person learned from facing these problems?

2. Compare your experience living in a new country with the experiences discussed in the Parrish article. Use the article for information.

3. Many people say that learning a new language is easier for children than it is for adults. Do you agree or disagree? Explain your point of view, telling about yourself and people you have known or read about. Try to convince your audience.

4. Write an essay in which you compare your first language with English. What are some of the similarities and differences? Be sure to mention word order, plurals, and questions.

5. Suggest to your readers ways to adjust to living in a different culture, using examples from your own experiences.

GETTING STARTED
Brainstorming with a Partner

One technique that writers use to get started writing essays, stories, or papers is brainstorming, as described on pages 52 and 53. Another related technique is brainstorming with a partner. Discuss with a classmate some of the writing topics that you are considering. Once you have each decided on a topic, ask each other the questions listed on page 74 and any others that relate to your particular topics. Write down ideas together for either partner's topic. Jot down words, phrases, or whole ideas that occur to the two of you as you talk. Brainstorm until you have filled a page with ideas that you have developed together. At that point, you have enough to begin your writing. When you are finished, share what you have written with your partner.

A Student Essay

English is a difficult language for me to learn, but I have to keep it up. I have found many difficulties in learning English such as the English spelling system, pronunciation, vocabulary and essay writing. However, I have to keep learning English if I want to reach my goal. Besides that, English is a good language to learn.

In order to reach my goal, I have to keep learning English because I live in Canada where most people speak English. Besides that the English language is one of the two official languages in Canada. Therefore, I keep learning English in order to get an office job in Canada. To get an office job, I have to begin with learning English before I take any other courses which can help me attain this.

As an international language, there are many advantages to learning English. For example when I visit another country, I will not have to worry about what language I should use. Everywhere I go, I can communicate in English since it is an international language. Moreover, if I had the ability to speak and write English when I was living in Indonesia, I could have had a higher salary than I used to earn. Nevertheless, I still have many difficulties in learning English.

The English spelling system is not easy to learn. I have to memorize a group of letters representing an English word. It is hard to guess how the English words are spelled. Sometimes there is more than one consonant or vowel in one word. For example the word 'professor,' I have to remember that there are two consonants, 's,' in it. Sometimes I forget how to spell it; instead I put one consonant 's' and two consonants, 'f.' Besides that, English spelling does not consistently represent sounds. For example, 'hear' sounds like 'fear,' but 'bear' sounds like 'fair.' Moreover, 'heard' differs from 'beard.'

Pronunciation is also a problem for me in learning English. It is hard for me to know where the stress is. Should I use the stress on the first syllable or the second syllable? Sometimes I find a real difficulty in understanding from native speakers because of my pronunciation. It might sound strange to them even though the word is used every day. For example, one day a Canadian friend invited me to come over to her house, and I told her that I would come over when she was not busy. It took a while for her to figure out what I was trying to say with the word 'busy.' Another example was when I was trying to order orange juice. The waitress did not understand what I ordered. She said, "I do not understand what you are saying." I was frustrated because I tried my best to pronounce 'orange,' but the waitress could not understand me.

Vocabulary is difficult because so many English words seem to come from Latin or French which I do not understand either. Besides that many words have different meanings. Sometimes it is hard for me to look for the meaning that best fits the context in which the word is used. It is impossible to memorize all the vocabulary and the meanings. Moreover, difficult vocabulary can affect my understanding in reading comprehension. Because of many new words in a story, sometimes I do not understand the content.

Writing an essay is the most difficult endeavour. It is because I have to deal with almost all the English problems. I have to think about the English grammar, spelling, and vocabulary I should use in my essay; also, I have to think about the writing organization. On top of that, I have to get the idea of what I am going to write about. Sometimes I want to quit going to school because of the English writing. I guess it is because I do not have the talent to be a writer. If I only had to express myself on a piece of paper without worrying about the organization, it might not be so bad. However, it is very hard for me to find good sentences to link ideas.

I have to keep learning English in order to reach my goal. Besides that, English is a good language to learn because it is already unsurpassed in international use. That's why I should keep learning English even though I find many difficulties in learning it.

Leliana Lavis

REVISING

With a partner, discuss Leliana Lavis' first draft, asking the following questions.

1. What specific words or ideas in the first paragraph make you want to read more?

2. What is the main idea that holds together the entire piece of writing?

3. What are the supporting details — facts, observations, and experiences that support the main points?

4. What in the final paragraph tells you as a reader that the piece of writing is complete?

5. What one idea will remain with you after reading this essay? Why did you choose this particular idea?

When you finish discussing Lavis' essay, reread your own essay. Keep in mind that your writing is not in its final form. With your partner, discuss your writing using the same five questions you used when discussing Lavis' essay. Then rewrite your essay, keeping your partner's suggestions in mind. Share your revision with your partner.

EDITING STRATEGIES

VOCABULARY DEVELOPMENT

in

Review the article "Between Two Worlds," noting how often the preposition *in* is used. This exercise will help you become familiar with the use of *in* in place expressions. Two examples have been chosen from the article.

in textile or plastics factories

in Canada

These examples show that *in* is used to give the feeling of being inside or within something, whether it be a country, a city, an apartment, or a box. We use the following expressions:

in class	in the fish tank
in a factory	in the car
in a small boat	(*but not* in the floor)

What is the difference in meaning between "*in* the refrigerator" and "*on* the refrigerator"? Between "*in* the desk" and "*on* the desk"?

A few special expressions involving transportation use *on*:

on the train

on the bus

on the plane
on the ship

EXERCISE

Fill in the blanks in the following sentences with either *in* or *on*.

1. Many of the women live ___in___ large Canadian cities, where they work ___in___ factories or ___in___ underheated buildings.

2. Every morning the worker gets ___on___ the bus to go to work ___in___ a factory where she gets minimum wage.

3. Some of the immigrants' children spend time ___on___ street corners when they aren't ___in___ school.

4. An immigrant woman who is not employed will often stay ___in___ her home rather than travel alone ___on___ a bus downtown.

5. The children of immigrants are encouraged to stay ___in___ school, because their parents want them to have high-paying jobs when they graduate, rather than working ___in___ other people's homes or ___in___ factories.

make and *do*

The words *make* and *do* have very special uses in English. As you read the following paragraph, underline *make* and *do* each time they appear, along with the words that directly follow them. The first three have been done for you.

When Lilia gets home from school, she helps her mother <u>do the cooking</u>. They <u>make an effort</u> to <u>make a meal</u> that everyone will enjoy. Usually it takes a while to <u>make dinner</u>, but at other times they <u>make do</u> with leftovers. After dinner, Lilia <u>does the dishes</u>. They <u>do without</u> television so that Lilia can begin to <u>do her homework</u> early. Lilia's mother tries to <u>make time</u> to <u>do some housework</u> after dinner, but she usually has to wait for the weekend. Then she and Lilia will <u>do the wash</u> at the laundromat. They will also <u>do all the floors</u>; they mop the kitchen and the bathroom and vacuum the living room and the bedrooms. Soon it is Monday morning again. When the alarm rings, they get out of bed, do a few exercises, <u>make their beds</u>, and make breakfast. Then Lilia rushes off to school and her mother rushes to work; as usual, they both always try to do their best.

Make a list of the *make* and *do* phrases you underlined. The first three have been done for you.

Make	*Do*
make an effort	do the cooking
	wash + dry.
make a meal *something that is inadequate*	*does the dishes*
	turn it off
make dinner	*do without television*
make do with leftovers	*do her homework*
make time = find time *Create some time*	*do some housework*
make their beds	*do the wash*
	do all the floors
	do a few exercise
	do their best.

to make do = manage, something, get by

Write five sentences using *make* and *do* to describe things that you typically do at home.

Note: *Homework* and *housework* are always singular, without a final *s*:

I do my homework for all my classes after I finish dinner.

He does all his housework on Saturday.

Fill in the blanks in the following sentences with *homework* or *housework*.

Homework is schoolwork, assignments for classes.

Housework is cleaning work done in a person's home.

Now answer these questions, using *make* and *do*.

1. In your family, who usually makes dinner?
2. Who usually does the dishes?

3. What time of day is best for you to do your homework?

4. Do you prefer to do your homework in a quiet atmosphere or with the radio or television playing?

5. Before you leave the house for school, do you usually have enough time to make breakfast? To do the dishes? To make your bed? To do exercises? To do housework? To do homework?

COMMONLY CONFUSED WORDS

they're/there/their

This exercise focuses on words that are often confused in writing because they are spelled differently but pronounced the same. These words are called *homonyms*. Looking at these words in context should help you understand how they are used.

> There *are many reasons why immigrant women find life in Canada difficult.* They're *afraid to talk to new people because of* their *English. They do not realize that* they're *not alone; many people in Canada are learning English as* their *second language.*

Examining this paragraph should help you complete the following definitions.

___They're___ means "they are."

___their___ means "belonging to them."

___there___ means "in that place or at that point."

Fill in the blanks in the following sentence with *they're, there,* or *their.*

Lilia and her friends would like to succeed in ___their___ education

so ___they're___ trying very hard, but ___there___ are many problems and responsibilities that are making it hard for them.

Now write sentences of your own using each of these words.

___Although they've received the student loading,___
___there are still many fanacial prombles in___
___their living.___

MECHANICS
Plurals

One common problem in editing writing and looking for surface errors is recognizing plural forms. Test your knowledge of plurals in the next paragraph by circling and correcting each singular noun that should really be a plural. There are nineteen missing plurals. Can you find them all?

Many man, woman, and child have left their homeland to come to Canada. They have had to leave their parent, friend, and family behind. When these person arrived, they suffered many crisis: often they found their life were difficult. They had to attend class to learn the new language, and they usually had to move to overcrowded city in order to get job opportunity. Traditionally, person have come to Canada from country all over the world. Despite the many difficulty of adjusting, these immigrant give a vitality to the country, and the country offers many possibility to these newcomer.

Turn to page 325 to check your answers. If you make more than two mistakes, review the following rules.

regular plurals

The regular plural of a word is usually formed by adding an *s* to the singular form. The article "Between Two Worlds" has many examples of regular plurals.

Singular	*Plural*
immigrant	immigrants
custom	customs
job	jobs

Can you find three more examples of regular plurals in the article? List them with the singular forms on the left.

_____parent_____   _____parents_____

friend   _friends_

new comer   _new comers_

special plurals

Many words follow special rules to form their plurals.

Words that end in a consonant (*b, c, d, f, g,* etc.) plus *y* form their plurals by changing the *y* to *i* and adding *-es.*

body	bodies
country	countries
baby	_badies_
library	_libraries_
city	_cities_
family	_families_

Words that end in a vowel (*a, e, i, o, u*) plus *y* form their plurals by adding *-s.*

journey	journeys
attorney	_attorneys_
ashtray	_ashtrays_
boy	_boys_
highway	_highways_

Words that end in *s, sh, ch, ss, zz,* or *x* usually form their plurals by adding *-es.*

plus	pluses	mattress	_mattresses_
brush	brushes	wish	_wishes_
patch	patches	watch	_watches_
class	classes	business	_businesses_

| fizz | fizzes | buzz | *buzzes* |
| wax | waxes | tax | *taxes* |

Words that end in one *z* usually double the *z* and add -*es*.

| quiz | quizzes | whiz | *whizzes* |

Words that end in *o* usually form their plurals by adding -*es*.

| tomato | tomatoes | hero | *heroes* |
| veto | vetoes | mosquito | *mosquitoes* |

Many words that end in *f* or *fe* form their plurals by changing the *f* to *v* and adding -*es*.

life	lives	housewife	*housewifes*
knife	knives	yourself	*yourselves*
leaf	leaves	wolf	*wolves*
calf	calves	half	*halves*

There are some exceptions to this rule, however.

| roof | roofs | *chief* | *chiefs* |
| belief | beliefs | *chef* | *chefs* |

irregular plurals

—vowel shifts

* Indo-European simplification

Some words have irregular plurals. This means that the plurals have special forms and do not use the regular -*s* form we have already learned. Here are some examples of irregular plurals:

man	men	woman	women
child	children	foot	feet
tooth	teeth	goose	geese
mouse	mice	ox	oxen

Here are some other words with special plurals:

datum   data

Singular	Plural
crisis	crises (crucial turning point in politics, story, play, or everyday life)
criterion	criteria (standard or rule to judge something by)
axis	axes (fixed or centre line about which things are arranged, as in a graph or on a globe)
medium	media (means or agency; instrument of communication)

false plurals

Some words that end in *s* are not plural. These words are treated as singular in sentences. They are followed by the singular form of the verb, as you can see in the following examples.

news   No news is good news.
             The news is on television at six o'clock.

me soes
measles   Measles is a very contagious disease, and many children get sick from it.

mumps   Even though it is usually not a serious sickness for children, mumps is often dangerous for adult males.

uninflected plurals

There are also a few words, mostly the names of animals, for which the plural form is the same as the singular form.

trout salmon tuna

sheep   One sheep always gets lost from the flock.
            There are millions of sheep in New Zealand.

fish   The shiny silver fish is swimming downstream.
         They saw hundreds of fish in the aquarium.

deer   The deer is a very graceful animal.
         Many deer live in the woods.

moose   The moose is a large animal that looks like a deer.
           Moose have large antlers.

EXERCISE

In the following paragraph there are nineteen missing plurals. Using what you have just practised, make the corrections.

Many family of young man and woman and sometimes even child from many country all over the world who are living in and trying to adapt to the city of Canada. At first, they get lost trying to find bus that will take them to job, library, movie, and school They have many difficulty communicating with their new neighbours Eventually, though, their life begin to make sense again. The successful one start their own business make new friend find new responsibility and develop new strategy for living in their new country.

EDITING PRACTICE

The following piece of writing would be easier to read if it were divided into sentences and paragraphs. Read it with a classmate and mark where new sentences should begin and where it should be divided into a second paragraph. Check your answers on page 326. As a second step, create your own compound and complex sentences, as described on pages 64 and 65 to help you practice sentence variety.

One part of learning a new language involves learning to use the language with others. Recently, a researcher in the way people learn languages wrote that if people want to learn how to talk in a second language, they should not be afraid to make mistakes, they should make contact with speakers of the new language, they should ask for corrections, and they should memorize dialogues if students want to learn to read, they should read something every day they should read things that are familiar they should look for meaning from the context without always looking at the dictionary to gain confidence, they should start by reading books at the beginner's level.

PAIRED EXERCISE

After reading and editing this paragraph about language learning, write an essay with a partner in which you describe which strategies mentioned in the paragraph would help immigrants gain in understanding of English. Include in your essay why you think these strategies would be helpful for students in particular, and which of them have been useful to you in learning English.

GRAMMAR STRATEGIES

THE PRESENT PERFECT TENSE

Examine the following sample sentences. Then fill in the blanks in the paragraph and sentences that follow.

She has not missed a day of school since she began.

She rarely goes out in the evening with friends and has only gone to a movie once in the last six months.

Lilia has been at the school for three years. It has taken her mother several years to get accustomed to the new lifestyle.

In the present perfect tense, the word __has__ follows the subject *she*.
(has/have)

The word __has__ follows the subject *it*. Since we know that *it* is
(has/have)

third person singular, we can assume that *he* is followed by the word

__has__. The third person plural, *they*, is followed by
(has/have)

the word __have__. The third person plural, *they*, is followed by
(has/have)

the word __have__.
(has/have)

To make the present perfect tense negative, add *not* between *have* or *has* and the past participle.

She has __not__ missed a day of school.

You have __not__ looked at the mail.

Adverbs such as *always, never,* or *rarely* belong between *have* or

has and the __noun, verb__.

She has never missed a day of school.
It has never snowed in Toronto in July.

To form a question, place *have* or *has* in front of the ___noun___.

Has she missed any days of school?
Have they been to Quebec?

The present perfect tense has two uses. The first is to embrace the past, the present, and the future all at once.

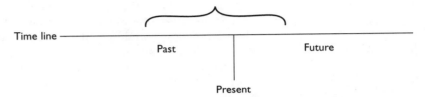

I have started each day in the same manner for the past eighty years.

The second use is to indicate the indefinite past. The present perfect tense is used in this case when the specific time when something occurred is not important; what is important is that it ever occurred at all.

They have learned to speak three languages fluently.

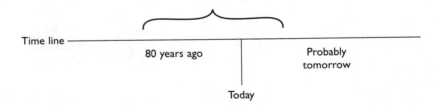

It does not matter when we heard this. If when we heard it is important, we use the past tense:

She played the piano last week.

Read the following dialogue, observing how the present perfect tense is used.

AN INTERVIEW WITH A SUCCESSFUL STUDENT

TEACHER: I noticed that your grades have improved recently and that you have become a more successful student. What have you learned that you think would help other students?

STUDENT: You're right. I have changed. When I think about it, I guess I have changed in three main ways.

TEACHER: What are they?

STUDENT: When I first came here, I used to look up every word that I didn't know in the dictionary. Many times I didn't understand the dictionary meaning, and even if I did, I would forget the new words very fast. Now I have learned to read the next few words or sentences before I go to the dictionary. I have found that sometimes I can figure out the word from the context of the rest of what I am reading.

TEACHER: That's interesting. How else have you changed?

STUDENT: At first, I was afraid to talk to my teachers when I had a problem. I thought that it was my fault and that they would think that I wasn't intelligent.

TEACHER: Oh.

STUDENT: I have discovered that in college in Canada teachers expect students to ask questions. In fact, I have learned a lot from asking questions. I also have gotten to know some of my professors too. I have also told a couple of professors that they were speaking a little fast for me to understand them. At first, I was nervous about this because I thought that they would get annoyed. But they didn't. One even thanked me for telling her, and she has begun to speak a little slower.

TEACHER: That sounds like good advice. What else have you learned that has helped you become more successful in college?

STUDENT: Well, I always used to study alone. Then one of my teachers suggested that a small group of us meet as a study group. At first, I didn't like it, and I didn't say much. But now I always try to say at least something each time we meet. Not only that, but I have discovered that I learn from listening and talking to other students.

TEACHER: Your advice sounds very important. I think that other students will learn from you.

STUDENT: I hope so. These things have made a big difference for me.

EXERCISES

1. Reread this interview, underlining each use of the present perfect tense. Decide with a classmate why that tense was used in each instance.

2. Discuss the following questions.

   a. What changes has the student made that have affected his college success?

   b. How does this student's experience in college compare with your own?

   c. What changes have you made in your own learning strategies that have helped you achieve success?

CONTRASTING TENSES

The Simple Present and the Present Perfect

Decide which tense you prefer in each of the following sentences.

1. She _feels_ angry all the time but _hasn't expressed_ her feelings openly.
   (feel)   (not express)

2. Even those who _are_ in the factory with her all day long _does not_ _has not done_
   (be)   (not do)

   understand the scope of the problems linked to her troubles

   learning English because she _does not express_ her frustration.
   (not express)

3. She _faces_ _always_ prejudice at school, which _makes_ her _wary_ _suspicious_ of friend-
   (face)   (make)   _untrustic_

   ships with both peers and teachers.

4. No child _wants_ to be different, so immigrant children often
   (want)

   hides the fact that their families _comes_ from elsewhere.
   (hide)   (come)

5. Although Mark _comes_ from elsewhere, he says his hockey
   (come)

   playing skill _do make_ _has made_ him a "true Canadian."
   (make)

describe _descripe_

The Present Continuous and the Present Perfect

Decide which tense you prefer in each of the following sentences.

1. Lilia's mother _is suffering_ from the shock of new customs, although
   (suffer)

   she _has tried_ to adjust.
   (try)

2. Lilia _has been_ at the high school for three years, and she _works_ hard
   (be)   *(work)*

   at all her subjects.

3. She _has felt_ angry since her first day on the job, and she _has isolated_
   (feel)   *(isolate)*

   herself from others.

4. Many immigrants _have found_ life in Canada to be too permissive; they
   (find)

   are trying to instil old-world values in their children.
   (try)

5. Because many immigrant women do not socialize, they _haven't met_
                                                       (meet, not)

   their neighbours, many of whom _are learning_ to cope with Canadian
                                   (learn)

   language and customs as well.

EXERCISE

Using the following sentence to begin your writing, write a paragraph about your own experiences learning English.

   I have studied English for _____ years, and I have found a few strategies that have helped me to improve.

SUCCEEDING IN SCHOOL

PREREADING ACTIVITIES

1. Spend about five minutes writing the answer to the question, "What is a Canadian?" Discuss your answers in class.
2. As a class, talk about your experiences with teachers in Canada and in any other country in which you have attended school. Discuss some of the differences in teaching styles that you have observed.
3. In a group, make a list of the characteristics that teachers should have to help their students to learn. If there was disagreement in your group, explain how you resolved the disagreement.

Adjusting to School in Canada

Iris Thomson-Glen has been the International Counsellor at Camosun College in Victoria, B.C., for many years. Among her duties, she helps students adapt to life in Canada and learn to understand and to cope with different patterns of behaviour in Canadian educational institutions.

"What are the classes like?" "What will the teacher expect of me?" These are typical questions new international students ask about attending a new college or university in Canada.

When international students first come to study in Canada they are often surprised by the variety of Canadian classroom settings. Formal lecture halls are common in universities, while colleges often offer smaller classes, labs, seminars, and tutorials. Because students attending colleges in Canada generally have smaller classes than in universities, they often have closer and more informal relationships with their instructors.

5

10

Different types of classrooms also suggest different types of teaching and learning styles. Teachers of seminars will have different expectations of students than those that lecture. Students are expected to participate actively in small seminars rather than mainly listen and notetake passively as they do in large lectures. 15

Students using an active style of learning usually ask questions and participate in class discussions. It is not considered rude to question the teacher regarding ideas raised in class. International students can sometimes find this a new and challenging aspect of classroom behaviour. Students who are able to adapt appropriately 20 to both active and passive styles of learning will be able to adjust to all types of classroom environments.

International students often say they want to improve in their courses but sometimes are not sure just how to do that. Being respectful to the teacher and smiling politely may feel appropriate 25 but will not let the teachers really know how they can help. Students in Canada are expected to ask for clarification and help, either during class time or office hours.

The relationship between students and their teachers, instructors or professors will vary depending upon the person, the situa- 30 tion, and the learning environment. In other words, some teachers will be comfortable with students calling them by their first names, while others will expect them to use a title like "Doctor," "Mr.," "Ms.," or even "Professor." In large classes there is most likely to be a more formal relationship where the teacher does not know stu- 35 dents by their first names and may or may not expect questions in class. It all depends on the person and the learning situation. There are, therefore, a variety of styles of teaching as well as classroom settings. It is important to learn what your teacher expects in each specific class. 40

While teachers in Canada play a big part in their students' education, it is expected as elsewhere that students also take on major responsibility for their own learning. This means working on homework assignments, doing extra work in areas that they have difficulty with, and, again, being active learners. Active learners not only 45 participate in classroom discussions, but they also take notes in class, meet with their teachers in their office hours, participate in study skills classes, and, in short, do everything they can to improve their ability.

It can take a period of adjustment to adapt to a new college or 50 university. By taking some time to learn *how* to learn in the Canadian classroom, students' efforts will be rewarded by academic achievements.

READING AND THINKING STRATEGIES

DISCUSSION ACTIVITIES

Analysis and Conclusions

1. What are the two questions students commonly ask? What are the answers Thomson-Glen provides?

2. From your own observation, what behaviours do teachers in Canada seem to value in students? What does this tell you about the culture in Canada? From your observation, what behaviours do teachers in other countries in which you have studied value in students? What does this tell you about the culture in that country?

3. In many classrooms in Canada today, the teacher is from one culture and the students are from many different cultures and countries. What effects might this have on the classroom? What suggestions do you have to help people in the classroom get to know each other better?

Writing and Point of View

1. In which paragraphs does Thomson-Glen answer each of the two questions she poses in the introduction?

2. What audience do you think Thomson-Glen is writing this for? If you were writing this to help teachers in Canada understand students from different cultures, what changes would you make?

3. What is Thomson-Glen's point of view about student-teacher relationships? Does she state this point of view? Why do you think this is so? What is the purpose of this piece of writing?

Personal Response and Evaluation

1. Thomson-Glen states that Canadian teachers often prefer informal relationships with their students. Have you found this to be true? If so, why do you think this is the case?

2. Thomson-Glen implies that students from some cultures have difficulty asking questions in class. Have you found this to be true? If so, what can these students do so that their teachers know that they are interested and involved in the class?

3. The words of a language are only part of what you learn when you live in a new country and learn a new language. What cultural differences have you observed?

GROUP ACTIVITY

After reading and discussing the Thomson-Glen article, as a group project, make a list of suggestions that will help a student become successful in an educational institution in Canada. When you have completed this list, you may want to share it with other classes and compare your ideas with the students in those classes.

JOURNAL WRITING

A primary reason for my success in the classroom was that I couldn't forget that schooling was changing me and separating me from the life I enjoyed before becoming a student.

RICHARD RODRIGUEZ, *Hunger of Memory*

What you write in your journal should come from inside you, from your own experiences. Here are some suggestions that may help you decide what you want to write:

Think about your experiences learning English. Think about the Rodriguez quote. Has it been easy for you? What kinds of problems have you had? Have you discovered anything about yourself by learning a new language? Do you like English? Do you feel or act differently when you speak English? When you dream, what language do you dream in?

One student wrote in his journal, "It hurts my ears to listen to English for a long time. The sounds are sharp and come by so fast that I get a headache listening to it." Have you ever felt this way?

WRITING STRATEGIES

ESSAY STRATEGIES
Specific Details

Writers use specific details to tell about experiences that they have had in their own lives, that other people they know have had, and that they have read about or seen in movies or on television. Writers often use direct quotations or detailed descriptions to make these specific details come alive to the reader.

EXERCISES

1. Reread Marty Chan's essay on pages 3 to 6, looking for specific details about his life.
2. Reread the article about immigrants' adaptations to Canadian life on pages 69 to 72, looking for specific details about their lives.

Generalizations

Writers sometimes use ideas or statements that emphasize the extensive or general qualities of a subject. These statements are broad and somewhat imprecise, so writers must be careful not to use *always* or *never* when they write such general statements. If they do, readers will think that the writers are exaggerating. When using generalizations, writers must support them with specific details to convince readers that their sweeping statements are logical and realistic.

EXERCISES

1. Reread the Thomson-Glen selection, looking for the words *often* or *generally*. Every time you find this word, underline the entire sentence. Explain why she used one of these words in each underlined sentence.
2. Reread the Parrish article on pages 69 to 72. What generalizations does Parrish make about immigrant women?
3. Reread the Lupri article on pages 22 to 23. What generalizations does Lupri make about families?
4. Reread the Chan essay on pages 3 to 6. What generalizations does Chan make in this essay?

ESSAY FORM
Using Inductive Reasoning

When writers support their ideas, they often begin with specific details and then use these details to lead to a generalization about an idea or a problem. The type of logical thinking that moves from specific details to a broad idea or belief is referred to as *inductive reasoning*.

Thomson-Glen uses specific examples of talk from students in the first paragraph to lead the reader to her generalizations in the following paragraphs.

Using Deductive Reasoning

Writers often vary their approach to ordering their ideas. They may begin with the general statement or assertion and then follow this with the specific details that support the main assertion. This type of logical thinking is referred to as *deductive reasoning*.

EXERCISES

1. Reread the Thomson-Glen article to find examples of inductive reasoning. Then find examples of deductive reasoning.
2. Review the Parrish article on pages 69 to 72 to find the specific details used to support the author's generalizations. Did she rely

on inductive or deductive reasoning in the examples you have identified?

3. Review the Chan essay on pages 3 to 6 to find the generalizations. Did Chan rely on inductive or deductive reasoning in the examples you have identified?

4. With a classmate, look at one of each other's essays and together decide where and why you used inductive or deductive reasoning.

SUGGESTIONS FOR WRITING

Before you begin to write, try brainstorming with a small group, as described below. You may also want to look in your journal for ideas. When you do begin to write, keep your audience in mind. Try to make your writing interesting to your readers as well as to yourself.

1. Write an essay titled "Student-Teacher Relationships," describing your observations attending school in a country other than Canada.

2. Write an essay comparing the schools in another country in which you were a student with the schools in Canada.

3. Write an essay in which you describe an effective teaching style and explain why you think that teaching style helps students.

4. Write an essay to other ESL students in your school who are trying to become successful in a Canadian college or university advising them what they should do to improve their chance for success.

5. Over a billion people in the world speak more than one language fluently, yet many people in Canada are reluctant to learn a second language. Based on your experience, write an essay convincing students in your college born in Canada that it is important to learn a second language.

6. Should everyone in Canada be fluent in both English and French? Give reasons for your opinion.

GETTING STARTED

Small Group Brainstorming

Meet in a small group to discuss possible topics for writing. Each person should have a notebook open to an empty page. As you are talking together, every time you hear an idea or a word that makes you think about writing your essay, jot it down. After several minutes of talking, each of you should have a list of ideas and words.

As you brainstorm in the group, ask each other *who, what, where, when, why,* and *how* questions about schools, teachers, and students. When each of you has enough ideas, read through your list of ideas and words and add any details that you will develop later in your writing.

REVISING

Writing is a personal experience, but it is also a communicative activity. One way to find out how your writing communicates your ideas is to share it with a peer. Practice doing the following revising activity using the draft of Hwan Lee's essay below. After reading Lee's essay, answer questions 1 to 5 below. When you finish discussing Lee's essay, reread your own essay with a classmate. Keep in mind that your writing is not in its final form. As you read now, you may want to make changes. You may add or delete ideas. You may want to move or remove sentences or paragraphs. You may decide that other words express your meaning better.

Ask your partner the following questions about your writing, and write the replies on a piece of paper that you will refer to when you revise.

1. What in the first paragraph makes you want to read more?
2. What specific details does the writer use?
3. What generalizations does the writer include?
4. Does the writer use inductive or deductive reasoning?
5. Does the draft have a clear ending so that a reader knows the piece is completed?
   Write your revision, and share it with your partner.

A Student Essay

Leadership in a Multicultural School

Let's suppose that you visit your new friend's home. If you are surrounded by his family, you will certainly feel quite uncomfortable at first. In this situation, whom do you think is more responsible for opening his mind first, you or his family members?

Obviously his family. Since it's his home and his family is the majority, they should try to make you feel comfortable. If all of them show indifference to you, how can you start a conversation? You will definitely expect his family to show some interest and friendliness toward you when you meet them for the first time.

Now let's think about students who speak English as a second language. Their problem is much bigger than the example that I mentioned. They are surrounded by people whom they not only don't know, but also whose language, culture, and appearance are different. In order to understand their problem, you need to put yourself in their place. Suppose that you were thrown into the middle of Korean society because your family had to move to Korea. Unfortunately, they do not speak English in Korea. Instead, they speak Korean. Suddenly you become a fool who cannot express an idea in your mind. Even if you have some explosive feelings and erudite knowledge, you cannot express them in Korean. Tearfully, you take all science subjects at school and you are branded as "a guy who is good at science but dumb at humanities."

On the street, let's suppose you want to ask the time of a stranger. Instead of saying, "excuse me," you might say "execute me," in Korean since you are not good in Korean pronunciation, and everybody will laugh at you. Even the sense of humour is different. When you laugh at something, nobody else will, and when everybody laughs at something, you won't. When you are lonely, when you are harried by day and haunted by night by the fact that you are a marginal person who can never get along with the Korean people around, you will definitely need somebody — somebody who can help you and understand you.

Each of you should be this kind of somebody in Canada for new Canadian students. You can show true leadership. How can you do this? If you know ESL students who cannot speak English properly, just approach them and ask if there is any way that you may help. You may say, "Do you want to know how to join clubs in school?" or "Do you want to play tennis with me after school?" or "Do you have any problems in your school work?" or "Is there anything about school that you want to know?" Students who have just arrived in Canada will be radiantly happy, since they will get not only practical knowledge about the school and subjects, but also friendliness, warmth, and caring from you. They will feel that they are not alone, that there are many people who will help, and they will gain more confidence.

A leader is like a conductor. When we listen to an orchestra, we feel a unity of sounds, and at the same time a variety of harmonies. The difference between the violin and the cello is not condemned, but respected. Therefore, when people from different cultures are well led and united, the harmony that they make cannot even be compared to one monotonous sound. That's why I believe that Canada has the greatest potential in the world.

Let's suppose that a conductor is also a violinist and says to the orchestra, "I am a violinist; therefore, I will only care about violins in our orchestra. I don't like other instruments. Get lost!" He is clearly forgetting his role as a conductor of the orchestra.

Native-born Canadian students! You are violinists; however, you should not forget that you are the leaders of the orchestra at the same time. You are Canadian students; however, you should not forget that you are also responsible for leading and understanding Chinese, Korean, Vietnamese, Indian, Iranian, and Japanese students since they have limited knowledge in your language and culture, since they have come here to be Canadians, and since they are going to live with you. Only the true leader can make the fantastic sound of an orchestra filled with variety and unity. If you do that, each of you is a true leader.

Hwan Lee, Korea

EDITING STRATEGIES

USE OF THE DEFINITE ARTICLE

a + million thousand hundred

the

Read the following paragraph from *Language Two* by Heidi Dulay, Marina Burt, and Stephen Krashen, noticing how the word *the* is used with country names.

> *Over a billion people in the world speak more than one language fluently. In the Philippines, for example, many people must speak three languages if they are to engage fully in their community's social affairs. They must speak the national language, Filipino; one of the eighty-seven local vernaculars; and English or Spanish. In small countries, such as the Netherlands or Israel,* foreign – Dutch language *most children are required to study at least one foreign language in school, and sometimes several. Most adults in the Netherlands speak German, French, and English in addition to Dutch. Throughout much of the world, being able to speak at least two languages, and sometimes three or four, is necessary to function in society.*

Find four country names in the excerpt you just read. Copy them in the spaces provided below. If *the* comes before the country name, copy it too. The first one has been done for you.

the Philippines ___French___

the Netherlands ___Israel___

Notice that some place names occur with *the* and some do not. *The* does not occur with names of continents:

Australia Africa
South America Europe

In general, *the* does not occur with country names:

France Turkey
Japan Chile

The sun never sets on the British Empire

unless the name of the country refers to a political union or association:

UAR
the United Arab Republic   the British Commonwealth

or unless it uses common nouns plus a proper noun with an *of* phrase:

*USSR
Union of Soviet Socialist Republics*

the Sultanate of Brunei   the Kingdom of Thailand

or unless it is plural:

the West Indies   the United States

In general, *the* does not occur with names of cities:

Montreal Paris
Bangkok Caracas

The is used for names of mountain ranges:

the Himalayas   the Alps

but it is not used with the name of a single mountain:

Grouse Mountain   Mount Everest

The is used with most bodies of water:

the Pacific Ocean   the Red Sea
the Mississippi River   *the Fraser River*

but it is not used with lakes and bays:

Lake Erie   Hudson Bay

unless they are plural:

the Great Lakes   the Finger Lakes

The is used with deserts, forests, and peninsulas:

the Sahara   the Black Forest
the Gobi Desert   the Iberian Pen<u>ins</u>ula

The is used with the names of geographic areas and points on the globe:

the Northwest   the Prairies
the South Pole   the equator

The is not used with names of languages:

~~But~~ Mandarin   Arabic   Spanish   Korean

I speak <s>the</s> Spanish <u>languages</u>

These are some of the rules for using *the* with place names and languages. Apply these rules to the following sentences. Write *the* in the space if it is needed; otherwise leave the space blank.

1. _____ English is the primary language spoken in

   _____ Australia, which is located between __*the*__

   Indian Ocean and ___*the*___ Pacific Ocean.

2. The enormous land mass extending from _____ Russia in *the*

   north to _____ Iran in ___*the*___ south and eastward via

   _____ Afghanistan and _____ Pakistan to

   __*the*__ northern India and _____ Bangladesh is pre-
   dominantly Indo-European in speech.

3. The Malayo-Polynesian language family includes languages spo-

   ken in _____ Indonesia, _____ Madagascar,

   __*the*__ Philippines, and other islands as far east as

   _____ Hawaii.

4. The Sino-Tibetan group is the second largest language family in
   number of speakers; the major languages in this group are

   _____ Burmese, dialects of _____ Chinese,

_____ Thai, and _____ Tibetan. However, the majority of speakers in this group speak _____ Mandarin and _____ Cantonese.

5. Some important language families are found on the continent of Africa and throughout ___*the*___ Middle East.

OPTIONAL EXERCISE

Use the rules you have just learned to correct the six *the* errors in the following paragraph. In some cases you will need to delete *the*, and in others you must add *the*.

My best friend moved to ~~the~~ British Columbia from the Philippines three years ago. Now she lives in ~~the~~ Vancouver and she can see Pacific Ocean and the ferry that travels to ~~the~~ Victoria each day. She has learned to speak ~~the~~ English and French and she plans to travel to ~~the~~ Quebec next year.

COMMONLY CONFUSED WORDS

advice/advise

"I would like to give you some advice *about how to act in your college classes, if you don't mind," said my new friend.*

"I would appreciate it if you would advise *me as to the best way to succeed in this school," I reassured my friend.*

Notice how *advice* and *advise* are used in the preceding sentences. Now complete the following definitions.

___*Advice*___ is a noun that refers to an opinion given to help or counsel someone.

___*Advise*___ is a verb that refers to the making recommendations to help or counsel someone.

Fill in the blanks in the following sentence with *advice* or *advise*.

1. Some people do not like to receive ___*advice*___ from strangers.

2. They believe that people who ___*advise*___ others often do not have enough experience with the situation themselves.

3. My experience is to listen to ___advice___ whenever it is sincerely

   offered, but I always maintain the right to reject the ___advice___,
   too.

4. She always likes to ___advice___ her friends, but she should listen

   to some ___advice___ herself, too.

EXERCISE

Write about the best piece of advice you have ever received and the worst piece of advice you have ever received. Explain how you made your choices.

MECHANICS
Capital Letters

When editing for surface errors, many writers have difficulty with capital letters. Test your knowledge of capital letters by trying to find the thirty missing capital letters in the following paragraph.

> Sung Hee moved to toronto from korea. She attended york university and lived in a dorm with her cousin. She began to work on saturday nights at eaton's, a big department store, and she practiced english with her customers. on sundays Sung Hee usually rented a little chevrolet from avis. Carrying a tourist book called inside toronto, she visited such famous sites as the c.n. tower and the royal ontario museum. She spent hours at the toronto public library looking at the emily carr paintings. She met tony at a midnight showing of casablanca, and last new year's they said "I do." Now she is teaching tony korean and planning to travel home to introduce him to her family.

Turn to page 326 to check your answers. If you had more than two mistakes, review the following rules.
Capital letters are used for the following terms:

1. The first word in a sentence, names of people, and the pronoun *I*:

   My friend thinks that I will be able to read Shakespeare soon.

2. Name of the months, days of the week, and holidays:

   Miguel was born in September, on the first Monday, Labour Day.

3. Names of particular places, languages, and nationalities:

The Brazilian girl in my class speaks French because she went to Le Havre High School in Montreal.

Note: Do not use capital letters if the specific names are not used:

He enjoys attending college and working in a store, but he likes to have time to visit museums and churches.

4. Titles of books, magazines, newspapers, stories, articles, films, television programs, songs, and poems:

When I saw Ida she was carrying *The Diviners*, *Chatelaine*, and *Pacific Yachting*.
She was going to see the movie *Hamlet* with her class.

5. The first word in a direct quote:

Ezra said, "You can really do a lot if you try."

6. Brand names of products:

The man bought Pampers and Pepsi-Cola at Thrifty's.

7. Names of religious and political groups, companies, corporations, and clubs:

Francoise joined the New Democratic Party when she was in university, but she became less active when she started to work for B.C. Tel because she was very busy with her job and her commitment to Unitarianism and to Greenpeace.

OPTIONAL EXERCISE

The following paragraph has thirty-three missing capital letters. Can you find them all?

when mikhail and fatima volunteered to work one afternoon in the western college post office, they were in for a surprise. in one corner, there were many boxes piled high. they found three heavy cartons of french language tapes addressed to professor maude cousteau, now of the canada council. she had left the school back in february and had moved to new brunswick. fatima accidentally opened a box filled with the lotus 1-2-3 programs needed for the college ibm computers. "mr. smith, this post office is a mess," mikhail told the postmaster. "i know it, son. we just have to get a little more organized. the mail has to go through, and we will do it. soon." mikhail and fatima left there wondering if the college mail would ever get through.

The answers are on page 326.

EDITING PRACTICE

All writers make surface errors in their first drafts. Sometimes it is difficult to find your own errors, but practice will help you improve your editing skills. Here we present a first draft that contains four subject-verb agreement errors, three preposition errors, four the errors, three plural errors, thirteen capital letter errors, and three inconsistencies in person. Find and correct these errors. Answers are on page 326.

Marie learn languages very easily. She was born on haiti and has spoken the french and the creole all her lives. Now marie also knows the english, spanish, and italian. She has a special technique that always work for her. At night you go to sleep by hypnotizing yourself as you stare at a poster of the stained-glass window of notre dame cathedral on the paris. Her sony walkman tape deck is in her head, and she listen to a different language tapes each night.

GRAMMAR STRATEGIES

POINT OF VIEW/VOICE

Everything that is written is written from someone's point of view or perspective. When we write, we must decide who will narrate or be the voice for what we write. We have several voices to choose from; we refer to these as "persons."

There are first person singular and plural, second person singular and plural, and third person singular and plural. First person singular is *I*. First person plural is *we*. Second person singular and plural is *you*. Third person singular is *she, he, it, one,* or a singular subject. Third person plural is *they* or a plural subject.

In general, first person is more personal and third person is more formal. We rarely use second person for essay writing. Whatever person is used, it is important to maintain a consistent point of view. If a writer moves from person to person in a single piece of writing, it can be confusing to the reader. In the following paragraph, the writer did not maintain a consistent person. Change the paragraph to make it consistent.

We can learn about language learning by observing yourselves. The problems that they have can probably be generalized to other language learners. Although they may think that English is more difficult to learn than another language, David Crystal, a noted linguist, tells us in his book *Linguistics* that there is no such thing as a most complex language. "A thing is more difficult to do depending on how much practice we have had at doing it and how used we are to doing similar things." Based on that statement, you can learn that if we really want to learn a new language, we must practise.

THE FUTURE TENSE

will

One of the most common ways of expressing the future and making predictions is to use *will* followed by the simple form of the verb.

	Singular	Plural
First Person	I will study	we will study
Second Person	you will study	you will study
Third Person	he will study	
	she will study	they will study
	it will study*	

*What is wrong with using *it will study?*

Here are some sample sentences using the future tense:

The teacher will *expect you to ask questions in class.*

Students will *dress casually in most classes.*

The Thomson-Glen article at the start of this chapter discusses some of the questions that students from other countries ask about Canadian classrooms. For the most part, the article is written in the present tense.

EXERCISES

1. As a group, change paragraphs 2 and 3 to the future tense. What changes did you have to make?

2. Use the information from the article and from your own experiences to write a letter of advice to a friend or relative who is about to embark on a program of further education in Canada. Tell that person what to expect in classes in Canada.

3. Use your own experiences to write a letter of advice to a Canadian friend who is about to travel to your home country and attend school there. Tell that person about the school and about teachers' expectations.

4. In the following paragraph, notice the patterns for creating negatives and questions with *will.*

Lecture classes will seem difficult to some students who are learning English. Often teachers will talk quickly unless you ask them to slow down. Many teachers will not explain difficult words and ideas. You will have to raise your hand or go to see them after class. During office hours, you will ask your teacher politely, "Will you explain Picasso's cubism again? I am a little confused about some of his paintings that you showed in class today. I will be glad to come back to see you if this is a busy time for you."

a. When you create a negative with *will,* where does *not* belong?

Note: The contraction *won't* is often used in writing and conversation instead of the full form *will not.*

b. When you ask a question with *will,* where does the subject belong?

5. Write two questions using *will* that you will ask of a classmate — for example, "What will you do this weekend?" Ask your questions of the person sitting to your right. (If there is no one to your right, ask the questions of anyone you choose.)

be going to

When we speak about the future, we often use *be going to*. This form is sometimes used in writing, but it is more common in speech. When you hear it spoken, *going to* may sound like "gonna" or "gunna." However, it means the same thing as *will* and can often be used interchangeably. However, there are some special uses for each. *Going to* is often used to express specific future plans or intentions, whereas *will* is almost always used to express promises, requests, offers, and predictions. *Will* is more often used in formal writing than *be going to*.

> *I* am going *to go to the movies tomorrow night.*
>
> *They* are going to *get married next month.*
>
> *He promises that he* will (is going to) *return the car tonight.*
>
> Will *you lend me $5?*
>
> Will *anyone trade a ticket to the rock concert for $50?*
>
> *It* will (is going to) *snow tomorrow.*

EXERCISES

1. Write a paragraph telling what you are going to do next weekend. (If you do not have any plans, you may want to write about what you are going to do next month or next summer.)

2. Imagine that you are a fortune teller who can make predictions about the future. Write a paragraph telling what you believe will happen in your family, your city, or your country in the next year. Or write a paragraph telling what will happen to some of the characters in a television program you have seen or a book or story you have read.

   another thing that would happen

PRONOUNS

The pronouns have been left out of the following sentences. On the basis of what you know about sentence structure, fill in the appropriate pronouns.

1. Many foreign graduate students have said, "___*my*___ adviser wants ___*me*___ to call ___*him*___ by ___*his*___ first name. ___*They*___ just can't do ___*that*___."

2. On the other hand, some professors have said of foreign students,

" _they_ keep bowing and saying 'yes, sir, yes, sir.' _we/I_ can hardly stand _it/that_ . _we/I_ wish _they_ would stop being so polite and just say what _they_ have on _their_ minds."

3. Graduate students typically have more <u>intense</u> <u>relationships</u> with

their professors than undergraduates do; at smaller schools student-teacher relationships are typically even less formal than

they are at larger schools.

4. Teachers generally expect students to ask _their_ questions or

even challenge what _we_ say.

5. Some teachers will be comfortable with students calling

them by _their_ first names, while others will expect

them to use a title like "Doctor," "Mr.," "Mrs.," "Ms.," or even "Professor."

If you had difficulty, refer to the pronoun chart that follows and do the Optional Exercise on page 113.

In general, a pronoun takes the place of a noun. To determine which pronoun to use, you need to know its referent, the noun to which it refers. For example, in the sentence before this one, to what noun does *it* refer?

Pronoun Chart ▶

Subject	Object	Possessive		Reflexive
I	me	my*	mine	myself
you	you	your*	yours	yourself
she	her	her*	hers	herself
he	him	his*	his	himself
it	it	its*	—	itself
we	us	our*	ours	ourselves
you	you	your*	yours	yourselves
they	them	their*	theirs	themselves

*These words are not used alone. They are followed by nouns or subject words.

PRONOUN RULES

1. **Pronouns take the place of nouns. Pronouns must refer clearly to the nouns they replace.**

   When she graduated from high school, they wanted her to go to college, but she thought she should get a job.

   Who is "she"? Who are "they"? You should make clear all the characters or topics in your story or essay before you use a pronoun.

2. **Pronouns should not shift point of view unnecessarily.**

   On the other hand, you know how important it is to get an education.

   Who is "you"? The reader, the writer, a friend of the reader? Unless there is a clear reason to use *you*, it can be confusing to the reader.

   Rewrite the sentence to make it clearer.

   On the other hand, she knows how important it is to get an education.

   She listened to it, and in the end I applied to college and got a job at night.

   Who is "I"? The paragraph is written in the third person. Why does the writer suddenly shift the point of view?

   Rewrite the sentence to make it clearer.

   She listened to them, and in the end she applied to college and got a job at night

3. **Pronouns must agree in number with the word or words they replace.**

   We want you to get that degree and have an easier life than we've had. She listened to it, and in the end I applied to college and got a job at night.

   What is "it"? Her parents are two people, and they said several things.

   Rewrite the sentence to make it clearer.

   Her parents want her to get that degree and have an easier life than they've had. She listened to it, and in the end she applied to college and got a job at night.

OPTIONAL EXERCISE

A fable is a fictitious story that is meant to teach a lesson called the *moral*.

The following is a famous fable told by Akiba Ben Joseph, a great scholar and head of the school for rabbis in Palestine in the first century. Fill in the appropriate pronouns. Answers are on page 326.

Once upon a time there was a smart young man who decided to trick a wise old man. ___He___ caught a little bird and held ___it___ in one hand behind ___his___ back. The boy approached the wise man and said, "Sir, ___I___ have a question for ___you___. ___I___ want to see how very wise ___you___ are. ___I___ am holding a bird in ___my___ hand. Is ___it___ alive, or is ___it___ dead?"

The boy thought that if the man said the bird was dead, ___he___ would open ___his___ hand to reveal the live bird, but if the man said the bird was alive, ___he___ would crush the bird, killing ___it___. The old man stared into the boy's eyes for a long time. Then ___he___ said, "The answer, my friend, is in ___your___ hands."

What is the moral of this fable?

ADDITIONAL WRITING PRACTICE

Writing a Fable

Every country in the world has fables or stories that are told to and read to children to help them learn the moral lessons of life. In some of these fables, the main characters are animals; in others, they are humans.

EXERCISES

1. Write a fable that you remember from your childhood to share with the other members of your class. You may write the moral at

the end of the fable, or you may ask members of your class to decide the moral.

2. Create your own fable to share with the members of your class. You may write the moral at the end of the fable, or you may ask members of your class to decide the moral.

3. Read the following fable, written by Jennifer Pram-On Korakot, a student from Thailand.

Berry Stupid

Strolling along by a tranquil river one morning, Billy Bob saw some berries on the water. He hadn't had breakfast that morning, so he was very hungry. Looking at the berries resting so peacefully on the water, his stomach started growling for food. Without hesitation, Billy Bob dived into the water to get the berries. Little did he realize that the water was shallow. As he crawled out of the water, the only berry Billy Bob had was a berry-sized bump on his head. As he sat by the riverbank rubbing his head, he looked up and realized the berries in the water were a reflection of the berries hanging from the tall berry tree above him.

Moral: Look before you leap.

6 COMMUNICATING & CARING

PREREADING ACTIVITIES

1. Did you ever get a special gift from a close relative when you were a child? What happened to that item as you grew older?

2. Do you recall any incidents of miscommunication with an adult when you were a child? Was the situation resolved? Share your recollection with your group.

3. Did you ever lose something of value to you as a child? What did you do about it?

Penny in the Dust

Ernest Buckler (1908–1984) was a Nova Scotia writer who wrote with sensitivity and psychological depth about his protagonists, set within detailed, realistic settings. The story "Penny in the Dust" illuminates a deep, yet unexpressed relationship between a father and his son.

My sister and I were walking through the old sun-still fields the evening before my father's funeral, recalling this memory or that — trying, after the fashion of families who gather again in the place where they were born, to identify ourselves with the strange children we must have been.   5

"Do you remember the afternoon we thought you were lost?" my sister said. I did. That was as long ago as the day I was seven, but I'd had occasion to remember it only yesterday.

"We searched everywhere," she said. "Up in the meeting-house, back in the blueberry barrens — we even looked in the well. I think   10
it's the only time I ever saw Father really upset. He didn't even stop to take the oxen off the wagon tongue when they told him. He raced right through the chopping where Tom Reeve was burning brush, looking for you — right through the flames almost; they couldn't do a thing with him. And you up in your bed, sound asleep!   15

"It was all over losing a penny or something, wasn't it?" she
went on, when I didn't answer. It was. She laughed indulgently.
"You were a crazy kid, weren't you."

I was. But there was more to it than that. I had never seen a shining new penny before that day. I'd thought they were all black. This
one was bright as gold. And my father had given it to me.

You would have to understand about my father, and that is the
hard thing to tell. If I say that he worked all day long but never once
had I seen him hurry, that would make him sound like a stupid man.
If I say that he never held me on his knee when I was a child and that
I never heard him laugh out loud in his life, it would make him
sound humourless and severe. If I said that whenever I'd be reeling
off some of my fanciful plans and he'd come into the kitchen and I'd
stop short, you'd think that he was distant and that in some kind of
way I was afraid of him. None of that would be true.

There's no way you can tell it to make it sound like anything
more than an inarticulate man a little at sea with an imaginative
child. You'll have to take my word for it that there was more to it
than that. It was as if his sure-footed way in the fields forsook him
the moment he came near the door of my child's world and that he
could never intrude on it without feeling awkward and conscious of
trespass; and that I, sensing that but not understanding it, felt at the
sound of his solid step outside, the child-world's foolish fragility. He
would fix the small spot where I planted beans and other quick-
sprouting seeds before he prepared the big garden, even if the spring
was late; but he wouldn't ask me how many rows I wanted and if he
made three rows and I wanted four, I couldn't ask him to change
them. If I walked behind the load of hay, longing to ride, and he
walked ahead of the oxen, I couldn't ask him to put me up and he
wouldn't make any move to do so until he saw me trying to grasp
the binder.

He, my father, had just given me a new penny, bright as gold.

He'd taken it from his pocket several times, pretending to examine the date on it, waiting for me to notice it. He couldn't offer me
anything until I had shown some sign that the gift would be wel-
come.

"You can have it if you want it, Pete," he said at last.

"Oh, thanks," I said. Nothing more. I couldn't expose any of my
eagerness either.

I started with it, to the store. For a penny you could buy the
magic cylinder of "Long Tom" popcorn with Heaven knows what
glittering bauble inside. But the more I thought of my bright penny
disappearing forever into the black drawstring pouch the store-
keeper kept his money in, the slower my steps lagged as the store
came nearer and nearer. I sat down in the road.

It was that time of magic suspension in an August afternoon. The lifting smells of leaves and cut clover hung still in the sun. The sun drowsed, like a kitten curled up on my shoulder. The deep flour-fine dust in the road puffed about my bare ankles, warm and soft as sleep. The sound of the cowbells came sharp and hollow from the cool swamp.

I began to play with the penny, putting off the decision. I would close my eyes and bury it deep in the sand; and then, with my eyes still closed, get up and walk around, and then come back to search for it. Tantalizing myself, each time, with the excitement of discovering afresh its bright shining edge. I did that again and again. Alas, once too often.

It was almost dark when their excited talking in the room awakened me. It was Mother who had found me. I suppose when it came dusk she thought of me in my bed other nights, and I suppose she looked there without any reasonable hope but only as you look in every place where the thing that is lost has ever lain before. And now suddenly she was crying because when she opened the door there, miraculously, I was.

"Peter!" she cried, ignoring the obvious in her sudden relief, "*where* have you been?"

"I lost my penny," I said.

"You lost your penny ...? But what made you come up here and hide?"

If Father hadn't been there, I might have told her the whole story. But when I looked up at Father, standing there like the shape of everything sound and straight, it was like daylight shredding the memory of a silly dream. How could I bear the shame of repeating before him the childish visions I had built in my head in the magic August afternoon when almost anything could be made to seem real, as I buried the penny and dug it up again? How could I explain that pit-of-the-stomach sickness which struck through the whole day when I had to believe, at last, that it was really gone? How could I explain that I wasn't really hiding from *them*? How, with the words and the understanding I had then, that this was the only possible place to run from that awful feeling of loss?

"I lost my penny," I said again. I looked at Father and turned my face into the pillow. "I want to go to sleep."

"Peter," Mother said. "It's almost nine o'clock. You haven't had a bite of supper. Do you know you almost scared the *life* out of us?"

"You better get some supper," Father said. It was the only time he had spoken.

I never dreamed that he would mention the thing again. But the next morning when we had the hay forks in our hands, ready to toss out the clover, he seemed to postpone the moment of actually

leaving for the field. He stuck his fork in the ground and brought in   115
another pail of water, though the kettle was chock full. He took out
the shingle nail that held a broken yoke strap together and put it
back in exactly the same hole. He went into the shed to see if the pigs
had cleaned up all their breakfast.

And then he said abruptly: "Ain't you got no idea where you   120
lost your penny?"

"Yes," I said. "I know just about."

"Let's see if we can't find it," he said.

"We walked down the road together, stiff with awareness. He   125
didn't hold my hand.

"It's right here somewhere," I said. "I was playin' with it, in the
dust."

He looked at me, but he didn't ask me what game anyone could
possibly play with a penny in the dust.

I might have known he would find it. He could tap the alder   130
bark with his jackknife just exactly hard enough so it wouldn't split
but so it would twist free from the notched wood, to make a whistle.
His great fingers could trace loose the hopeless snarl of a fishing line
that I could only succeed in tangling tighter and tighter. If I broke the
handle of my wheelbarrow ragged beyond sight of any possible   135
repair, he could take it and bring it back to me so you could hardly
see the splice if you weren't looking for it.

He got down on his knees and drew his fingers carefully
through the dust, like a harrow; not clawing it frantically into heaps
as I had done, covering even as I uncovered. He found the penny   140
almost at once.

He held it in his hand, as if the moment of passing it to me were
a deadline for something he dreaded to say, but must. Something
that could not be put off any longer, if it were to be spoken at all.

"Pete," He said, "you needn'ta hid. I wouldn'ta beat you."   145

Beat me? Oh, Father! You didn't think that was the reason ...? I
felt almost sick. I felt as if I had struck *him*.

I had to tell him the truth then. Because only the truth, no matter how ridiculous it was, would have the unmistakeable sound
truth has, to scatter that awful idea out of his head.   150

"I wasn't hidin', Father," I said, "honest. I was ... I was buryin'
my penny and makin' out I was diggin' up treasure. I was makin'
out I was findin' gold. I didn't know what to *do* when I lost it. I just
didn't know where to *go* ..." His head was bent forward, like mere
listening. I had to make it truer still.   155

"I made out it was gold," I said desperately, "and I — I was
makin' out I bought you a mowin' machine so's you could get your
work done early every day so's you and I could go in to town in the

dreaming good things of his father

big automobile I made out I bought you — and everyone'd turn around and look at us drivin' down the streets ..." His head was perfectly still, as if he were only waiting with patience for me to finish. "*Laughin'* and *talkin'*," I said. Louder, smiling intensely, compelling him, by the absolute conviction of some true particular, to believe me.   160

He looked up then. It was the only time I had ever seen tears in his eyes. It was the only time in my seven years that he had ever put his arm around me.   165

I wondered, though, why he hesitated, and then put the penny back in his own pocket.

Yesterday I knew. I never found any fortune and we never had a car to ride in together. But I think he knew what that would be like, just the same. I found the penny again yesterday, when we were getting out his good suit — in an upper vest pocket where no one ever carries change. It was still shining. He must have kept it polished.   170

I left it there.   175

READING AND THINKING STRATEGIES

DISCUSSION ACTIVITIES

Analysis and Conclusions

1. What was the relationship between Pete and his father? Use excerpts from the story to support your statements.

2. Why do you think Pete didn't immediately tell his parents about losing the penny? Why was losing the penny such a terrible loss to him?

3. What do Pete's dreams of buying a mowing machine and an automobile tell about him? About his feelings about his father?

Writing and Point of View

1. How does Buckler lead into the story? Is this an effective technique of introducing a narrative? Explain.

2. Does Buckler help you to picture the boy and his father? How did you see them? Describe what the father looks like. Describe what the boy looks like. Give examples from the text that describe their personalities. When you read, do you usually picture the characters inside your head? Does it help if the author describes the characters carefully, or do you prefer to use your imagination?

3. Buckler pays close attention to setting in his stories. Describe the setting. How does the setting enhance a particular mood or feeling? What is the mood of this story? What elements or parts of the story create this mood? Some things to think about are these: What is the time of year? Where does it take place? What does the father do for a living? Are other characters important to the story, or does it deal mainly with the boy and the father?

Personal Response and Evaluation

1. If you were Pete's father or mother, how would you have handled the situation?
2. Have you had any similar experience with a child?
3. If Pete were a girl, would the story change? Why? If the relationship described were between a child and a mother, would the story be different? Why?

RESPONSE PARAGRAPH

1. As soon as you finish reading "Penny in the Dust," write a paragraph describing how the story made you feel and what personal memories it brought to mind. Share your paragraph with a classmate.
2. Narrate an incident in your experience where communicating what you really felt was really important to you. Use dialogue. Share your paragraph with others in a small group.

JOURNAL WRITING

First, I do not sit down at my desk to put into verse something that is already clear in my mind. If it were clear in my mind, I should have no incentive or need to write about it …. We do not write to be understood; we write in order to understand.

C. DAY LEWIS, *The Poetic Image*

Writing in a journal, whether it is shared or kept for yourself, is powerful. It is a means of touching on feelings and experiences hidden inside yourself. Allowing the journal to express your deepest self will have a positive effect on all your writing.

"Penny in the Dust" is about both a boy's unexpressed fear and his unexpressed love as well. Have you ever felt afraid? Have you ever felt it difficult to express your love? What events in your childhood did this story make you think about?

WRITING STRATEGIES

is a whirlwind of energy
simile — like
metaphor

ESSAY STRATEGIES

Developing Your Writing Using Sensory Details

In Chapter Five, we discussed the use of details to support the main idea or to help form generalizations. Details are also used to make writing vivid and exciting, to help the reader fully experience what is being described.

Sensory details come to us through our senses — sight, smell, hearing, touch, and taste. When we write, we carefully choose words that describe our sensory experiences. Look at the differences in these two pairs of descriptions:

My bedroom is pretty, and it is my favourite room. *kind of simple*

My bedroom is painted lavender, except for the windows, which are white. There is a big, fluffy rug on the floor where I usually lie down to do my reading and homework.

My sister's baby is cute and cuddly.

My sister's baby has big, brown eyes and soft, dark hair. His skin is as soft as a pile of cotton balls. His fingers are so strong that when he holds on to my hair, I have to pull with all my strength to get it away from him.

As a reader, which of each pair of descriptions is easier to picture? As a writer, when would you use the shorter description and when would you use the more detailed description?

EXERCISES

1. Write two descriptions of a room that you know well — your living room, kitchen, or bedroom, for example. Write a short description and then a detailed description. Share both with a classmate. Discuss the differences and how you decide how much detail to include in your writing.

2. Write two descriptions of a room from your past — your fifth grade classroom or your old bedroom, for example. Follow the same steps as in Exercise 1.

3. Write two descriptions of scenes from nature — a sunset, a day at the beach, or a snowy day, for example. Follow the same steps as in Exercise 1.

4. Discuss what you have learned about your own writing from doing the practice writing in Exercises 1–3.

ESSAY FORM
Describing a Place

When writers use description, they paint a picture with words. They try to present a clear and vivid picture of what they have experienced. In "Penny in the Dust," Ernest Buckler writes:

> *It was that time of magic suspension in an August afternoon. The lifting smells of leaves and cut clover hung still in the sun. The sun drowsed, like a kitten curled up on my shoulder. The deep flour-fine dust in the road puffed about my bare ankles, warm and soft as sleep. The sound of the cowbells came sharp and hollow from the cool swamp.*

1. What picture forms in your mind as you read this paragraph?
2. What senses does Buckler appeal to?

In Emily Carr's autobiography *Growing Pains* she describes, in a short segment, a train trip across Canada:

> *Canada's vastness took my breath. The up-and-downness of the Rockies, their tops dangled in clouds, thrilled and were part of natural me, though I had to steel myself as we glided over trestle-bridges of great height spanning gorges and ravines with rivers like white ribbons boiling far below, and lofty trees looking crouched and squat down there in the bottom of the canyon while we slid over their tops. We squeezed through rocky passes, hid in tunnels, raced roaring rivers, slunk through endless levels of dead, still forest, black-green and mysterious, layer upon layer of marching trees, climbing trees, trees burned, trees fallen, myriad millions of trees and loneliness intertwisted. Our engine gulped endless miles, each rail-length one bite. On, on, till the mountains ended and the train slithered over level land munching space rhythmically as a chewing cow. Was there never to be an end? Did our engine spin track as she advanced like a monster spider? Would we finally topple over the brink into that great bonfire of a sunset when we came to the finish of this tremendous vastness? — No rocks, no trees, no bumps, just once in a great, great way a tiny house, a big barn, cattle in that great space sizing no bigger than flies — prairie houses, cows, barns, drowned in loneliness.*

> *When at last we came to Canada's eastern frontier, just before she touched the Atlantic ocean, she burst into a spread of giant cities, clean, new cities. The greedy, gobbling train turned back to regobble Canada's space, while we launched into sea-bounce that*

grieved the stomach, wearied the eye.— Nothingness, nothingness, till your seeing longed and longed — whale, bird, anything rather than nothing piled on top of nothing!

1. What picture forms in your mind as you read this excerpt?
2. What do you learn about the geography of Canada from this reading?

A student from Afghanistan, Zelimin Sarwary, writes about a visit to the home of a family friend, Nasema:

The dining room was in a square shape about 18 feet wide. Nasema, as was customary, had no dining table or cabinet in her dining room. Instead of a cabinet for china wares, the dining room had four shelves which Nasema decorated with antique things such as ancient spoons, plates, glasses, teapots, cups, china, and so on. The decoration of the dining room made my mother enjoy Nasema's delicious home-cooked meals even more. Because Nasema had no dining table, she had to use a cloth on the floor and place the food on it.

There were three bedrooms of equal size, one white, one pink, and one light green. Nasema and her children slept on the soft comfortable cotton mats, the "toshaks," that the Afghan people sleep on. The colours are sometimes coordinated with the walls. The bathroom was large and was without a shower. Seldom did Nasema wash herself and her children at home. Regularly they went to a "hammom" or sauna because it was warm and more comfortable than home where there were not so many people.

The simple hammom Nasema used held about four hundred people. It had five different rooms for different purposes. The very first room was used by those who paid money to the cashier and their clothes were kept there. The second was used for changing clothes. It had about twenty benches. Each bench seated about ten people. In the third room, people washed their bodies. It had two white and black stone "Dake Done" or communal bath tubs, one for hot water and the other for cold water. Against the wall, there were two cubicles. For some reason, the people called those two cubicles the "Bride's House." They had only cold water. People usually went there at the very end and took a cold shower. After that, they went to the dressing room to get dressed. There were a few masseuses for the customers. The women's hammom was separated from the men's but up to five-year-old boys were allowed to go with their mothers. People in Afghanistan believe that up to five-year-old boys are not mature enough to think about sex.

After the hammom, Nasema and my mother stayed up half the night talking about the Soviet invasion of Afghanistan. They both cried. Night passed and the following morning came.

1. What picture forms in your mind as you read this descriptive essay?
2. What do you know about Nasema and Afghanistan from reading this essay?

SUGGESTIONS FOR WRITING

Before you begin to write, you may want to review your journal or any other writing you have done for this chapter. Try clustering to help you get ideas, as described in the "Getting Started" section below. Always spend some time thinking before you begin to write.

1. Retell the story from Pete's father's point of view, making whatever changes you think should occur.
2. Have you ever had an experience like Pete's in which you were afraid to reveal your true feelings to an adult? Tell the story of this experience, and tell what you learned from it.
3. Write a description of someone you know with an interesting or complex personality.
4. Reread Zelimin Sarwary's essay about Afghanistan (page 123). Write an essay describing a familiar place that you know well from your past. Use many sensory details so that your reader can experience the place as fully as possible.
5. Write a story that teaches other students in your class something about your culture or background that they do not know. In the story, carefully describe the setting or place where the story occurs.

GETTING STARTED
Clustering

Sometimes even though we have ideas about a subject, we cannot seem to write them down. The blank page fills us with fear. One technique that may help you overcome this problem is clustering. It is a simple but effective method to get started writing.

First, begin with a blank notebook page. In the middle of the page, write your nucleus word (the key concept you will be writing about) and circle it. (In our example, the nucleus word is *father*.)

Then write down any other words that occur to you; circle these words and draw arrows connecting your original word to them.

Write the words down quickly, just as they occur to you. Connect words where you think they belong together. When something new occurs to you, go back to the nucleus and draw a new arrow and circle. You can have as many circles as you have ideas. Don't try to make sense, and don't worry if the clustering doesn't seem to be going anywhere. If you temporarily run out of ideas, doodle a little bit by drawing your circles or arrows darker. Keep clustering until you get a sense of what you are going to write. Then stop clustering, read the ideas in the circles, and start to write.

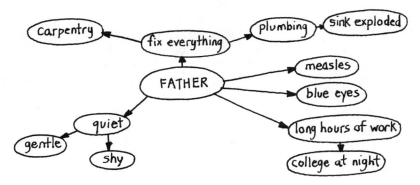

There is no right or wrong way to form clusters. When you start to write, the words will come and begin to take over; the writing will come easily. Don't stop yourself. Let it happen and see what occurs in your writing.

EXERCISES

1. Begin with a clean page. Write the word *fear* in the middle of the page and circle it. Let your mind begin to make connections. You may want to close your eyes. When a word comes to you, write it on the page, circle it, and draw an arrow to it from your nucleus or from its connecting word. Let yourself go, and do not judge or even really think about what you are writing. You will know when to stop when you feel a strong urge to write, when you suddenly know what you want to say. Then glance at your word clusters and begin writing on a new page. Write until you feel that you have written out all your ideas. You may want to look at your clustering again to see if you had any ideas that you did not develop. Then read what you have written, and spend a few minutes making any changes that you think will improve the piece of writing.

2. Do the same with the word *father* or *mother*.

REVISING

When you have finished writing your essay, separate yourself from your writing by reading the following student essay. Then practice by revising this essay.

A Student Essay

Nine years ago, I used to play with my friends in the playground in front of my school. We were sitting down in the grass. Where I was sitting, I didn't see a big green insect near my hands. Suddenly, the insect bit me in my right palm. Since I was with my friends, I didn't cry because they might think I am a "cry baby."

I ignored the pain. When I got home, I acted like nothing happened to me, but I was hiding my hand because it was swollen. My big brother came home from school, and he started to play a joke on me. He grabbed my right hand and said, "You're getting fat," and then I told him an insect had bitten me. I asked him not to tell my mother, but he took my other hand and compared the two. He said that my right hand was swollen and I would have to go to see a doctor. He ran into the kitchen and told my mother. My mother called me and looked at my hands. The colour of my hand had changed to yellowish because of the pus and probably the poison from the insect.

My mother took me to a doctor. The doctor gave me a big, long needle and then stuck another needle in my hand to suck out all the pus and poison. My mother was watching, and then she fainted because she has high blood pressure. After a few minutes she got up, and I was sitting next to her. When she asked me if I was all right, I said, "I'm fine."

On our way home, I was thinking that maybe it would be better not to tell her something like this if it happened again. I realized that some people who have illnesses get sicker when they panic. So either I will tell her, but she will not go to the hospital with me, or I will not tell her at all. What do you think?

Marina Ibea, The Philippines

Write the following questions on a separate piece of paper and answer them first about either Marina Ibea's or Zelimin Sarwary's writing. When you have finished thinking about either of these student essays, you will have given yourself time to separate from your own writing so that you can look at it now from a fresh perspective. Copy the questions again, and write the answers to them after reviewing your own essay.

1. What is the main point of the draft?
2. What is the best sentence in the entire piece of writing?
3. What is the weakest sentence in the entire piece of writing?
4. Are the same words used over and over? How can some variety be added to this writing?
5. Is there any place in the writing where the ideas do not connect? If so, how can this be improved?
6. Does the conclusion work; does it tie the ideas together?

EDITING STRATEGIES

IDIOMATIC EXPRESSIONS

Each of the following paragraphs contains a context clue that will help you understand some of the idiomatic expressions used in the Buckler short story. Find these context clues in the story. Then use the expressions in a sentence of your own.

1. *they couldn't do a thing with him* (lines 14 and 15)

   Pete's father was so upset about his son's disappearance that he looked for him frantically, without heeding anyone's advice to be more cautious.
   Your sentence:

   _____

   _____

2. *take my word for it* (line 33)

   Pete says that the reader will have to believe that his description of his father is accurate; words simply cannot describe the man's complex personality.
   Your sentence:

   _____

   _____

3. *there was more to it* (line 33)

   Pete's description of his father is incomplete; one would have to know the man to fully understand the positive qualities of his

personality. He is not simply what he seems to be to a casual observer.
Your sentence:

_____

_____

4. *making out* (line 157)

Pete was pretending that he had bought his father a car and a mowing machine, and that the two of them led a totally different existence from their reality.
Your sentence:

_____

_____

COMMONLY CONFUSED WORDS

your/you're

"You go up to bed," I said, *"you're sick."*

"Your temperature is all right," I said. *"It's nothing to worry about."*

Notice how *your* and *you're* are used in the preceding sentences. Now complete the following definitions.

_____ is a contraction of the words *you are.*

_____ means "belonging to you."

Fill in the blanks in the following sentences with *your* or *you're.*

1. "Did you lose _____ wallet?" the waitress asked, holding it in her hand.

2. "_____ going to have to practice every day if you want to compete in the Olympics," the coach announced.

3. "_____ visiting the C.N. Tower on _____ trip to Toronto, aren't you?" Willie asked.

MECHANICS
The Apostrophe

The apostrophe creates an editing problem for many writers. In the following sentences, underline the words that have an apostrophe ('). Then examine the sentences to decide how it is used.

1. "What's the matter, Pete?"
2. "I've lost my penny."
3. Pete's father found his son's penny.
4. I read aloud from Ernest Buckler's "Penny in the Dust."

An apostrophe can be used in two ways:

1. It can be used in contractions to show that part of a word is missing.
2. It can be used to show possession, that something belongs to someone.

The apostrophe in sentences 1 and 2 is used to show _____.

The apostrophe in sentences 3 and 4 is used to show _____.

Note: Contractions are found mostly in dialogue and informal writing. The uncontracted forms are usually used in formal writing and speech. In the Buckler story, contractions are used in the dialogue, but uncontracted forms are used in the narration and description.

EXERCISES

1. In each of the following sentences, the apostrophe is used to indicate that part of a word is missing. In the blank, fill in the complete word. The first has been done for you.

_____is_____ a. "What's the matter, Pete?"

_____have_____ b. "I've lost my penny."

_____am_____ c. "I'm all right."

_____would_____ d. "I'd rather go to bed."

_____had_____ e. "He'd better help him find it."

_____ *has* f. "He's got one more penny."

2. The second use for the apostrophe is to show possession, that something belongs to someone. Fill in the blanks showing the possessive form.

   a. the penny that belongs to the boy   *the boy's penny*

   b. the father of Pete   *Pete's father*

   c. the car that belongs to Papa   *Papa's car*

   d. the toy that belongs to Pete's sister   *Pete's sister's toy*

3. In the following paragraph, fill in the ten missing apostrophes and twelve quotation marks. Answers are on page 327.

Ernest Buckler's story, "A Penny in the Dust," tells about a young boy who loses a prized penny. "I'd better hide," he thinks, and crawls under the covers of his bed. From there, he doesn't hear his parents voices as they call: Pete, where are you? While playing with the shiny penny, Pete had been dreaming of telling his father: I'm going to buy you a new mowing machine and a car. When he finds Pete, the boy's father is still upset. What's the matter, Pete? he asks. I wouldn't have beat you. The next day Pete's father easily finds his son's penny in the dust.

EDITING PRACTICE

The following paragraph is a first draft that has not yet been edited for surface errors. Correct the eleven capital letters errors, one missing set of quotation marks, four preposition errors, four *the* errors, and one *they're/their/there* error. Answers are on page 327.

My sister, hilda, lives on an apartment in the top of a high hill in the west vancouver. She works as a computer operator on a big bank their, and when she looks out her window, she sees the granville street bridge. She loves heights. She even flew on a private airplane over rocky mountains. Once she said to me, I saw both pacific and atlantic oceans in one day. She would like to travel around the world someday.

GRAMMAR STRATEGIES

ADJECTIVE WORD ORDER

When we describe, we use adjectives — sometimes series of adjectives. In English, there is a required order for these adjectives. Below is a chart illustrating adjective word order. After studying the chart, read the sentences that follow it, using the words provided to fill in the blanks in the proper order. The first one has been done for you. Check your answers by referring to the chart. This chart is meant to help you when you write, but you do not have to memorize it. The more you write, the more familiar you will become with word order, and it will eventually become natural to you.

Articles and Possessives	Numbers: Ordinal and Cardinal	General Descriptive Adjectives and Some Adjectives Ending in -ed, -ing, -y, -ful, -ous*	Size*	Shape	Age	Colour	Adjectives of Nationality and Religion and Some Adjectives Ending in -ic, -al, -ed, -y	Noun Adjuncts	Nouns
the	two		big	angular	old	green	air-conditioned	convertible	cars
her	three	lovely	little	slender	newborn	grey	Burmese		cats
Louise's		famous		long		blue	lacy	evening	gown
						blue and			
a		chipped	huge	square		white	English	soup	bowl
a		weeping	tiny	round	old	grey-haired	French		lady
a	first	quick					comic		scream

(handwritten annotation next to "Ending in": "good, bad")

* These positions are sometimes interchangeable.

1. My sister and I were walking through *the old, sun-still fields.*
   (sun-still, old, fields, the)

2. I had never seen _____ before that day.
   (penny, a, new, shining)

3. The more I thought of _____ disappearing forever in
   (penny, my, bright)

   _____, the slower my steps lagged.
   (drawstring, the, pouch, black)

4. _____ in the road puffed about my bare ankles.
   (dust, deep, the, flour-fine)

5. His great fingers could trace loose _____ of a fishing
   line.   (snarl, the, hopeless)

   The following sentences are not from the story. Fill in the adjectives in the order required. Refer to the chart if you have difficulty.

6. Pete's father climbed _____ to the boy's
   bedroom.   (winding, the, staircase, long, dark)

7. He sat at _____ and began to write.
   (desk, old, wooden carved, his)

8. Staring at his son's picture, he held _____ in
   his hand.   (old, his, pen, green, fountain)

9. He wanted to write, but suddenly he felt very tired; he sat on

   _____ and fell asleep.
   (plaid, the, soft, old, brown)

EXERCISE

Describe a person you saw on the street today, using long strings of descriptive words. After you have finished, refer to the chart to check the order of your adjectives.

SOCIETY AND
PLAYING ROLES

DATING PRACTICES

PREREADING ACTIVITIES

1. In a group, discuss your observations about dating in Canada. Think about what you have seen on your campus, on the streets, and at parties. What patterns have you observed in relation to who asks for the date, who pays, and how people act on dates?

2. In a group, discuss the way dating is portrayed on television, in books, and in the movies. What patterns have you observed in relation to who asks for the date, who pays, and how people act on dates?

3. Compare your personal observations with what is presented in the media. What differences do you find? How do you explain these differences?

Who Pays the Cheque When You're Dating?

The following article from Chatelaine *was written by Barbara MacKay, based on research by counsellors, in order to examine the dilemma of how to share the expenses when dating.*

On their first date, Maureen and Dennis ate at one of the most popular Italian restaurants in town. The two, who had met at a fitness club, enjoyed each other's company at dinner, but when the waiter later placed the cheque between them, the relaxed mood of the evening seemed to vanish. Who would pay the cheque? Dennis had 5 asked Maureen out, but she had been the one to suggest dinner and at this particular restaurant. He seemed to hesitate, then reached for the bill. "Oh, no, he wanted me to offer," Maureen thought. "Is it too late now — how much should I pay?"

The days when men were the only ones to ask for dates, and 10 women had their evenings paid for, seem to be on the wane, but there are no new rules about who pays for what when couples go out. Instead, many women and men tend to play it by ear, often trying to

°Figure out what the other
wants to do

°expensive

second-guess° each other. For instance, a woman may wonder: "Should I pay for half for the sake of equality and to avoid any notion that I owe him anything?" A man may wonder: "Should I pick up the tab on the first date and hope she'll get it the next time?"

Who pays for a date can establish or reflect the roles of each person in the relationship. Dr. Catherine Gildiner, a Toronto psychologist, says money gives a person a measure of power. If a man asks a woman out and picks up the entire tab, it casts the couple into traditional roles, which some women and men now find unsuitable. In some cases, a woman resents a date if he feels that, by paying, he has more power — e.g., to choose the restaurant and meal — or he mistakenly assumes that she is obliged to him in some way. Or a man may resent a date who automatically expects him to be entirely responsible for the bill.

Splitting the cheque on the first few dates can help start the relationship as one between two equals, Dr. Gildiner suggests. It also allows you to evaluate each other more objectively. For instance, it helps to prevent any notion that you're obliged to your date in some way merely because he picked up the tab for an expensive evening. And it may reassure him that you're dating him to spend time with him — not to eat for free. It may also mean the two of you can afford to go out more often.

When possible, it is best to deal with dating expenses in the beginning, according to Bruce Barnes, a Toronto psychotherapist. For example, suppose that you like to pay your way on a first date and a man invites you to dinner at his favourite restaurant, which you know is pricey.° You might reply, "I'd love to go out with you, but that restaurant is too expensive for me." Then, you could suggest another place. This way, "you can both sit back and enjoy the meal without any hidden expectations or assumptions," Barnes says.

Sharing dating expenses needn't involve using a calculator to tabulate who drank more wine or who had dessert. If you want to split a cheque, 50–50 is probably best, despite who ate what. Barnes says that other egalitarian methods of dating, such as paying on alternate dates or reciprocating with home-cooked meals, can also help you maintain an equal balance in a relationship. For example, some women and men feel that the person who initiated the date — regardless of whether it was the man or the woman — should pick up the tab the first time, then the other person can reciprocate next time.

Barnes says some men who are insecure feel that their masculinity is threatened when a woman picks up the tab. If your date always insists on paying the entire bill and you prefer to share the cost at least sometimes, you might say, "I wouldn't have accepted your invitation unless I wanted to go out with you and pay for half."

On the other hand, some women who insist on paying 50 percent of everything on every date may be revealing their own insecurity: they may be unsure of their independence and need to prove it all the time, according to Dr. Gildiner. She says that the 50–50 arrangement need not be a rule "for all times and forever." As you become more secure in a relationship and see each other more often, you can work out arrangements that suit each of you.   65

Indeed, splitting the bill 50–50 is sometimes unfair. For example, Barnes suggests that you assume your date is picking up the cheque if he asks you out, then chooses a restaurant without consulting you, and orders an expensive entree and a bottle of wine to match, while you're modest in your meal selection. In this situation, if your date   70 looks at the cheque and says, "Your half comes to…," he's not a liberated man who is treating you as an equal — he's just plain cheap, says Barnes.

READING AND THINKING STRATEGIES

DISCUSSION ACTIVITIES

Analysis and Conclusions

1. What were the traditional rules of dating with regard to payment of the cheque? In what ways have those rules now changed?

2. What are some of the motivations behind someone wanting to pay for a date?

3. What advice do Dr. Gildiner and Bruce Barnes give about paying the cheque?

Writing and Point of View

1. MacKay starts her article with a brief narrative or anecdote. Do you think this is an effective introduction to the subject? Explain your point of view to your group.

2. Notice the way in which MacKay uses expert opinions to provide information on the topic. Why is this effective?

3. Does MacKay display a personal point of view on the subject of who should pay the cheque, or does she mainly report objectively on the current social situation?

Personal Response and Evaluation

1. Do you think women and men should equally share the costs of a date? Explain, using your observations or experiences.

2. Should women ask men out on dates? Explain, using your observations or experiences.

3. Explain the dating patterns in your country. Who asks for the date? Who pays? Which system do you prefer? Why?

SMALL GROUP DISCUSSION

In a small group, discuss the best way to deal with one or more of the following situations.

1. Someone asks you on a date and you do not want to go, but you want to be polite to the other person.

2. Someone asks you on a date and your parents do not allow you to date yet.

3. Many of your friends are dating, and one of them wants to set up a date for you. However, in your culture, people do not date casually.

4. You ask someone on a date. The person refuses and tells you that you two should just be friends.

As a class, discuss the results of your discussions. Some groups may role-play some of these situations for the entire class.

JOURNAL WRITING

It is well to understand as early as possible in one's writing life that there is just one contribution which every one of us can make; we can give into the common pool of experience some comprehension of the world as it looks to each of us.

DOROTHEA BRANDE, *BECOMING A WRITER*

Each of us has a unique vision of the world. We have all dreamed a personal dream of the person we will love. In addition to that dream, we have had real experiences. In your journal, write about the characteristics that you value in a friend or a date. Are these characteristics different from what you would value in a husband or a wife? Can men and women be just friends? Should men and women be friends before they get married? Do people who have arranged marriages fall in love? Is love necessary in order for a marriage to survive and be successful? Write about as many of these ideas as you choose.

WRITING STRATEGIES

ESSAY STRATEGIES

Use of the Anecdote or Short Narrative

Reread the first paragraph of MacKay's essay. Her essay begins with an anecdote or short story taken from personal experience. Many writers use anecdotes or short narratives to enrich and personalize their writing. Using anecdotes or narratives is also an effective way to engage the reader — that is, to get the reader interested in reading what you have written.

Audience engagement is an important aspect of successful writing. If the reader is interested in your writing, then communication is going on between writer and reader. This is the real purpose of writing.

Any anecdote or narrative you use should relate to the topic of your essay. Be sure you make a smooth transition from the story to the body of your essay.

EXERCISES

1. Reread "Between Two Worlds" on pages 69 to 72 to find narratives about immigrants' daily lives. In what ways do these short narratives enrich the essay?

2. Reread the Chan essay on pages 3 to 6. What anecdotes or short stories does he tell that relate to his main idea? How do these anecdotes affect you as a reader?

3. Choose one of the student essays that have appeared so far in this book. Read it with a partner. Does the writer use anecdotes? If so, what is the purpose of the anecdotes? If not, what kind of anecdotes would you suggest that the writer add to make the piece more effective?

ESSAY FORM

Writing an Explanation

at least 2 pages (choose one topic)

In the MacKay essay, the author is explaining common patterns of sharing the expenses when dating in order to offer some advice to her readers. When you explain something in writing, you are making it clearer to a reader. Some of the steps that are useful in helping a writer to explain or teach something to a reader include these:

1. *Look around you* as you did in the "Prereading Activities" on page 135. Observe patterns in the way people act and think in relation

to the subject you are going to explain. Or carefully observe the process you are going to explain in your writing. What in the MacKay essay tells you that she looked around her before she began writing?

2. *Define* your subject. Some writers use the dictionary or another source book to help them define the process or pattern that they are writing. What does MacKay define in this essay?

3. *Describe* in detail the steps that are needed to understand the process or pattern. Readers see the picture through your words, so make them clear and direct. What specific descriptions did you find in the MacKay essay? How do they add to the overall effectiveness of the essay?

4. *Compare* your subject to others. What payment patterns does MacKay compare in this essay? Why does she make these comparisons?

5. *Analyze* the parts or steps of the pattern of process you are explaining. Then tell how these steps work together. What does MacKay include about traditional patterns in relation to her subject? What other payment arrangements does she describe in detail?

6. *Evaluate* the reasons why the pattern or process you are explaining is important for the reader to think about and know. What does MacKay write to convince you that the issue she is explaining is important to you as a reader?

You will not need to use all six of these steps in every essay that you write, but keeping them in mind can help you write clear and effective essays. Reread other essays in this book to evaluate which of these steps the writers used and how effectively they used them.

SUGGESTIONS FOR WRITING

Choose one of the following topics to write about. Before you start writing, you may want to try the paired clustering activity in "Getting Started" on page 141.

1. Describe a first date, real or imagined. Use lots of detail to make the experience come alive for the readers. What made this date unique? Why did you choose to write about this particular date?

2. "There is no such thing as love at first sight. For love to be real, people must know each other for a long time and have many shared experiences." Do you agree or disagree? Support your point of view with your own experiences or observations.

3. Compare a casual date with a formal date. Consider such things as where people go, what they wear, and who pays for the date.

4. On the basis of your own observations, do you think that dating patterns have really changed in recent years? If you are a woman, would you ask a man out? If you are a man, would you go out with a woman who invited you? Would you split the cheque? Should the man always treat?

5. "When a man wants to show a woman that he cares and respects her, he pays for their date." Do you agree or disagree with this statement? Support your point of view with your own experiences and observations.

6. Many people believe that men and women cannot really be friends. They feel that there is always an attraction between people of the opposite sex. Write an essay analyzing your feelings on this subject. Give examples from your experiences and observations.

GETTING STARTED
Paired Clustering

In Chapter Six, you used clustering to help you think of ideas and get started writing. In this chapter, you will use a similar technique, except that you will work with a partner. One of you should write the word *dating* on a blank piece of paper. Draw a circle around the word and say all the words that come to your mind about dating. Each of you writes down words on the page as quickly as they occur to you. After about five minutes, stop and look at the cluster you have created.

Next each of you should choose as many of the words and ideas from the big cluster as you need to form your own personal cluster, which you will use when you begin to write.

A Student Essay

In recent years, dating patterns have changed. There are many things such as girls paying for the guys, girls asking guys out, and girls are not shy anymore.

In my family, my mom doesn't agree with girls paying for guys. However, it doesn't always go the old way anymore. When I go out with my girlfriend, she sometimes pays for the date. She doesn't believe that guys should pay all the time. She said that by letting guys pay, they tend to get the wrong ideas. By paying for the date, the guy would not have any wrong ideas.

When I was growing up, girls were not supposed to ask guys out. They would have to wait until guys asked them out. But now that has changed. My friend, Peter, was asked by a girl to go out on a date. He told me he was surprised to hear a girl ask him out, but he liked the idea of girls asking guys out.

Today's girls are not shy anymore. They see guys who are good-looking and they go to ask them out. In the old days, it was shameful to see girls asking guys out. Today it's not shameful, it's courageous.

I feel it is a good change for the girls because it gives them the right to choose anyone they want to go out with. There are many ways that dating has changed, some bad and some good, but I think girls asking out guys is good.

Koan Ung, Cambodia

REVISING

With a partner, answer the following questions, looking at Koan Ung's essay on dating.

1. What in this essay tells you that the writer looked around and observed the way people act and think?
2. Did the writer define any terms or ideas?
3. What specific descriptions do you find in this essay? How do they add to the overall effectiveness of the essay?
4. What specific comparisons can you find in this essay?
5. Does the writer tell you about the history and the future of the subject of the essay? If not, would this add to your understanding of the subject?
6. Where in the essay does the writer evaluate the reasons why the subject is important for you to know about?

Next, with your partner, answer the same questions, looking at the draft of the essay that you have just written. Do the same with your partner's essay. Revise your draft, keeping in mind what you have discussed. Then share your revision with your partner.

EDITING STRATEGIES

WORD DEVELOPMENT

adverbs using *-ly*

One way to enhance your vocabulary is to learn new word forms based on words you already know. A common occurrence in English is for an adverb (a word that modifies a verb, an adjective, or another adverb) to be formed by adding *-ly* to an adjective. The following examples show how to combine sentences and change adjectives into adverbs.

He hesitated.
He was anxious.
    He hesitated anxiously.
    Anxiously, he hesitated. (**Notice the comma.**)

She wants to ask him out.
She is desperate.

    She *desperately* wants to ask him out.

desperately she wants to ask him out.

She accepted his suggestion.
She was gracious.

— good manner

She graciously accepted his suggestion.
Graciously, she accepted his suggestion.

She asked a question.
She was polite.

she politely asked a question
Politely, she asked a question

He kissed her.
He was tender.

she tenderly kissed her.
tenderly, he kissed her.

He spoke to her about where they would go.
He was quiet.

He quietly spoke to her about where they would go.
Quietly, he spoke to her about where they would go.

She flung her money on the table. *(fun.)*
She was careless.

[handwritten: fling flung flung]

[handwritten: she carelessly flung her money on the table]
[handwritten: Carelessly, she flung her money on the table.]

He told her he wished he hadn't paid for dinner.
He was angry.

[handwritten: He angrily told her he wished he hadn't paid for dinner]
[handwritten: Angrily, he told her he wished he hadn't paid for dinner]

Now use these adjectives and adverbs in sentences of your own.

IDIOMATIC EXPRESSIONS

Each of the following paragraphs contains a context clue that will help you understand some of the idiomatic expressions used in MacKay's article. Underline these context clues; the first has been done for you. Then use the expressions when you answer the questions that follow each paragraph.

1. *play it by ear* (line 13)

   [handwritten: flexible   instant / instinct reaction]

   When an unexpected situation occurs, you must <u>accommodate yourself to it and act appropriately</u>.
   Have you ever been in a situation in which you had to abandon your previous plans and play it by ear?

2. *pick up the tab* (line 17)

   When people go out together for a meal or snack, <u>one person might pay for everyone</u>.
   Describe an occasion in which you would pick up the tab.

3. *splitting the cheque* (line 28)

   When friends go out together, or when some couples date, they usually split the cheque. In this way, <u>each person pays for himself or herself</u>.
   Sometimes women prefer to split the cheque on dates. Why might a woman prefer this arrangement? When would you choose to split the cheque?

4. *pay your way* (line 38) *[handwritten: being control of your finance.]*

When each person pays for his or her own part of the cheque, they are paying their way. Do you believe individuals should pay their way when dating? When students are at college or university, should parents pay their way, or should students pay their own way?

COMMONLY CONFUSED WORDS

though/thought/through

Read the following paragraph; then complete the definitions that follow.

> *Even* though *Maureen's family would have* thought *it improper, she decided to pay the cheque. She* thought through *exactly what she would say. She asked Dennis if this arrangement would suit him,* though *she was afraid he would be insulted. When she was* through, *he smiled and accepted, saying: "I'll pick up the tab next time." She* thought *she had succeeded.*

thought is the past tense of *think*.

though means "even if" or "and yet."

through means "in one side and out the other" or "from the first to the last of."

Fill in each of the following blanks with *though, thought,* or *through.*

1. She _thought_ he would say no, even _though_ she hadn't even asked him yet.

2. As she watched him walk _through_ the door into the restaurant,

   she felt unsure of herself _though_ her friends told her everyone did on their first date.

3. He helped her get _through_ the ordeal by smiling at her.

   Now write your own sentences using *though, thought,* and *through.*

EXERCISE

Choose the present, past, or present perfect tense for each of the following sentences. Be prepared to explain your choice of tense.

1. Since coming to Canada, I _have observed_ many different kinds of
   (observe)

   dating patterns.

2. Last week, a girl in my math class *asked* me to meet her in the
   (ask)

   library to go over our homework.

3. She *enjoys* the freedom of being able to ask a guy out.
   (enjoy)

4. We *went* to the cafeteria and *talked* about math for almost an hour.
   (go)   (talk)

5. I guess dating *has changed* in the past few years on many college and
   (change)
   university campuses.

6. Now almost everyone in my school *feels* comfortable about

   informal study dates.

7. However, when it *comes* to formal parties and dinners, some of
   (come)

   my classmates *do not approve* of girls asking guys out. ~~of girls ask-~~
   (not approve)
   ~~ing guys out.~~

8. What do you think the students in your school *feels* about dating?   (feel)

MECHANICS
The Comma

All the commas have been left out of the following letter. Fill in the
commas where you think they belong. Then check your answers on
page 327.

May 14 1995

3778 Hudson Street
Victoria B.C.
V8S 3H8

Dear Aunt Millie,

   *I think you should sit down before you read this letter, and I
think you should have your handkerchief handy. I am sitting here
in Santo Domingo with Luis, your favourite nephew. He was*

happy to see me, and he wants you to know how much he misses seeing you and the rest of the family. Luis said to give you 10,000 kisses when I get home, so I know I will be busy. I am sure you want to know how everyone else is, but I have not travelled out to see the rest of the family yet. Well, Luis says they are all fine. By the way, he is married and he has a little girl. Just like that, you are a great aunt. Even though you have never seen her, her name is Millie. Standing there with her short curly hair, she looks just like you. Millie your new 4-year-old niece says, "Hi!" I will bring you a picture of her, some homemade candy, and a crocheted scarf. I guess I will see you soon, won't I?

something over the week
to open the wine

Always,

Carmen

Carmen

Commas are used in a great many ways.

1. Commas are used with dates:

   May 14, 1995.

2. Commas are used with openings and closings of letters:

   Dear Aunt Millie,
   Always,

3. Commas are used with addresses:

   3778 Hudson Street, Victoria, B.C. V8S 3H8

4. Commas are used with numbers:

   10,000
   1,000,596

5. Commas are used between complete thoughts that are connected by coordinating words such as *for, or, and, yet, not, so,* and *but*:

   I think you should sit down before you read this letter, and I think you should have a handkerchief handy.
   He was happy to see me, and he wants you to know how much he misses seeing you and the rest of the family.

   Note: If the complete thoughts are very short, no comma is necessary:

   I arrived and he met me.

6. Commas are used to separate introductory material from the rest of the sentence:

Well, Luis says they are all fine.
Suddenly, the door opened.
Just like that, you are a great aunt.
By the way, he is married, and he has a little girl.

7. Commas are used after introductory clauses beginning with *after, although, as, as if, because, before, even, even though, if, since, so that, though, unless, until, when, whenever, whichever, while,* and *whoever*:

When she got the good news, Millie seemed happy.
When she finally let me inside, she looked strange.
Even though you have never seen her, her name is Millie.
As she grabbed me around the waist, she looked deep into my eyes.

Note: If these introductory clauses are short, the comma may occasionally be omitted:

As she entered she looked at us in amazement.

8. Commas are used after introductory *-ing* phrases:
Standing there with her short curly hair, she looks just like you.

9. Commas are used to set off words that identify or repeat something in a sentence; these words could be omitted without changing the meaning of the sentence:

Millie, your new 4-year-old niece, says ...

10. Commas are used to set off quotations:

Millie says, "Hi!"

11. Commas are used between items in a series:

I will bring you a picture of her, some homemade candy, and a crocheted scarf.

12. Commas are used before tag questions (short questions added to a statement to seek confirmation):

I guess I will see you soon, won't I?

EXERCISE

Insert commas where they are necessary in the following paragraph.

Travelling to a different country, whether it is returning home, or going to a new destination, is exciting. When the airplane arrives in the airport safely, even people who travel often are glad. Suddenly, they are in a new, exciting world. Feeling tired, they get off the plane, and they head for their destination. They convert their money, wait in line for taxis and spend too much money on foolish things. On the way home they feel mixed emotions but overall most of them are glad they took the chance and travelled.

Check your answers on page 327.

EDITING PRACTICE

The letter on pages 146 and 147 is all one paragraph. Decide where there should be paragraph breaks. Rewrite the letter, inserting the paragraph indentations and all necessary commas.

GRAMMAR STRATEGIES

MODAL AUXILIARIES

Modal auxiliaries are a special group of words including *can, could, have to, may, might, must, shall, will, would, should,* and *ought to.* These words are followed by the simple form of the verb ("I can *swim,*" "He ought to *go*"). To make a modal negative, add *not* after the modal and before the verb ("I *will not* swim," "They *should not* eat that apple"). Modal auxiliaries are not usually indicators of time and tense, although "I can swim" has a different time meaning than "I could swim."

Some of the uses for modals are as follows:

1. To make general requests *(can, could, will, would)* and to request permission *(may, might)*:

   Can/Could/Will/Would you help me revise my essay?
   May/Might I borrow that book?

2. To show inference or prediction:

   Someone's ringing the doorbell.
   It *could/might* be Marie (It's a possibility.)
   It *may* be Marie. (It's a strong possibility.)
   It *should* be Marie. (It probably is Marie.)
   It *will* be Marie. (It is definitely Marie.)

3. To show ability *(can, be able to)*:

   I *can* swim.
   I *am able to* swim.

4. To offer advice *(might, could, should, had better, must, have to, will)*:

   He *might/could* study English in school. (It's possible.)

He *should* study English in school.
He *had better* study English in school.
He *must* study English in school.
He *has to* study English in school.
He *will* study English.

5. To show desire *(would like to):*

She *would like to* learn English more quickly.

6. To present an offer *(would like):*

Would you *like* something to eat?

7. To show preference *(would rather, would prefer to):*

I *would rather* drink tea *than* coffee.
I *would prefer to* drink tea instead of coffee.

EXERCISE

Read the following paragraph about the MacKay article, and underline any of the following modal auxiliaries you find: *can, can't, has/have to, had better, may, might, must, ought to, should, will, won't,* and *would rather.*

MacKay writes that women may now ask men out on dates and share the expenses. They can feel comfortable doing so because it is done all the time. Men ought to feel flattered, not threatened, when they are asked out by women. Some women would rather have men ask them out and pay the tab, but they realize they had better initiate the relationship sometimes, too. MacKay thinks that the decision as to who pays the cheque should be casual and relaxed. If neither feels comfortable sharing the expense, it might be better if one will pay when dining out; then the other has to reciprocate with a home-cooked meal. In a modern relationship, the man can't be expected to take care of all the expenses, or he won't feel it is an equal partnership. The arrangement must enable both the man and woman to feel

they are on an equal footing.

Examine the use of the modal auxiliaries in the paragraph; then answer the following questions.

1. Is there any ending on the verb that follows the modal auxiliary? *No*
2. In a group, reread each of the sentences and decide the meaning of each modal auxiliary.
3. In a group, rewrite this paragraph in the past tense. What changes would you have to make in the sentences and in the modal auxiliaries? Why would you make those changes?

COUNTABLES AND UNCOUNTABLES

Examine the following two sentences:

People have fewer anxiety attacks when they share the cheque rather than one paying the tab all the time.

People have less trouble when they share the cheque rather than one paying the tab all the time.

In the space provided, copy the words that are different in these two sentences.

Countable fewer anxiety attacks

uncountable less trouble

One of these is countable and the other is uncountable.

Which is countable? _____

Which is uncountable? _____

If you had any difficulty, read the explanation that follows.

In English, certain nouns are uncountable. An article *(the, a, an)* is usually not used with an uncountable noun. Two basic types of uncountable nouns are *mass nouns* and *abstract nouns*. Mass nouns include liquids such as water, milk, soda, coffee, tea, rain; solids that are made up of many small particles such as sand, salt, pepper, snow; and gases such as air, hydrogen, oxygen, smoke.

Abstract nouns include concepts such as love, hate, anger, fear, beauty, ugliness, intelligence, life, freedom, success, truth, and peace; and categories such as money, furniture, merchandise, food, vocabulary, equipment, luggage, homework, advice, and information.

Uncountable nouns are treated as singular subjects and take singular verbs. They do not use an -s ending to show the plural.

> So much information is reported each day that no one can keep
>   track of it all.
> Water is finite, and we must conserve it.
> Her vocabulary seems excellent.
> The new furniture looks beautiful in the living room.

Here are some uncountable and countable nouns.

Uncountable	Countable
water	five bottles of water
clothing	a coat, ten shirts, a pair of socks
furniture	a couch, two couches, four tables
information	a fact, two ideas, three opinions
homework	three pages of assignments
housework	washing dishes, mopping floors
laundry	two loads of laundry

Style. The woman one dresses is casual (handwritten note in margin next to "clothing")

Using the uncountable and countable nouns in the lists, fill in the blanks in the following sentences.

1. I did lots of _homework_ for my math class.

2. My husband washed two _loads_ of _laundry_ in the machine when he came home from work.

3. The bride and groom bought new _furniture_ for their apartment.

4. Watching the news on television provides most people with _information_ about what is going on in the world.

5. The hall closet was filled with _shirts_ and _clothes_. It was so full that some of the _clothes_ fell on the floor.

EXERCISE

In the following paragraph, fill in each blank with a verb that makes sense to you as a reader. Think about countables and uncountables when you decide if verbs need an -s ending or not.

Life __is__ confusing when students first __start__ college. Although academic freedom __allows__ students to choose some of their own courses, placement tests __prevent__ them from taking some of their favourite courses. Those first weeks, homework in each class _____ due every day. New students __have__ lots of questions, but fear __holds__ them back from asking them the first few days. A tremendous amount of information __is__ available if students _____ where to find it. Signs __are__ all over the college walls. The best advice __is__ not to give up. Success __comes__ with perseverance.

THE GERUND (-ING) VERB FORM

When we write, we decide which verb form (-s, -ed, -ing) to use on the basis of the tense of the verb. In addition, when we have two verbs together, we must decide which form to use for the second verb. Usually the preposition to is followed by the simple form of the verb; for example, "I like to sing." There are special rules for the verb form that should follow some verbs. We see some examples of these in the article:

> If your date always insists on paying the entire bill and you prefer ... (paragraph 7)

> Women who insist on paying 50 percent of everything on every date may be revealing ... (paragraph 8)

Here is a list of some of the verbs that require the verb that follows to be in the -ing (gerund) form:

| alternate | deny | miss | report |
| appreciate | dislike | postpone | resent |

avoid	enjoy	practice	resume
consider	escape	quit	stop+
delay	finish	regret*	

The verb form that should follow most prepositions (*on, in, off, up, by, about, from, of*) is the *-ing* gerund form.

In the following sentences, underline the preposition and the verb that follows it. The first one has been done for you.

1. Instead <u>of splitting</u> the cheque, she allowed him to pick up the tab.
2. Many women have enriched their social lives by taking the initiative with men.
3. We can go out together more often by sharing dating expenses.
4. She keeps their relationship equal by reciprocating with home-cooked meals.
5. If she goes on a date, she insists on splitting the bill 50–50.
6. I don't know if I'll deny you pleasure or offend you by insisting on paying for myself. (There are two examples in this sentence.)

There is a special list of expressions after which *to* is followed by the *-ing* gerund form. This is very unusual. *To* is almost always followed by the simple form of the verb with no ending. However, the following expressions are following by the *-ing* gerund form:
I *stopped to talk* to my best friend. (We spent some time talking.)

admit to	be used to*
confess to	get used to*
look forward to	

Here are some examples of how these words are used in sentences:

The young man admitted to asking *his brother's girlfriend out on a date.*

She confessed to plagiarizing *the essay.*

*In a formal letter, regret is followed by the infinitive form of the verb (*to* plus the simple form of the verb): "I regret to tell you ..."

+*Stop* can be followed by either the *-ing* form or the *to* form, but the meaning changes:
I *stopped talking* to my best friend. (We no longer talk.)
I *stopped to talk* to my best friend. (We spent some time talking.)

*Notice that the meaning of *be used to* and *get used to* is different from *used to,* which we studied in the student essay in Chapter 6. *Be used to* and *get used to* mean "to get accustomed to."

Maureen looks forward to having *dinner with Dennis.*

Maureen is not used to asking *men out on dates. She says that she will try to* get used to doing *this so she can improve her social life.*

EXERCISE

In the following sentences, fill in each blank with a verb that makes sense to you as a reader.

1. The teacher finished _checking_ and then asked for questions about the examination ~~that~~ *on* Thursday.

2. The students appreciated _knowing_ about what would be on the test.

3. One of the students asked the teacher to postpone _having_ the test until Monday.

4. The teacher told the students that they had to get used to _taking_ *having / writing* tests every week.

5. A few students considered _gathering together_ after class to study together in small groups. */staying / meeting*

COMBINING SENTENCES

As discussed earlier, combining sentences is a way of making sentences longer and more interesting. Writers vary the length of their sentences by combining shorter sentences into a variety of longer sentences. Here we will practise writing sentences that begin with *-ing* phrases. For this to be effective, the subject in the two sentences must be exactly the same.

I grew up.
I learned that men call, ask, and pay for the date.
    Growing up, I learned that men call, ask, and pay for the date.

I wait for you to get to the restaurant.
I am incredibly impatient.

    Waiting for you to get to the restaurant, I am _incredibly impatient_

She treasures her femininity.
She also believes in equality.

    Treasur~~es~~ing her femininity, she also _believes in equality_

He feels shy.
He hasn't asked her on a date yet.

_____ feel _____ ing _____ shy _____ , he *hasn't asked her* . on
a date yet

He slides into his desk.
He taps her shoulder and says, "Hi."

_____ sliding into his desk *he taps her should* _____ .
says, "Hi."

Now write a sentence of your own using this pattern. Notice
where the comma goes in this type of sentence.

_____

_____

_____

COMPARING THE SEXES

PREREADING ACTIVITIES

1. The title of the textbook excerpt you are about to read is "How Different Are the Sexes?" What do you expect will be some of the differences mentioned in the article?

2. In a small group, discuss whether you feel that males and females are treated differently in your home, in school, in your neighbourhood, and in society in general. Each group should present its ideas to the class as a whole.

3. In a small group, discuss the advantages and disadvantages of being a male or being a female. Each group should present its ideas to the class as a whole.

How Different Are the Sexes?

The following excerpt is from Ian Robertson's 1989 textbook Society: A Brief Introduction. *The excerpt is about differences between males and females. Before you read this, discuss in what ways, if any, girls should be raised differently from boys and why.*

Throughout the world, the first question parents ask at the birth of a child is always the same: "Is it a boy or a girl?" The urgency of the question reveals the great importance that all human societies attach to the differences between men and women.

The division of the human species into two fundamental cate- 5
gories is based on sex — the biological distinction between males and females. All societies, however, elaborate this biological fact into secondary, nonbiological notions of "masculinity" and "femininity." These concepts refer not to sex but to *gender* — the culturally learned differences between males and females. In other words, male or 10
female is what, by birth, you are; but masculine or feminine is what, with appropriate socialization, you may *become.* Gender thus refers to purely social characteristics, such as differences in hair styles, clothing patterns, occupational roles, and other culturally learned activities and traits. 15

Biological Evidence

Men and women are different in their *genes*, which provide the inherited blueprint for their physical development. Females have two similar chromosomes (XX), while males have two dissimilar chromosomes (XY). Except in the area of short-term feats of physical strength, the male's lack of a second X chromosome makes him in many respects the weaker sex. Male infants are more likely than females to be stillborn or malformed. Throughout the life course, the death rate for men is higher than it is for women. Women are more resistant than men to most diseases and seem to have a greater tolerance for pain and malnutrition.

Men and women also have differences in their *hormones*, chemical substances that are secreted by the body's various glands. The precise effects of hormones have not been fully determined, but it is known that they can influence both physical development and emotional arousal. Both sexes have "male" as well as "female" hormones, but the proportion of male hormones is greater in men and that of female hormones is greater in women. The present consensus among researchers is that hormonal differences probably do have some influence on the behaviour of men and women but that this influence varies greatly — not only among individuals, but also within the same person over time.

Psychological Evidence

Although there are many differences among both individual men and individual women, the typical personality patterns of adult men and women are clearly dissimilar in many ways. For example, men tend to be more aggressive and to have greater mathematical ability; women tend to be more nurturant and more emotional. But are these differences inborn or learned? In the case of adults, this question cannot be answered, since it is impossible to untangle the effects of biological and social influences on personality. Psychologists have therefore focused much of their research on very young infants, reasoning that the earlier sex-linked differences in behaviour appear, the more likely they are to be the result of inborn factors.

Many studies of young infants have found sex-linked personality differences early in life. Even in the cradle, for example, male babies are more active than females; female babies smile more readily and are more sensitive to warmth and touch than males. But these are only general tendencies. Many male babies show traits that are more typical of female babies, and vice versa. These and other findings seem at first sight to indicate some inborn personality differences between the sexes, but it is possible that even these early variations are learned. From the time children are born, parents and others treat them in subtly different ways according to their sex. In fact, experiments have shown that if adults are told that a girl infant is a boy, they will respond to her as if she were a boy — for example, by commenting on the infant's sturdiness and playing with her vigorously. But if they are told the same child is a girl, they are likely to remark on her prettiness and to touch her more gently. Infants may therefore learn to behave differently even in the first few weeks of life. 60

65

READING AND THINKING STRATEGIES

DISCUSSION ACTIVITIES

Analysis and Conclusions

1. What is the difference between sex and gender?
2. What evidence does Robertson provide to prove that males are the weaker sex?
3. Why is it difficult to answer whether differences between the sexes are inborn or learned?

Writing and Point of View

1. On pages 75 and 76, several essay types are defined. Which of these types best describes the Robertson article?
2. Robertson defines several words in this excerpt. What words does he define, and how does he let the reader know that these words are important?
3. Reread the excerpts on pages 22 and 157. In what ways are these excerpts similar, and in what ways are they different? What characteristics do you notice that make textbook writing different from other writing?

Personal Response and Evaluation

1. In almost all societies, women live longer than men. Why do you think this is so?
2. Compare gender — the culturally learned differences between males and females — in Canada and in any other country you have lived in or visited.

3. Are boy babies treated differently from girl babies? Describe some differences in treatment that you have observed. Think of colours that babies are dressed in, the toys they are given, how much they are held, and the way people play with them.

DEBATE

While working on this chapter, it might be interesting to have several class debates. Divide the class into men and women, or use any other division that seems to work. Each group is given a point of view on a topic. Together the group members create an argument based on facts and observations. Then the actual debate can begin. It might be useful to audiotape or videotape the debate for later class discussions.

The following are some points of view that might be considered for debate.

Team A

Women are the weaker sex.

Children should be brought up as equals; there should be no differences in treatment.

Women are not psychologically equipped to hold positions of power.

There can never be true equality between men and women.

Team B

Men are really the weaker sex.

Boys and girls should be brought up differently. This is necessary for their future roles in life.

Women can deal with positions of power as well as men can.

Men and women must develop true equality.

NOTE TAKING

For practice in taking notes from a lecture class, your teacher will read several paragraphs from "How Different Are the Sexes?" aloud to the class. Take notes as if you were planning to study from them. Then meet in a small group to compare your notes. Discuss how you decided what to write down. What do you think are the most important ideas? Justify your choices.

JOURNAL WRITING

"If each man did for himself the work he expects of his woman, there would be no wealth in the world, only millions and millions of poor, tired men."

CHARLOTTE PERKINS GILMAN

When you write in your journal, think about what it means to be a male or female in our society today. Have your views about relationships between men and women changed since you learned English? Have your views changed since you started college? Write about what it means to be a man or a woman in today's society. Write about the ways in which your ideas have changed about male and female relationships.

WRITING STRATEGIES

ESSAY STRATEGIES
Using Definitions in Your Writing

As part of writing this selection, Robertson defined several words or terms that he thought would not be familiar to his readers. Many writers use definitions as part of their writing no matter what type of writing they are doing. Whether they are creating an explanation, a comparison, an analysis, or a persuasive piece of writing, a definition may add substance and believability.

The purpose of defining a word or a term is to make it more understandable to the reader. A few steps can assist you in defining terms in your writing. One way is to place the term to be defined in a broader context of related things. The next is to look for the special characteristics that make this term different from other related terms. For example, in paragraph 1 Robertson defines *sex* by broadening it into the class of "distinctions." He breaks this down into distinctions that are "biological" and finally into "male and female."

The division of human species into two fundamental categories is based on sex — the biological distinction between males and females.

When Robertson defines *gender*, he places this in the broad class of "differences." He breaks this down into differences that are "culturally learned" and finally into "male and female."

These concepts refer not to sex but to gender — *the culturally learned differences between males and females.*

Reread the Robertson article to find any other terms that he has defined. Notice how he indicates to his readers that he is about to define a term. Look carefully at how he breaks the term down into an explanation in simpler, more easily understandable words.

ESSAY FORM
Comparison and Contrast

In "How Different Are the Sexes?" Robertson compared and contrasted males and females. When a writer compares two things, the writer looks for the similarities. When a writer contrasts two things, the writer looks for the differences. We compare and contrast things every day. We may compare how quickly the bus came this morning with how quickly it came yesterday. We may contrast the experience of walking to school with the experience of taking the bus. It is a human activity to compare and contrast. We do it in our minds, and we do it aloud with our friends. For many writers, however, the comparison-and-contrast essay can create problems.

Comparison-and-contrast essays may follow two basic patterns of organization. Both may contain the same information, but it is presented in a different manner. In the first method, the writer follows this basic pattern:

Introduction
Body Paragraph(s) A — presents all the information about A
Body Paragraph(s) B — presents all the information about B
Conclusion — sums up and makes final comparisons and/or contrasts

The second method involves alternating within each paragraph. It is organized as follows:

Introduction
Body Paragraph — about one aspect of the comparison
Point A
Point B
Point A
Point B

Body Paragraph — about another aspect of the comparison

Point A
Point B
Point A
Point B

Conclusion

Many writers find the first method, the block approach, easier to organize. In this method, all the information about one side of an issue or problem is presented, and then all the information about the other side is given. Using this method, it is also possible to present all the similarities and then all the differences. In the second method, the alternating method, a point from one side is given, then a point from the other side. This is a good method to use for longer pieces of writing because it is easy to follow. For this reason, readers may prefer this method.

The following paragraph is from an essay that uses the block form; it presents the information about women's physical superiority. We can assume that the writer will next give us all the information about the areas of male superiority.

> *Women, on the average, have a better sense of smell than men. Women hear better at the upper range. Women have more physical endurance than men. They generally live longer and do not usually suffer from hypertension and heart disease.*

Using the alternating method, the writer of an essay about male and female differences makes the comparison within the paragraph itself. The paragraph that follows uses the alternating method to compare the health problems of men and women.

> *Women, on the average, have a better sense of smell than men. Men, however, have keener eyesight. Women hear better at the upper range, whereas men often have more acute hearing at the lower range. The estimated life span for men is seventy-four years; for women it is seventy-eight years.*

The comparison-and-contrast essay is a popular form of writing. The following student paragraph is written in the comparison-and-contrast mode. Does it follow the block pattern or the alternating pattern?

There are differences between men and women. Men usually live a shorter time than women. Women have a higher range of hearing. Men have a lower range of hearing, but they can see better for a long distance. Women have long-term strength. At night they take care of the baby and then go to work the next day. Men have short-term strength. They go to work during the day and then when they get home, they complain that they are very tired. Most men spend their time outside the house. Women stay home and do the chores. Men are usually taller and women are shorter. More crimes are done by men, but women commit crimes, too. Both women and men have vices like gambling and smoking. Both genders often marry more than once.

Marina Ibea, The Philippines

In comparison-and-contrast writing, we use special transition words:

To compare	*To contrast*
also	but
as . . . as	not as . . . as
as well as	however
likewise	nevertheless
similarly	conversely
too	in contrast

EXERCISES

1. Write a paragraph comparing and contrasting the behaviour of males and females in college.
2. Write a paragraph contrasting living in your native country with living in Canada.
3. Write a paragraph comparing and contrasting a book with the movie made from that book.
4. Write a paragraph comparing and contrasting the teaching methods of two teachers you have had.

SUGGESTIONS FOR WRITING

Before you start to write your essay, try making quadrants, as shown in the "Getting Started" section below, to help you develop ideas for writing.

1. Write an essay comparing and contrasting the way girls are raised with the way boys are raised. Use your own observations and experiences as evidence.

2. Write an essay comparing and contrasting the teaching methods in your native country with those in Canada.

3. What are some of the differences between men and women? Include information from the Robertson article, as well as your own observations and experiences.

4. The characteristics that a person looks for in a friend may be very different from the ones that are important in a future husband or wife. Compare and contrast these characteristics.

5. Each language is unique, although there may be some similarities between certain languages. Compare and contrast your first language with English. Consider such characteristics as the ways in which questions are constructed, where adjectives are placed, the use of articles, how nouns are made plural, and whether or not the language is phonetic.

6. If you were a scientific researcher, what would you research and why? In an essay, explain the details of your research proposal. Imagine that your reader gives grants of money to researchers, and you are trying to convince that person that your idea is worthwhile.

GETTING STARTED
Making Quadrants

Before you begin to write, spend some time thinking of ideas that relate to the process or pattern you are writing about. To help you come up with ideas, fold a piece of paper into four sections.

In one section, write the word *Describe*. In that section, write the following four questions:

What do you see?
What do you hear?
What do you feel?
What do you taste?

In another section, write the word *Compare*. Then write the following questions:

What is it similar to?
What is it different from?

In the next section, write the word *Analyze*. Then write the following questions:

What parts does it have?

How do they work together or not work together?

In the remaining section, write the word *Argue*. Then write the following questions:

Why is it a good idea?

Why would people think it is a bad idea?

In each of the sections, think about the process or pattern you are going to write about; then write answers to the questions. Reread these answers when preparing to write your essay.

A Student Essay

Thailand is the country where I was born. I was taught differently from my brothers in regard to the way we were brought up. Thai boys are taught to be strong and brave. The boys participate with their fathers doing the same activities such as playing football, watching a boxing match and helping their fathers to earn money for the family. On the other hand, Thai girls are brought up like their mothers. They learn to do housework and how to take care of the family at home.

Thai men are the leaders of the family, the leaders of the communities and the leaders of the country. The men take responsibility for the family finances. However, Thai women take good care of the family, doing all kinds of household activities. For example, the women mostly bring up the children, prepare the meals, clean up the house, wash all the clothes and so forth. Consequently, Thai men and the women play different roles.

In Canada, men and women are relatively equal. Men not only have responsibility for earning money but also helping the family bring up the children and doing some housework. Likewise, women work outside the house to make money to support the family besides carrying on household duties. Sharing the life means sharing everything. Canadian men and Canadian women have similar social status, educational status and occupational status. Still, the issue of women's rights sometimes becomes controversial.

I like some aspects of the Canadian way of life; nevertheless I like men to be the leaders of the family and main economic support. At the same time men should appreciate the efforts and support of the women in the family and treat all members of the family kindly and respectfully.

Thai society is gradually changing; more people are accepting the western way of life. Women are receiving higher education and gaining higher status. The role of women is changing as well. Men and women are earning the same salaries and filling the same positions. However, women who live in the larger cities are more likely to have better opportunities than women who live in more remote areas. In short, Thai culture is still quite strong in terms of family values. Thai men are still respected as the leaders of the family, although women, especially in urban areas, are gaining equality, specifically in the workplace.

Subaida Poteh, Thailand

REVISING

With a partner or in a small group, reread the student essay; then answer the following questions about it.

1. What is the main idea of this essay? How did you know?
2. Which method of comparison did the writer use in this essay?
3. What do you like about this essay? Why?
4. What would you like to add to this essay? Why?
5. What would you like to delete from this essay Why?
6. Try to move one sentence in the essay. Which sentence did you move? Why? How does it change the rest of the essay?
7. What is the best sentence in the essay?
8. What audience do you think the writer had in mind? What in the essay told you this?

Working with a partner or in a small group, use these same questions to discuss your own draft and to help you prepare to revise it. After you have revised your writing, share it with the same classmate or group again.

EDITING STRATEGIES

IDIOMATIC EXPRESSIONS

Each of the following paragraphs contains a context clue that will help you understand one of the idiomatic expressions used in "How Different Are the Sexes?" Underline these context clues; the first one has been done for you. Then use the expressions when you answer the questions that follow each paragraph.

1. *in other words* (line 10)

   Another way of saying that sex and gender are different is to make an analogy with something that is comparable, such as the beauty of a baby and the beauty of an elderly person. The first occurs as a gift of birth and youth; the second a person may or may not achieve because of his or her attitude or life experiences. Can you think of an analogy with something else in life that expresses in other words that the differences between the sexes are not purely biological?

2. *in many respects* (lines 21–22)

   Robertson claims that the male's lack of a second X chromosome makes him in several ways weaker than the female. Male babies either die at birth or are born with physical problems more often than female babies. Males usually die earlier than females.

   In many respects, when writers report information, they present what they believe to be the most effective support for their main idea, even if others may not always agree with them. What other kinds of information would you have liked Robertson to include to convince you that males are weaker than females in many respects?

3. *in the case of* (line 44)

   Many questions about sexual differences will remain mysteries because it is impossible to be sure whether certain behaviour was taught or was present at birth. For example, researchers cannot be sure if the fact that girl babies smile more than boy babies is a response to inborn personality or life experience.

   In the case of babies, what differences have you noticed between boy and girl babies? What do you think explains these differences?

4. *at first sight* (line 56)

   It may seem initially that parents teach their children the behaviour that is expected of them. However, if you watch many children together and observe certain tendencies, you may begin to think that the behaviour is inborn.

   The Robertson article at first sight suggests that people in our world make differences between males and females. In your experience in college classes, are males and females treated differently automatically, or are they given a chance to show their individual abilities?

LEARNING NEW VOCABULARY

One way to learn new vocabulary is to identify words that relate to a particular field of study. In "How Different Are the Sexes?"

Robertson uses some vocabulary that relates to biology and psychology. Although each discipline has its own particular jargon or terminology, the words we shall focus on are words that you will encounter again in some of your other classes.

Paragraph 2

species: a fundamental classification of a biological group whose members have a high degree of similarity and can reproduce among themselves

Paragraph 3

gene: the basic unit of heredity, which is a segment of the DNA molecules that transmit and determine all bodily characteristics
chromosomes: rod-shaped bodies that carry the genes that convey the hereditary characteristics; each species has a specific number of chromosomes
malformed: abnormally formed (said of a part of the body)
malnutrition: poor nourishment resulting from insufficient food

Paragraph 4

hormones: secretions of the glands that influence most activities carried on in the body

Paragraph 5

nurturant: feeding, educating, caring for, and otherwise promoting the development of children
inborn: present at birth
sex-linked: determined by genes carried on one of the sex chromosomes and therefore linked to the sex of a person

Paragraph 6

trait: distinguishing characteristic or quality

To make the meaning of these words clearer, reread the Robertson selection, concentrating on the meaning of these words and how they are used.

COMMONLY CONFUSED WORDS

accept/except

Read the following paragraph, observing the use of *accept* and *except*.

> *Many people automatically* accept *the idea that males are stronger than females. However,* except *in the area of short-term feats of physical strength, females are the stronger sex. Many men say they can* accept *the fact that males die earlier than females in*

almost all societies, except *that it makes them wonder if the problem is that they are just working too hard.*

From what you observed in this paragraph, can you determine the difference in meaning between *accept* and *except*? Complete the following definitions:

_____ means "agree to or receive."

_____ means "but" or "aside from the fact that."

Now use these two words in sentences of your own.

MECHANICS

A Different Use for Quotation Marks

Quotation marks are most often used to indicate the exact words of a speaker and to set off the title of a short story or other short work.

However, the Robertson selection illustrates another use for quotation marks in writing. Notice the purpose of quotation marks in the following sentences taken from the excerpt.

All societies, however, elaborate this biological fact into secondary, nonbiological notions of "masculinity" and "femininity."

Both sexes have "male" as well as "female" hormones, but the proportion of male hormones is greater in men and that of female hormones is greater in women.

In these sentences, the quotation marks are used *to set off special words* from the rest of the sentence. When writers do this, they add extra emphasis to those words. Why do you think Robertson put the words *masculinity* and *femininity* in quotation marks in the first sentence illustrated here? Why do you think he put the words *male* and *female* in quotation marks? What effect did that have on you as a reader?

EDITING PRACTICE

The following paragraph is a first draft that contains many surface errors: one comma error, two preposition errors, four subject–verb agreement errors, one possessive error, one *the* error, two tense consistency errors, and two *there/their/they're* errors. Find and correct all the errors.

Sociologists examines how people live in groups. They examined phenomena such as peoples' behavioural patterns in relation to love and marriage. They want to know if people on Italy celebrate marriage in the same way as people on Philippines. They're studies show some customs and traditions is similar from place to place. For example people usually get married with some kind of ceremony. They usually get dressed up for there wedding. However, there are some differences. In some places marriages are arranged. In other places people meets and falls in love. In general, everyone hoped that the marriage will be happy and long-lasting.

Answers are on page 328.

GRAMMAR STRATEGIES

COMPARATIVES AND SUPERLATIVES

One of the most basic uses of language is to express similarities and differences, to compare and contrast. Comparisons can be expressed using adjectives, adverbs, nouns, and verbs.

1. Comparisons using adjectives:
   COMPARATIVE: Rose is *smarter than* Marie (is).

   SUPERLATIVE: Rose is *the smartest* student in the room.

   COMPARATIVE: Harry is *less competitive than* Roland (is).

   SUPERLATIVE: Harry is *the least competitive* one in his family.

2. Comparisons using adverbs:
   COMPARATIVE: Han walks *slower than* Thuy (walks, does).

   SUPERLATIVE: Han walks *the slowest* of all the students in the class.

   COMPARATIVE: Mimi talks *less frequently than* Jenny (talks, does).

   SUPERLATIVE: Mimi talks *the least frequently* of all the girls.

3. Comparisons using nouns:
   COMPARATIVE: Li has *more* books *than* Ping (has, does).

   SUPERLATIVE: Li has *the most* books of all the students.

COMPARATIVE: Sam has *fewer* books *than* Howard (has, does). (*Books* is a countable word.)

SUPERLATIVE: Sam has *the fewest* books of all the brothers.

COMPARATIVE: Sam has *less* money *than* Howard (has, does). (*Money* is an uncountable word.)

SUPERLATIVE: Sam has *the least* money of all the brothers.

4. Comparisons using verbs:
COMPARATIVE: Hong weighs *more than* Pedro (weighs, does).

SUPERLATIVE: Hong weighs *the most* of all the fighters.

COMPARATIVE: My book cost *more than* your book (cost, did).

SUPERLATIVE: My book cost *the most* of all the books in the store.

The rules for using *-er* or *more* and for using *the ... -est* and *the most* are as follows:

1. Use *-er* or *-the ... -est* with one-syllable adjectives and adverbs and with two-syllable adjectives that end in *y* (which changes to *i*), *ple*, *ble*, and sometimes *tle* and *dle*.

2. Use *-er* or *more* or *the . . . -est* or *the most* with two-syllable adjectives that end in *ly, ow, er*, and *some*.

3. Use *more* or *the most* with other adjectives and with adverbs of two or more syllables.

Irregular Comparative and Superlative Forms▶

Base Form	Comparative Form	Superlative Form
much	more	the most
many	more	the most
little	less	the least
good	better	the best
bad	worse	the worst
far	farther (literal) further (figurative)	the farthest the furthest

EXERCISES

1. Fill in the blanks, using the examples as your guide.

Base Form	Comparative Form	Superlative Form
cute	cuter	the cutest
nice	_____	_____

pretty	prettier	the prettiest
happy	_____	_____
ample	ampler	the amplest
simple	_____	_____
lovely	lovelier	the loveliest
manly	_____	_____
friendly	_____	_____
hollow	hollower	the hollowest
mellow	_____	_____
handsome	handsomer or more handsome	_____
beautiful	more beautiful	_____
intelligent	_____	the most intelligent

2. Several sentences from the selection are reproduced here with the comparatives omitted. Fill in the blanks with the words needed to make the sentences comparative. Refer to the article to check your answers.

   a. The male's lack of a second X chromosome makes him in many

   respects the _____ sex.
   (weak)

   b. The death rate for men is _____ than it is for women.
   (high)

   c. Both sexes have "male" as well as "female" hormones, but the

   proportion of male hormones is _____ in men and that of
   (great)

   female hormones is _____ in women.
   (great)

d. Men tend to be _____ and to have _____ mathematical
(aggressive)   *(great)*

ability; women tend to be _____ and _____.
(nurturant)   *(emotional)*

e. Male babies are _____ than females; female babies smile
(active)

_____ and are _____ to warmth and touch than males.
(readily)   *(sensitive)*

ACTIVE VOICE AND PASSIVE VOICE

Underline the verbs in the following sentences. The first has been done for you.

1. It is <u>known</u> by most researchers that hormones can influence both physical development and emotional arousal.

2. The male is observed by doctors to be more active than the female at birth.

3. Females are expected by most teachers to have greater verbal ability.

4. If parents are told by a nurse that the baby is a girl, they are observed to touch her more gently.

According to the first sentence, who knows that hormones can influence physical development and emotional arousal? _____

According to the second sentence, who observes that the male is more active than the female at birth? _____

According to the third sentence, who expects women to have

greater verbal ability?_____

According to the fourth sentence, who tells parents that the baby is a girl? _____

All four sentences were written in the passive voice. Fill in the following blanks to change them to active voice. The first one has been done for you.

1. Most researchers *know that hormones can influence physical ...*

2. Doctors observe _____

3. Most teachers expect _____

4. If a nurse tells _____

Compare the passive voice sentences to the active voice sentences. What differences do you observe?

> PASSIVE: *It* is known *by most researchers that hormones can influence both physical development and emotional arousal.*

> ACTIVE: *Most researchers know that hormones can influence both physical development and emotional arousal.*

In the passive construction, the verb *be* and the past participle are used. In present passive, we use *am, is,* or *are* plus the past participle. In the past passive, we use *was* or *were* plus the past participle. The preposition *by* is often used in the passive construction.

The passive voice is frequently used when the performer of the activity is unknown or unimportant. This technique emphasizes the receiver of the action rather than the doer of the action.

Both active voice and passive voice are correct forms of English. They offer the writer variety in creating sentences. You may notice that textbooks use the passive voice more frequently than newspapers. It is a more formal style. Many modern writers prefer the active voice.

EXERCISE

The following paragraph is written entirely in the passive voice. Add variety to the paragraph by changing some of the sentences to the active voice.

In the past in many countries around the world, marriages were arranged by a matchmaker hired by the family. This matchmaker was expected to make a lasting match. An unhappy marriage was feared by many young people. However, the parents' wishes were respected by the children. Young people were reminded of their obligations by their family and their community. It was expected by everyone that the marriages would lead to love and mutual respect. Divorce was looked down on by most of the community and by religious leaders. Marriage was regarded as a lifetime commitment by most people in those days. As a result, golden anniversaries were celebrated by many more couples then than at present.

ADVERBIAL CONJUNCTIONS

In the following paragraph, connecting words such as *however, moreover, otherwise,* and *therefore* have been left out. Rewrite the paragraph, adding these words. There are many possible ways to correct this paragraph. Share your rewritten paragraph with a classmate or with your teacher.

In this chapter, we looked at some of the ways that researchers compare males and females. Women have XX chromosomes. Men have XY chromosomes. The male's lack of the second X chromosome makes him the weaker sex. Sex is determined at conception. Gender is learned throughout our lives. Robertson explained that boy and girl babies are treated differently. Boy babies and girl babies behave differently. Men are often more aggressive than women. They tend to have greater mathematical ability. Women tend to be more emotional. They often have greater verbal ability than men. These differences may be inborn or learned. No one knows for sure. Research asks questions. Research answers questions. There will always be more research needed in this field.

We can connect the sentences in this paragraph with adverbial conjunctions such as those listed here. When we use these adverbial conjunctions to connect two complete sentences, we must use a semicolon before the conjunction and a comma after it:

Men have XY chromosomes; however, women have XX chromosomes.

Here is a list of these adverbial conjunctions or joining words:

Conjunction	*Meaning*
in addition to	combined or associated with
also	in addition
furthermore	in addition
moreover	in addition
as a result	due to that fact
consequently	as a result
therefore	as a result
hence	as a result
however	but
nevertheless	but
on the contrary	but
on the other hand	but
indeed	in fact
instead	as a substitute or an alternative
meanwhile	at the same time
otherwise	under other conditions

Let's look at some of the ways in which the sentences in the paragraph above could have been connected.

1. **Men tend to have greater mathematical ability. Women tend to have greater verbal ability.**

We can connect these sentences using any of the words that show contrast or mean almost the same thing as *but*:

Men tend to have greater mathematical ability; on the other hand, women tend to have greater verbal ability.

Men tend to have greater mathematical ability; however, women tend to have greater verbal ability.

2. **Robertson explained that boy and girl babies are treated differently. Boy and girl babies behave differently.**

We can use any of the words that mean "as a result" to connect these sentences:

Robertson explained that boy and girl babies are treated differently; consequently, boy and girl babies behave differently.

Robertson explained that boy and girl babies are treated differently; hence, boy and girl babies behave differently.

3. **Men are often more aggressive than women. They tend to have greater mathematical ability.**

We can use any of the words meaning "in addition" to connect these sentences:

Men are often more aggressive than women; furthermore, they tend to have greater mathematical ability.

Men are often more aggressive than women; they also tend to have greater mathematical ability. (Note that *also* is treated as an adverb, not as a conjunction.)

CHAPTER 9

AGING AND LIVING

PREREADING ACTIVITIES

1. The following excerpt is from an autobiography written by a 93-year-old man. Before you read it, what do you expect him to write about in this piece, titled "Age and Youth"?

2. Pablo Casals, the writer of "Age and Youth," was a famous musician who travelled all over the world. Discuss your ideas about the life of a professional musician. Do you think professional musicians should retire when they reach a particular age?

3. Pablo Casals lived his last years in Puerto Rico. Where is Puerto Rico? What do you know about its land and climate?

Age and Youth

"Age and Youth" is an excerpt from Joys and Sorrows, the autobiography of the great musician Pablo Casals. An autobiography is a nonfiction account of a person's life. This excerpt reveals Casals's feelings about his life at the age of 93.

On my last birthday I was ninety-three years old. That is not young, of course. In fact, it is older than ninety. But age is a relative matter. If you continue to work and to absorb the beauty in the world about you, you find that age does not necessarily mean getting old. At least, not in the ordinary sense. I feel many things more intensely   5 than ever before, and for me life grows more fascinating.

Not long ago my friend Sasha Schneider brought me a letter addressed to me by a group of musicians in the Caucasus Mountains in the Soviet Union. This was the text of the letter:

°distinguished conductor, composer, or performer of music

Dear Honourable Maestro°—   10
I have the pleasure on behalf of the Georgian Caucasian Orchestra to invite you to conduct one of our concerts. You will be the first musician of your age who receives the distinction of conducting our orchestra.

Never in the history of our orchestra have we permitted a man   15
under one hundred years to conduct. All of the members of our
orchestra are over one hundred years old. But we have heard of your
talents as a conductor, and we feel that, despite your youthfulness,
an exception should be made in your case.

We expect a favourable response as soon as possible.   20

We pay travel expenses and of course shall provide living
accommodations during your stay with us.

Respectfully,
Astan Shlarba
President, 123 years old   25

Sasha is a man with a sense of humour; he likes to play a joke.
That letter was one of his jokes; he had written it himself. But I must
admit I took it seriously at first. And why? Because it did not seem
to me implausible° that there should be an orchestra composed of
musicians older than a hundred. And, indeed, I was right! That por-   30
tion of the letter was not a joke. There is such an orchestra in the
Caucasus. Sasha had read about it in the *London Sunday Times*. He
showed me the article, with photographs of the orchestra. All of its
members were more than a hundred years old. There were about
thirty of them — they rehearse regularly and give periodic concerts.   35
Most of them are farmers who continue to work in the fields. The
oldest of the group, Astan Shlarba, is a tobacco grower who also
trains horses. They are splendid-looking men, obviously full of vitality. I should like to hear them play sometime — and, in fact, to conduct them, if the opportunity arose. Of course I am not sure they   40
would permit this, in view of my inadequate age.

There is something to be learned from jokes, and it was so in this
case. In spite of their age, those musicians have not lost their zest° for
life. How does one explain this? I do not think the answer lies simply in their physical constitutions or in something unique about the   45
climate in which they live. It has to do with their attitude toward life;
and I believe that their ability to work is due in no small measure to
the fact that they do work. Work helps prevent one from getting old.
I, for one, cannot dream of retiring. Not now or ever. Retire? The
word is alien and the idea inconceivable to me. I don't believe in   50
retirement for anyone in my type of work, not while the spirit
remains. My work is my life. I cannot think of one without the other.
To "retire" means to me to begin to die. The man who works and is
never bored is never old. Work and interest in worthwhile things are
the best remedy for age. Each day I am reborn. Each day I must   55
begin again.

For the past eighty years I have started each day in the same
manner. It is not a mechanical routine but something essential to my

°unbelievable

°enthusiasm

°opening sections of musical compositions
°type of musical composition
°Johann Sebastian Bach (1685–1750), a great German composer
°blessing

daily life. I go to the piano, and I play two preludes° and fugues° of Bach.° I cannot think of doing otherwise. It is a sort of benediction° on the house. But that is not its only meaning for me. It is a rediscovery of the world of which I have the job of being a part. It fills me with awareness of the wonder of life, with a feeling of the incredible marvel of being a human being. The music is never the same for me, never. Each day it is something new, fantastic and unbelievable. That is Bach, like nature, a miracle! 60 65

I do not think a day passes in my life in which I fail to look with fresh amazement at the miracle of nature. It is there on every side. It can be simply a shadow on a mountainside, or a spider's web gleaming with dew, or sunlight on the leaves of a tree. I have always especially loved the sea. Whenever possible, I have lived by the sea, as for these past twelve years here in Puerto Rico. It has long been a custom of mine to walk along the beach each morning before I start work. True, my walks are shorter than they used to be, but that does not lessen the wonder of the sea. How mysterious and beautiful is the sea! How infinitely variable! It is never the same, never, not from one moment to the next, always in the process of change, always becoming something different and new. 70 75

READING AND THINKING STRATEGIES

DISCUSSION ACTIVITIES
Analysis and Conclusions

1. What attitude does Casals have toward life? Give examples from the text to support your point of view.

2. What does retirement mean to Casals? Support your answer with examples from the text.

3. Why does Casals live by the sea? What effect does the sea have on him?

Writing and Point of View

1. Why do you think Casals included the letter in this essay instead of just telling the reader about it? What effect did reading the letter have on you?

2. The excerpt is from an autobiography. What is the difference between an autobiography and a biography? If you could meet with any famous person to write that person's biography, whom would you most want to meet with? Explain why.

3. In lines 60 to 63 of the essay, the pronoun *it* is used four times. What does each *it* refer to?

4. If this had been a biography, would it be written in the first person or the third person? Why? What biographies or autobiographies have you read that you would recommend to your classmates?

Personal Response and Evaluation

1. Have you ever known any older person with an especially positive attitude toward life? Describe that person.

2. Casals discusses his love of music. How has music influenced your life? Do you like classical music, jazz, rock 'n' roll, or country and western music? If not, what kind of music do you like?

3. Some people believe that Canadians do not respect older people enough and do not treat them with enough care and kindness. In your experience, does this seem to be true? Explain.

INTERVIEWING

Ask a classmate the following questions and any others about this topic that you think would be interesting. Take notes about what your partner tells you.

1. Who is one older person that influenced your life?

2. How old was the person?

3. What memory about this person stands out in your mind?

4. What did you learn from knowing this person?

5. How would you describe this person so that I can see him or her through your eyes?

Then reverse the process, with the classmate asking you questions and taking notes. After you have finished your interview, write a report of what you learned from your partner. Share your report with the class.

JOURNAL WRITING

The journal is an excellent tool with which the writer may begin to see his or her experience as unique in the world. Although we may focus on the same aspect of life in our journals, each of our views of the world will be personal and distinctive.

Your representation of the world differs from mine, and this is not only insofar as the world has used us differently — that is to say we have had differing experiences of it. It is also because your way of representing is not the same as mine. We are neither of us cameras. ... I look at the world in the

light of what I have learned to expect from past experiences of the world.
                    JAMES BRITTON, *LANGUAGE AND LEARNING*

Let us examine age and the aging process in our journals. Although we are not necessarily old, we are all constantly aging. Casals tells us that age is relative. "If you continue to work and to absorb the beauty in the world about you, you find that age does not necessarily mean getting old." He encourages us to question what it means to be old and what it means to be young. Imagine yourself as an old person. Imagine yourself as a young child. How does this make you feel? Think about this when you write in your journal.

WRITING STRATEGIES

ESSAY STRATEGIES

Finding a Controlling Idea

One technique that can help focus your writing is to concentrate on a few words or a theme that illustrates the main idea of your essay. In your writing, you may not actually state this theme, but you will think about it in deciding on appropriate supporting details. For example, Pablo Casals never writes that "life is a great gift," but every example he provides about the orchestra, his music, and the beach are illustrations of this controlling idea or theme. Sometimes these controlling ideas are clichés or overused expressions, so you should not include them in your essay. However, keeping them in mind as you write can be useful to help you focus and decide on appropriate supporting details. Here are some examples of controlling ideas:

You learn from adversity.

Persistence is rewarded.

Wealth isn't always measured in terms of money.

EXERCISES

1. Choose one of the themes just listed, or write your own theme that will assist you in describing a person. Make a list of supporting details that illustrate the theme and also create a picture of the person you want to describe.

2. Write a description of the person, keeping the theme in mind but never stating it. Share your writing with a classmate, and ask the classmate to tell you what your theme was.

ESSAY FORM

Description: Writing about an Event

When Casals writes about receiving the letter, his daily routine, or walking on the beach, he is writing about important events that define who he is as a person. When you write about an event, you can focus on the *person*, the *place*, or the *feelings* associated with the event. First, you must decide what to concentrate on to describe the event from your own perspective. Once you have decided on your focus, in your first draft, practise using the four processes listed here as you write your essay. When you write your final draft, you may find that you do not need all the steps, and you may delete some or add others that work better for you.

1. *Observe.* Look closely at the event in your memory, in pictures, or in real life. Notice the specific or unusual details, the moments that stand out, so that your readers will be able to see and feel the event through your words.

2. *Describe.* Use the journalistic technique for writing described on page 74 and ask yourself the *who, what, where, when, why,* and *how* questions about the event. Write out your answers, and include in your essay as many as seem necessary to show your reader the event.

3. *Compare and contrast.* Tell the reader what event yours is similar to or different from and why. Tell your reader why this is important to understanding the event.

4. *Evaluate.* Tell your readers why this event is important to you or to others.

EXERCISES

1. Reread the Casals excerpt to determine which of the listed steps he used in his writing.

2. Reread another selection in the book to determine which steps the author used.

3. Reread one of your own essays describing an event to determine which steps you used. Rewrite one of your own essays, adding information using one of the steps you did not use in your earlier version. Reread both versions. Which version of your essay do you prefer? Why?

SUGGESTIONS FOR WRITING

Choose one of the following topics that interests you. Before you begin to write, try the "Getting Started" suggestion below.

1. Describe an older person who has had an important influence on your life. Include a lot of detail so that the reader can picture the

person. Tell a story about the person so that the reader can understand why this person means so much to you.

2. "Work helps prevent one from getting old," Casals writes. Do you agree or disagree? Support your point of view with your experience or observations.

3. Should people be forced to retire at the age of sixty-five to give opportunities to young people? Support your point of view with your experience or observations.

4. Casals says that no day passes in his life in which he fails to look with amazement at the miracle of nature. Analyze his statement and explain whether you have ever felt inspired by the "miracle of nature." Give examples from your own life.

5. There are now more people in Canada over the age of sixty-five than there have ever been before. What types of problems can this create? What are some ways of dealing with these problems?

GETTING STARTED
Directed Freewriting

Before you begin to write your essay, take a blank piece of paper. Write the title or the main idea of your essay at the top of the paper. Close your eyes for about a minute, concentrating on those words at the top of the page. Open your eyes and begin to write anything at all that comes into your mind. Write for at least ten minutes without putting down the pen, even if what you are writing seems unrelated to the topic. Just keep writing until you have filled one to two pages with ideas. Then stop writing and read what you have written, underlining any idea that relates to your topic. When you begin to write your essay, read your freewriting again. You may find other connections with your topic, or you may decide to change your essay topic to one you find more interesting.

A Student Essay

The following student essay was written in response to suggestion 3. Read it and think about how well it answers that question.

Should People Be Forced to Retire?

People should not be forced to retire at the age of sixty-five. Even if this gives opportunities to young people, it is not fair to the elderly.

Older people should decide for themselves when it is time to retire. The government or big companies should not have the right to force them to retire just to give way to the younger ones. If they are physically well enough to do their work, they should be allowed to continue. Older people are often more talented and more experienced than younger people.

If they are forced to retire, it could lead the old people into a forced hell of loneliness, sadness, and death. Giving them a chance will add to their lives because they love their work and enjoy what they have been doing. For some of them, their work is the only thing that keeps them from dying.

I think older people should be left alone by people who want them to retire. They have their own lives to lead, just as the younger generation does. The elderly should decide for themselves when they want to retire. People should not force them to do something they are not ready to do for themselves. They can still be talented and well experienced at doing their work. They should have their own freedom which no one should take away. They deserve some rights for all the hard work they had been doing for years. They also deserve to keep their dream and protect something that keeps them alive.

Monica Boateng, Guyana

REVISING

Ask yourself these questions about Monica Boateng's essay. Then meet with a classmate to discuss what you have written. Ask your classmate to write out answers to the same questions regarding your draft. Study your classmate's responses.

1. What is the purpose of this essay? What was the writer trying to say?

2. Which ideas or examples best support the main point of the writing?

3. In which part of the essay would you have liked more information? Did you have trouble following the writing? Where?

4. Is there anything else that you would like to know about this topic that is not included? Is there anything that would make the essay more interesting to you as a reader?

After you have discussed your writing with your classmate, revise it. Then share your revision with the same classmate.

EDITING STRATEGIES

THE PHRASE *USED TO*

Casals tells us that he used to take long walks on the beach, but now his walks on the beach are shorter. Looking back on our lives, we

remember many things that we used to do that we no longer do.
Write two sentences describing things you used to do that you no
longer do.

> *I used to eat eggs for breakfast every day, but now I eat cereal and
> whole wheat toast.*
> *I used to live in a houseboat, but now I live in an apartment.*

_____

_____

Note: In the phrase *used to, used* always ends in *-d. Used to* is
always followed by the simple form of the verb with no *-s,
-ed,* or *-ing* ending.

EXERCISES

1. Underline *used to* and the verb that follows it in each of the sentences you wrote.
2. We often follow a *used to* phrase with "but not anymore." Change
   each of the preceding sentences to read "but not anymore."

   I used to eat eggs for breakfast, but not anymore.

_____

_____

_____

3. Write a paragraph about yourself and your family describing
   something you used to do but do not do anymore.

PREPOSITIONS

in/on/at (time)

In Chapter Three, we looked at the use of *in, on,* and *at* in relation to
place. These prepositions are also used idiomatically in relation to
time. For example, Casals begins, "On my last birthday I was ninety-
three years old." It would be incorrect to use *in* or *at* in this sentence.
We will examine the uses of *in, on,* and *at* as they are used to describe
time.

In is usually used for a large block of time:

in a million years	in the fall
in my lifetime	in the winter
in 1992	in June

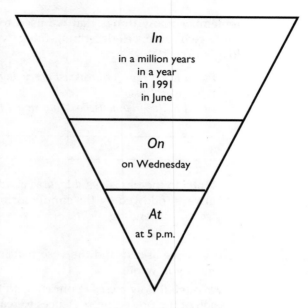

in the spring   in a week

in the summer   in the second week in April

On becomes a little more specific:

on December 27   on the First of July

on the eighteenth of the month   on Thanksgiving

on weekends   on Tuesday

on the weekend   on the day

on my birthday

At is the most specific of all; it is used to pinpoint an exact time:

at midnight   at 6 p.m.

at dawn   at 10:15

at noon   at 2 o'clock

A birthday would be expressed in one of the following ways:

I was born in 1970, in May, on the tenth of the month at 9:15 p.m.

I was born on May 10 in 1970 at 9:15 p.m.

However, there are some special expressions using *in*. We say, "I'll be there in a minute" or "in a second" when someone asks how long we will be. If someone asks when he or she will see us again, we say:

"in a minute"   "in a month"

"in a week"   "in a year"

EXERCISE

On the basis of what you have learned about prepositions so far, fill in each of the following blanks with *in, on,* or *at*.

1. Pablo Casals was born _____ 1876, _____ Vendrell, Spain, _____ December 29.

2. He lived _____ Puerto Rico for many years of his life.

3. _____ a typical day _____ his life, he got up _____ dawn.

4. He made his debut _____ the age of twenty-two _____ Paris 1898.

5. Casals founded the Barcelona Orchestra _____ 1919.

6. _____ 1950, he organized and played _____ the first of the chamber music festivals _____ Prades, France.

7. He also founded the Casals Festival _____ Puerto Rico _____ the 1950s.

COMMONLY CONFUSED WORDS

its/it's

Notice how *its* and *it's* are used in the following paragraph. Then, on the basis of what you have observed, complete the definitions that follow.

The Casals reading is remarkable for many reasons. First, *it's* written by a 93-year-old person who is youthful in mind and spirit. *Its* main idea is work and the value of remaining busy and active.

Casals writes of an orchestra and tells us that all *its* members are over 100 years old. *It's* inspiring to know that such a man as Casals and such an orchestra as the Georgian Caucasian Orchestra ever existed.

_____ means "it is."

_____ means "belongs to it."

Fill in each of the following blanks with *it's* or *its*.

1. _____ a rare opportunity to meet someone as positive as Pablo Casals.

2. Time goes by very quickly, and many people fear _____ passage. They think that _____ too late to fulfil their dreams.

3. _____ true that music has filled Casals's life. He loves sounds, rhythms, and _____.

4. Casals would probably say that _____ never too late to enjoy life and all _____ pleasures.

Now write your own sentences using *it's* and *its*.

MECHANICS
The Semicolon

Lines 26 and 27 of "Age and Youth" contain two semicolons. Circle each of these semicolons, and copy the sentences in which they appear in the space.

_____

_____

_____

Notice that the semicolons are used each time to connect two complete sentences. Writers use semicolons to join two sentences when the idea in the second sentence is a continuation of the idea in the first.

In the following exercise, write a second related sentence that will make sense when connected to the first.

1. Pablo Casals lived in Puerto Rico; _____

_____

2. His friend played a joke on him; _____

_____

3. Casals received a letter; _____

_____

4. He loved music; _____

_____

EDITING PRACTICE

The following paragraph is an unedited first draft that contains many surface errors: two subject-verb agreement errors, one spelling error, three *the* errors, and four preposition errors. Find and correct the errors. The answers are on page 328.

Like Pablo Casals; Marc Chagall was a remarkable man who lived a long and productive life. He was born on 1887, and he died on 1985. Chagall lived for almost a century. His paintings makes people feel happy. They usually shows dancing figures such as flying cows and pigs, playful lovers, and bright coloured flowers. Chagall was born in the Russia on Jewish quarter of town of Vitebsk. He had eight brothers, and sisters. Chagall knew he wanted to be an artist when he was a little boy. However, he did not become famous until he was on his fiftys.

GRAMMAR STRATEGIES

FINDING AND CORRECTING RUN-ONS

A run-on occurs when two or more complete sentences are joined with no punctuation or connecting word. Another type of run-on is the comma splice, in which two complete sentences are joined only by a comma. Run-ons present editing problems for many writers. In the following paragraph, there are four run-ons. Underline each one.

People in Canada are getting older, today approximately 10% of the population is over 65. In 1971 only 8.1% of the population was this old, and it is predicted that 27% of the population will be 65 or older by the year 2031. Approximately 30% of these people live on their own the rest live in institutions or under the care of children or other relatives. An ever-growing number of Canadian adults are caring for a parent this can create a very stressful situation. Adult children are becoming parents to their parents, however, this can be overwhelming. The older parents also feel the need for some independence and for the right to make decisions about their own lives.

FROM *CANADA AND THE WORLD* MAGAZINE
AND STATISTICS CANADA.

If you had any difficulty identifying the run-ons in the paragraph, read the following explanations.

There are five basic methods for correcting run-ons:

1. Use a period to end the first sentence and a capital letter to begin the next.

People in Canada are getting older. Today approximately 10% of the population is over 65.

	Subject	Verb	Complete Thought
People in Canada are getting older,	x	x	x
today approximately 11% of the population is 65 or over.	x	x	x

(This is a run-on because two complete
sentences are connected only by a comma.)

About 30% of these people live on their own	x	x	x
the rest live in institutions or under the care	x	x	x
of children or other relatives.			

(This is a run-on because two complete sentences
are linked with no sign to connect them.)

An ever-growing number of Canadian adults			
are caring for a parent	x	x	x
this can create a very stressful situation.	x	x	x

(This is a run-on because two complete sentences
tences are linked with no sign to connect them.)

Adult children are becoming parents to their	x	x	x
parents, however, this can be overwhelming.	x	x	x

(This is a run-on because two complete
sentences are linked by a comma.
However is a transition word.)

2. Use a subordinating word such as *when, because, if, although, as,* or *since;* or a relative pronoun such as *who, which,* or *that.*

   Although about 30% of these people live on their own, the rest live in institutions or under the care of children or other relatives.

3. Use a comma and a coordinating word: *for, or, and, yet, nor, so,* or *but.*

   An ever-growing number of Canadian adults are caring for a parent, and this can create a very stressful situation.

4. Use a semicolon to connect two sentences when the second sentence begins with a transition word such as *however, therefore,* or *furthermore.*

   Adult children are becoming parents to their parents; however, this can be overwhelming.

5. Use a semicolon or a colon to connect two sentences when the idea in the second sentence is a continuation of the idea in the first sentence.

   Adult children are becoming parents to their parents; this can be overwhelming.

   People in Canada are getting older: today approximately 10% of the population is over 65.

EXERCISE

Correct the following run-ons, using any of the illustrated techniques. Try several approaches, as this helps to create variety in your writing.

1. He always loved music Pablo Casals learned to play the cello.

2. His friend Sasha Schneider played a joke on him Schneider sent Casals a letter inviting him to conduct an orchestra.

3. Casals liked to live near the sea he enjoyed early morning walks on the beach.

4. Looking at nature makes Casals very happy he feels connected to life in that way.

5. Some elderly people continue to work and absorb beauty around them they feel that aging does not mean getting old.

6. Casals had a routine he started every day by walking on the beach and playing the piano.

7. He went to the piano he played two preludes and fugues by Bach.

8. Casals believes there is something to be learned in jokes it was true of Schneider's joke as well.

9. All the members of the orchestra are healthy they are all over 100 years old.

10. The oldest of the group is Astan Shlarba he is a tobacco grower and a horse trainer.

PARAGRAPH COHERENCE

Each paragraph should contain one basic idea that is developed by the writer. Some writers add ideas that do not belong; when they edit, they are unable to recognize these unrelated ideas. In the following paragraphs, cross out any sentences that do not belong.

1. The elderly couple sat together on the park bench. They held hands as they watched the young people pass them. Sometimes they would look at an especially affectionate young couple, and they would smile at each other as if remembering something from their own past. It was a very special day for them. It was their fiftieth anniversary, and that night they would celebrate with their children and friends. Fiftieth anniversary parties mean a lot to the families, and everyone looks forward to the parties. They had looked forward to this event for a long time. They had discovered that as the years went by, they had grown closer together and their love had grown deeper. This love showed in their faces, and it made everyone who saw them that day feel a part of their happiness.

2. Freedom has a different meaning for each person. For one person, it might be the feeling that comes when one can say whatever one feels, whether at home or on the street, without fear of arrest. For

another, it might be "a room of one's own" where no one else can enter without permission. Apartment rents are very high in most major cities right now, and it is hard to find a big apartment that is affordable, so a room of one's own is usually just a dream. For some people, freedom means the ability to love a person regardless of that person's race, sex, or religion. For others, it is the right not to love anyone and still be accepted by society. For Pablo Casals, freedom meant the right to be himself and the right to continue to play his music.

U N I T

4

FINDING A JOB
AND WORKING

10 WORKING WITH PEOPLE

PREREADING ACTIVITIES

1. In a small group, discuss the characteristics of a good salesperson in Canada. Discuss whether these characteristics are different for a salesperson in a department store, a fast-food restaurant, a fruit store, and a big corporation.

2. Discuss with your group the way you expect to be treated by a college official, a government official, and a boss. Have your experiences corresponded to your expectations? Explain.

3. Discuss with your group the differences in expectations between bosses and workers in your country and in Canada. How do you explain the differences?

Toss Out the Hard Sell, It's Time to Get Intimate with Customers

Randy Boswell wrote this article for the Ottawa Citizen *in 1994. It deals with treating customers in a friendly way.*

°fashionable terms
°common language used by a particular group
°pressure techniques used to sell a product

It may be time to get intimate with your customers.

Business buzzwords° are a dime a dozen° in the post-synergy age of management lingo,° but customer intimacy is catching on like wildfire.

The hard sell° is out.   5

The human touch is in. And the secret to success for businesses in the '90s is to build relationships with customers that, "are like really good marriages," says Jim Clemmer, a management consultant and author of several books preaching the primacy of customer service.   10

He says the best way to get customers to buy things is to get them first to buy into "a long-term relationship."

"It's one thing to talk about customer-driven organizations," said Clemmer. "But it's quite another to make changes that really create a company that puts customer service first."   15

Clemmer doesn't advocate assigning that task to one department or senior employee. He emphasized that most companies need a "revolution in corporate culture" so profound that a customer-driven ethic pervades every activity and the thinking of every employee.   20

Leonard Lee, founder of Lee Valley Tools, says he's built his successful woodworking and gardening supply business on a foundation of customer confidence.

"You have to find ways of developing customer loyalty, or you risk having them teased away with a 10-cent saving somewhere   25
else."

That threat looms as U.S.-based giant Home Depot prepares to head north to expand its do-it-yourself empire. But Lee said mega-stores° that bank on° low price and mediocre service are no match for his customer-driven operations.   30

His seven stores across Canada are staffed mainly by hobby woodworkers and gardeners who can relate to what customers need and who maintain records that provide "an intimate portrait" of every buyer's interests.

The employees aren't on commission,° so they don't hassle° any-   35
one to boost sales: "You don't sell everything you can. You sell what the customer expects you to sell."

His workers are on a profit-sharing program, so they still have a general stake in maintaining high sales as well as cutting costs. But they're encouraged — if it seems better for the customer — to send   40
him or her to another store. Customer complaints are handled swiftly, said Lee. He once sent a $100 gift certificate to a man who griped about a faulty honing guide, forcing the company to recall 1,400 products.

"In the end, he saved as money, so I said thanks," said Lee.   45

The drive to become customer-driven will only get stronger among all kinds and sizes of business, said Peter Cleveland, an executive in the Ottawa office of accounting firm Ernst & Young.

He predicted that within a decade, increasingly powerful consumer lobbies will be publishing lists of major companies, rating   50
their customer-service programs and reputation.

°large stores
°depend on

°wages paid according to amount an employee has sold
°bother

READING AND THINKING STRATEGIES

DISCUSSION ACTIVITIES

Analysis and Conclusions

1. What is a "customer driven" operation? How does this type of service differ from that experienced in a megastore?

2. How do you think Boswell would define customer service? What elements of social interaction contribute to good customer service?

3. In what ways would salespeople working on commission differ in their interactions with customers from those who are paid a regular salary?

Writing and Point of View

1. Boswell introduces his subject in three short paragraphs, utilizing idiomatic expressions. What is the effect on the reader of his method of introduction?

2. What examples can you find in this article of quotations from statements made by authorities? How did these quotes affect your understanding of the article?

3. If you were to write an essay like this one, what position would you take on the issue of customer service vs. lower prices at megastores? What details would differ from Boswell's essay?

Personal Response and Evaluation

1. Do you agree with Boswell's opinion on the value of customer service? Have you had a particular positive or negative personal experience in a Canadian store? Share it with your group.

2. In Canada, smiles, eye contact and friendly conversation are considered appropriate behaviour in employee-customer relationships. How are employees expected to behave in your country?

3. Would you prefer getting a job in which you had regular contact with the public or not? Why or why not?

CLASS PRESENTATION

1. Select an occupation that interests you, and do research on it in the library. Write one or two pages describing the education needed, the kind of work, the beginning salary, and any other

information that you think would be useful to someone interested in that job. Present your findings to the class in a short oral report.

2. Interview someone who works in a job that interests you. Ask questions to find out about both the positive and the negative aspects of the job. Present your findings to the class in a short oral report.

JOURNAL WRITING

Reading about jobs makes us think about our own future. What will we do with our lives? Is it important to make a lot of money? Is it important to help people? Is it possible to do both? How do we decide on a job for the future?

This journal entry should focus on jobs, decision making, and finding your way in the world. What jobs have you considered for yourself? Why are these jobs attractive or meaningful to you? Did any one person influence you in your ideas about a future occupation? Did any experience in your life influence you in your ideas about a future occupation?

WRITING STRATEGIES

ESSAY STRATEGIES
Quoting from Other Sources

Writers use quotations for a number of purposes. Writers may use quotations to convince readers that other people have the same opinion about the subject, that the subject is important, or that the writer has read and thought about the subject before writing about it. However, the main purpose of using quotations is to persuade readers of the credibility or believability of the piece of writing.

Randy Boswell used quotations throughout "Toss out the hard sell, it's time to get intimate with customers." List some of the quotations that appeared in the article, noting the source of the quotation next to it.

_____

_____

_____

_____

_____

Look at the quotations and the sources. What do these quotations have in common? What publication did the Boswell article appear in? Who is the audience for this publication? How might the audience have affected the choice of quotations? What is Boswell's purpose for using these quotations? Which quotation is most effective to you as a reader? Which quotation is least effective? Why?

ESSAY FORM

Persuasion: Writing to Prove a Point or to Clarify an Issue

When we write to prove a point or to clarify an issue, we are trying to persuade our readers to rethink a subject from our point of view.

The techniques for writing a persuasive essay include the following five steps:

1. *Propose.* In your first paragraph, write a clear statement or proposition that contains your main point:

   All companies should teach courtesy to their employees.
   Our relationships with our family and friends should be more important than our relationship with our jobs.
   People should not be forced to retire on the basis of age.

2. *Describe.* Describe the problem in detail. Use evidence, including facts, examples, and quotations, to convince your readers that the problem needs to be discussed or solved.

3. *Analyze.* Break your subject down into parts. Explain how the parts work together to form a whole. Include the important history or future developments relating to your problem. Review deductive and inductive reasoning on page 97 to help you decide how to organize your writing.

4. *Compare and contrast.* Compare your solution to others, and explain why your solution is the preferred way to resolve the problem.

5. *Evaluate and recommend.* Conclude your essay with a strong example or reason. Restate your proposition differently but powerfully.

EXERCISES

1. Reread persuasive essays that you have written to analyze your writing in relation to the five steps. Which ones did you use? What might have made your essay more effective?

2. Reread other essays in this book to decide which are persuasive and which serve other purposes. What is the author trying to persuade you about? Does the writing make you rethink your ideas? Why or why not? What advice would you give the writer to make the writing more effective?

SUGGESTIONS FOR WRITING

Before you begin to write, look at your journal or other writing done for this chapter for ideas. If you have difficulty getting started, try the "Getting Started" activity below. Or try clustering (pages 124 and 125), brainstorming (pages 52 to 53), or freewriting (page 30) to help you get ideas.

1. Write a narrative that tells about an employee-customer interaction that started out with a problem and was resolved because of the employee's reaction. Think of descriptive words and the dialogue that the two people used.

2. Some people believe that large companies should teach courtesy to their employees who are in contact with the public and that these companies should reward courteous employees. Do you agree or disagree? Support your point of view with your own experience or your observations of others.

3. Write an essay in which you compare how employees and customers are expected to act in your native country with behaviour that you have observed in Canada. How do you explain the differences in the two countries?

4. Describe a person who is very satisfied with a job or is very dissatisfied with a job. Explain why the person finds the job so fulfilling or unfulfilling. Include enough details so that the reader will get a picture of the person you are describing and be persuaded that the job is either rewarding or difficult to bear.

5. Some people think that people work too hard in Canada. They believe that it is just as important to enjoy life as it is to work hard. Do you agree or disagree? Support your point of view with your own experience or your observations.

GETTING STARTED

Creating a Dialogue with Yourself

Before you write your essay, write a dialogue with yourself in which you ask yourself questions about your topic. Write down your answers, and then challenge those answers with more difficult questions. Keep challenging yourself until you think you have asked and answered the difficult questions about your subject. When you have answered the difficult challenges, you will have thought about your topic, and you will be prepared to write a thoughtful and credible essay.

REVISING

After you finish writing your first draft, give yourself some time to separate from your words and ideas so that you will be able to view your writing from a new perspective.

During this time, read the student essays that follow. These students were responding to writing assignment 4. Answer the following revision questions about these essays. After you have practised utilizing these questions, use them to help you revise your first draft.

1. Does the introduction make you want to read more? Is it clear what the essay will be about?

2. What connects the first paragraph to the second paragraph, the second to the third, and so forth?

3. Are there enough details and information to support the ideas?

4. Is there any place in the draft where the writing seems confused or disconnected from the main idea? If so, how can it be improved?

5. Does the conclusion tie together the ideas of the essay?

After you have answered these questions, revise your essay, keeping your ideas in mind. Share your revision with a classmate.

Student Essays

John Wong and Lois Chan describe work experiences which, though unpleasant at the time, taught them important lessons about life.

Two Managers

Three years ago, I got my first job at McDonald's as a cashier. All I had to do was to take the customer's order and to collect the money. Maybe you think that it was an easy job. What was difficult for me was not the sore back or strained face muscles from smiling. What was really difficult was to work with two managers at my back.

In a situation where one manager told me to fill up the ice while the other manager told me to sweep the floor, it was always hard to decide what to do first. Sometimes I planned to fill up the ice first and then sweep the floor, but the manager who told me to sweep the floor always got angry because he thought that I was not doing what he told me to do. One manager told me to fill the soft drink cup right up to the yellow line of the cup. Another manager told me to fill it up above the yellow line. Therefore, I was always being blamed for not doing the "right" thing!

Once I was really frustrated. One day when it was not very busy, there was a customer in my line who ordered two hamburgers and two large fries. The hamburgers were not ready at the time he ordered and they took about fifteen minutes instead of the usual five minutes. At the same time, I was making the fries. I had the fries ready just before the two hamburgers were up. While I was filling up the fries, the manager said to me, "You should have the fries prepared ahead of time because the man has been waiting for almost fifteen minutes." I was really angry and said, "The fries only take two or three minutes to cook and I am already filling them up." I thought, "What takes 15 minutes is your hamburgers!"

Although I did not seem to have a very good time at McDonald's, it was a worthwhile experience. I learned a lot from my job. For example, I learned how to work and communicate with people. I also learned some slang words even though sometimes the slang words "screwed me up" a little. Furthermore, I think my English improved.

John Wong, Hong Kong

Not a Princess

When I was 15 years old, I had my first part-time job. My experience might be very common to many people, but it was really an unusual experience for me.

When the manager of Harvey's restaurant phoned and told me that I could work in his restaurant, I was very excited. At first I thought I should tell my family about this news, but I changed my mind after a few seconds. It was because I knew that they would look down on me. I don't mean they would feel my job was bad. I just mean they would think I did not have any ability to do this job because they thought I was very careless. In my family's eyes, I was weak, afraid of everything, and shy, just like a princess.

In fact, I do not believe I am this kind of person. Therefore, I changed my mind again. I decided to tell my family about working at Harvey's, because I wanted to show them my ability and courage to do this job.

When I was working at Harvey's Restaurant, I often met terrible customers. One time a lady came in. "Hi, can I help you?" I said politely.

"Yes, I want to buy a coffee. How much is it?" The lady's voice was very sharp.

"Fifty cents," I replied.

After I finished making the coffee, I gave it to her and took the change.

"Oh, sorry. You just gave me thirty cents. The coffee costs fifty cents," I said.

"What? I only gave you thirty cents! You're wrong. I'm sure I gave you fifty cents," the old lady said loudly and angrily. All the customers in the restaurant began to look at us.

"No, you ..." At that time the manager came out from the kitchen.

"What's wrong?" the manager said.

"She just paid thirty cents. It's supposed to be fifty cents," I said.

"No, I've already given her fifty cents," the lady spoke more loudly.

"Okay, I don't think it's your mistake. I'm sorry," the manager said to the lady.

I was very angry and choked back my reply. At this point I could see the manager did not believe me. I was insulted. Everyone really thought it was my fault.

I worked at Harvey's only one month. At the beginning I thought that working was easier than studying in school. We did not have any tests or homework. In fact, I was wrong. It was not easy at all. Also I understood that school and society are two different worlds. In school, people are simple and honest, but in society, there are many dishonest people. This was really a good lesson to learn.

Lois Chan, Hong Kong

EDITING STRATEGIES

LEARNING NEW VOCABULARY

Classifying

One way to learn new vocabulary is to classify words, terminology, or concepts in relation to a particular field. This article contains many words that relate to business and jobs.

1. Make a list of all the words in this article that are used to describe activities (for example, *gardening*).

2. Make a list of the words that describe emotions (for example, *intimacy*).

Synonyms

Each of the words in column A means almost exactly the same as one of the words in column B. Words that have almost the same meaning are *synonyms*. Draw a line from each word in column A to its synonym in column B. The first one has been done for you.

A	B
1. customer	a. job
2. success	b. complained
3. activity	c. second-rate
4. mediocre	d. achievement
5. hassle	e. consumer
6. profit	f. consumer
7. griped	g. financial gain
8. buy	h. both
9. task	i. action

COMMONLY CONFUSED WORDS

Modals

may and *can*

Read the paragraph that follows. Underline *can* and *may* and the verbs that follow these words. Then fill in the blanks in the sentences below the paragraph.

> *If you look in the "help wanted" section of your local newspaper, you can see that there are many jobs available requiring different kinds of skills. People try to get jobs that they can do with confidence. Even though occasionally a person may find a job that involves a lot of training, this is not usually a job hunter's goal. This is a personal decision. Some people can cope with a lot of challenge in their work, but many workers want predictability. They do not feel confident thinking that their job may change from day to day. Moreover, the type of work that people want to do varies greatly. Some people may find one type of job interesting, though to someone else that job may seem boring.*

Choose *may* or *can* to complete the following sentences.

_____ means "to be able to."

_____ is used to express possibility.

Now use these words in sentences of your own.

Words to Express the Future

In addition to using *will* and *be going* to express the future, we sometimes use the simple present tense and the present continuous tense. The time context and the time expression indicate that the event is taking place in the future. Verbs such as *arrive, come, go,* and *leave* are often used in the present tense even when they have a future meaning.

The plane arrives at 6 o'clock.

The baby-sitter comes at 7 tonight.

We go on vacation after the children finish school.

They leave for Montreal in June.

They are arriving late tonight.

She is coming over when she finishes her homework.

We are going out tonight.

They are leaving after the third of the month.

EXERCISES

1. Write sentences using the present and present continuous tenses of *arrive, come, go,* and *leave* to express future time.

2. Where will you be five years from now? What will your life be like? Write a paragraph describing your future, using *will* and *be going to*.

MECHANICS
The Colon

The colon is used at the end of a complete sentence for the following purposes:

1. To introduce a list:

   I bought the following items for school: a loose-leaf notebook, two pens, five pencils, computer disks, a pair of gym shoes, and books for all my classes.

2. To introduce a quotation:

   Boswell writes about customer service: "The human touch is in."

3. To emphasize a word, phrase, clause, or sentence that adds emphasis to the main clause:

It means delivering smiles, eye contact, and friendly chitchat to a stranger: customer service.

4. To separate minutes from hours in expressions of clock time:

12:30 p.m.   9:45 a.m.

5. To end the salutation of a business letter:

To whom it may concern: Dear Ms. Daughtry:

6. To separate a title from a subtitle:

A Canadian Writer's Workbook: An Interactive Writing Text for ESL Students

Which of these uses for the colon does the following sentence illustrate?

The idea sounds fine: customers deserve good feelings as much as they do a quality product or competent service.

EXERCISE

Place colons where they are needed in the following sentences.

1. According to Randy Boswell, customer service in Canada should include the following skills listening, selling only products that consumers want, and building long-term relationships.
2. In Canada, many companies are now putting their efforts into monitoring employees' interactions with customers and rewarding the right behaviour customer service.
3. Jim Clemmer, a management consultant, says "It's one thing to talk about customer-driven organizations, but it's quite another to make changes that really create a company that puts customer service first."

Which of the uses for the colon does each sentence illustrate?

EDITING PRACTICE

The following first draft needs editing for surface errors. Rewrite the paragraph, correcting all the errors. The errors include: one run-on, four *they're/their/there* errors, three subject-verb agreement errors, six plural errors, two pronoun reference errors, and one *live/leave* error. Answers are on page 328.

Reading about the differences between men and woman can help people learn a lot that will help them in there everyday lifes. Many scientists are conflicted about whether these differences are caused by nature or nurture. No one know for sure how much in-born genetic characteristics determine people's lifes. Man and women may be influenced by they're environment as much as there genetics. According to research, the brain changes, they can change because of many things, such as diet, the air, handedness, etc. It make sense that one should take good care of yourself by eating right, exercising, and trying to leave healthy lifes. However, despite everything people does, they're will always be some difference between the sexs.

GRAMMAR STRATEGIES

INDIRECT SPEECH

Sometimes when we report what another person has said, we use direct quotations, the exact words that a person has spoken. To do this, we use quotation marks and appropriate capital letters and punctuation marks.

The child said, "It is snowing."

We can also restate what the person has said without quoting the exact words. This is referred to as indirect or reported speech.

The child said that it was snowing.

The use of indirect speech has particular rules to help readers understand what they are reading.

In indirect speech, the tense changes:

1. From present to past:

Mei Mei said, "The clock *is* broken."
She said that the clock *was* broken.

2. From past to past perfect:

Jose said, "I *bought* a new television."
He said that he *had bought* a new television.

In indirect speech, the modal auxiliary changes:

1. From *may* to *might*:

Lynn said, "It *may* rain."
She said that it *might* rain.

2. From *can* to *could*:

Pak said, "I *can* speak Mandarin."
He said that he *could* speak Mandarin.

3. From *will* to *would*:

Reinaldo said, "I *will* go to the movies.
He said that he *would* go to the movies.

4. From *must* to *had to*:

Estelle said, "I *must* finish my paper."
She said that she *had to* finish her paper.

In indirect speech, the demonstrative changes:

1. From *this* to *that*:

Will said, "I can't carry *this* table alone."
He said that he couldn't carry *that* table alone.

2. From *these* to *those*:

Sonia said, "*These* books are overdue at the library."
She said that *those* books were overdue at the library.

In indirect speech, the adverbials of time and place change:

1. From *today* to *that day*:

Leslie said, "I want to leave *today*."
She said that she wanted to leave *that day*.

2. From *tomorrow* to *the following day* or *a day later*.

3. From *yesterday* to *the previous day* or *the day before*.

4. From *next month* or *next year* to *the following month/year* or *a month/year later*.

In indirect speech, the word order of questions changes:

1. To a statement word order:

   Maria asked, "What time *is it?*"
   She asked what time *it was.*

2. *If* or *whether* is added if there is no question word:

   Michael asked, "Is it raining?"
   He asked if it was raining.

Using the information just given, change the following direct quotations to indirect quotations. The first one has been done for you.

1. Randy Boswell says, "It may be time to get intimate with your customers."
   <u>Randy Boswell said that it might be time to get intimate with your customers.</u>

2. "I don't think it's your mistake," the manager said to the lady.

   _____

   _____

   _____

3. John Wong says, "I was always being blamed for not doing the 'right' thing!"

   _____

   _____

   _____

4. "In the end, he saved us money, so I said thanks," said Lee.

   _____

   _____

   _____

For additional practice, with a partner, try changing the dialogue in "Not a Princess" on pages 205 and 206 from direct quotations to indirect statements. You can try this again with another article or story that uses direct quotations if you so desire.

USE OF THE INFINITIVE

In Chapter Seven, we examined verbs that are followed by the *-ing* form of the verb. In this chapter, we will look at verbs that are followed by the infinitive, which is *to* plus the simple form of the verb.

Here are some examples.

Many employees have to learn to deal *with irate customers. When they* decide to work *in a job in which they are on the "front line," they* choose to deal *with people and problems every day. Some employees* need to learn *how to expend emotional labour on their jobs. They* want to find out *the best way to listen to a resentful customer, negotiate the difficulty, and solve the problem without* forgetting to appear *courteous.*

These are the most commonly used verbs that are followed by an infinitive:

agree	deserve	learn	refuse
appear	expect	manage	seem
ask	forget	need	try
attempt	have	plan	wait
choose	hope	prepare	want
decide	know	promise	would like

EXERCISES

1. Read the following sentences, underlining each verb and the infinitive that follows it. The first one has been done for you.

a. He <u>agreed to work</u> as a secretary during the summer, but he <u>forgot to tell</u> his boss that he was majoring in accounting.

b. There appear to be many job openings in the fast-food industry.

c. The recent college graduate asked to meet the president of the company.

d. He chose to work in a big city because he wanted to meet many new people.

e. The advertisement attempted to make the job sound challenging and interesting.

f. The new driver managed to get a job as a taxi driver.

g. The waiter deserved to get a big tip, but his customers refused to give him anything.

h. She planned to go back to school in September even though she expected to keep her job.

2. In the following sentences, fill in each blank with a verb in the infinitive form. There are many possibilities; no one answer is right. Decide what sounds good to you. The first one has been done for you.

a. The man decided _to ask_ for an application.

b. He knew he needed _____ a high school diploma, and he was prepared _____ the interviewer about the other job qualifications.

c. His friend promised _____ a copy of the records from his country.

d. He had _____ his birth certificate, his work permit, and his passport for the interview.

e. Even though he knew how _____ many machines, he hoped _____ some training on the job.

f. In his country he had learned _____ a computer, and that knowledge seemed _____ important to the company.

g. As he waited _____ called for an interview, he tried

_____ his nervousness.

h. The first thing he said to the interviewer was, "Good afternoon,

I would like _____ for your company."

3. Fill in each of the following blanks with an appropriate verb. Choose either the infinitive or the *-ing* form of the verb.

a. The woman learned _____ the phone right away.

b. She enjoyed _____ to new people every day.

c. Still she missed _____ her own language.

d. She needed _____ with old friends at night.

e. She tried _____ together with them, but some nights she

had _____ the date.

f. She always appreciated _____ friends for lunch, though.

4. Write a paragraph describing a job. Use both verbs that are followed by the infinitive and verbs that are followed by the *-ing* form of the verb.

PARAGRAPH COHERENCE

Each paragraph should have internal coherence; the ideas should be connected so that they flow one to the next.

The following sentences form a paragraph describing a person's first day in a new job. Arrange the sentences in the order that makes the most sense to you. The first sentence has been marked for you. (Some readers think this should be two paragraphs. Where would you divide it into a second paragraph?)

_____ *"Mr. Western's office," I said meekly and then pushed the wrong button and lost the call.*

__**1**__ *When I began working for the Smith Western Company as a secretary, I was nervous.*

_____ *He told me that we should get acquainted and that I should begin to learn the office routine.*

_____ I agreed with him and listened as he began a long series of explanations about how everything worked.

_____ I opened the glass door and stared in amazement; the office seemed enormous, and there were so many people whose names I would have to learn.

_____ There was a large computerized typewriter and a telephone with about 30 buttons.

_____ Little by little, though, it began to fall into place, and at the end of the first week, I had actually begun to like the place.

_____ My boss, Mr. Western, called me into his room right away.

11

ENJOYING YOUR WORK

PREREADING ACTIVITIES

1. In a group, make a list of the qualities you would like to find in a job while you are a college student.

2. In a group, make a list of the qualities you would like to find in a job (or career) after you have completed college. What differences are there in the two lists? How do you account for the differences?

3. What do you think are the most important general qualities that make employees satisfied with their jobs?

The Work Itself: A Social Psychologist Looks at Job Satisfaction

The following excerpt is from a textbook called Applied Social Psychology *by Stuart Oskamp. It presents research exploring the variables that influence job satisfaction.*

The Work Itself

Research has shown many work attributes to be related to job satisfaction. Locke (1976) concluded that most of them have in common the element of mental challenge.

Probably the most basic attitude here is that the work must be personally interesting and meaningful to the individual in question 5 (Herzberg, Mausner, and Snyderman, 1959; Nord, 1977). Obviously, this specification makes work satisfaction subject to a wide range of individual differences, for individuals with one set of values, abilities, and backgrounds may find a particular kind of work personally interesting, while people with different values, abilities, and 10

°bolting together

°repeated

°improvement; expansion

°mechanical; without thought

°deal with; handle

°responses

°involving relations between people

backgrounds may find the same work completely unmeaningful. A more objective aspect of meaningfulness is task significance — the impact of the work on the lives of other people (Hackman, Oldham, Janson, and Purdy, 1975). For example, a worker riveting° aircraft wings has a more significant job than one riveting trash containers and is likely to feel more satisfaction with it.   15

Application of skill is another job attribute that contributes to work satisfaction (Gruneberg, 1979). On assembly lines and other jobs that involve much repetitive° work, the amount of variety in the job has frequently been found to be positively related to job satisfac-   20
tion (Walker and Guest, 1952; Hackman and Lawler, 1971; Kremen, 1973). "Utility workers" and others who rotate from job to job usually show higher satisfaction than workers who perform only one operation all day long, and this finding has been the basis of many "job enrichment°" schemes. Again, individual differences are impor-   25
tant, for not all workers value more varied or challenging jobs (Hulin, 1971).

Another job aspect related to skill is job autonomy — the worker having a say in when and how to perform the job. A somewhat similar work attribute is task identity — doing a "whole" job, or at least   30
a portion where one's personal contribution is clear and visible. Both of these factors have been found to be positively related to job satisfaction (Hackman and Lawler, 1971).

Too little challenge in the work, as in completely automated° tasks, generally leads to boredom and lowered satisfaction.   35
However, so much challenge that the worker cannot cope with° it may lead to failure and frustration, also an unsatisfying state of affairs. Thus success or achievement in reaching an accepted standard of competence on the job is an important factor in satisfaction (Locke, 1965; Ivancevich, 1976), though again individual differences   40
make this a less important factor for individuals with a low need of achievement (Steers, 1975). Although success can generally be judged by workers themselves, external recognition confirms the worker's success and also provides feedback° about the level of achievement. Of course, recognition, in the form of awards, promo-   45
tion, or praise, is also part of the general working conditions and of the interpersonal° aspects of the job, and so it has multiple implications for satisfaction.

A final task attribute that contributes to satisfaction is the relative absence of physical strain (Chadwick-Jones, 1960). This is one   50
major advantage of automation in heavy industrial jobs; for some jobs and some individual workers it can offset automation's disadvantage of promoting boredom.

°outside the person

Working Conditions (Impersonal)°

Pay. Pay is one of the most important working conditions for 55
almost all occupational groups (Smith, Kendall, and Hulin, 1969;
Lawler, 1981). Yet even here there is conflicting evidence, for some
studies have found pay to be relatively unimportant in determining
job satisfaction for certain groups of workers (Opsahl and Dunnette,
1966). Gruneberg (1970) concluded: 60

> It appears that money means different things to different groups,
> and is likely to have greater importance for individuals who can-
> not gain other satisfactions from their job ...

Another aspect of pay is the system by which wages are determined. Most studies have found that hourly pay is preferred to 65
°work paid for item by item
°motivation; the most work
produced, the higher the salary
piecework° systems by most workers, and straight salaries are preferred to incentive° schemes (Opsahl and Dunnette, 1966; Schwab
and Wallace, 1974). One reason for this is that piecework systems
tend to disrupt social relationships on the job, which are another
major source of worker satisfactions. However, there is an interest- 70
°a contradiction that is
nevertheless true
ing paradox° here, for wage incentive schemes generally result in
greater productivity than does hourly pay (Warr and Wall, 1975).

READING AND THINKING STRATEGIES

DISCUSSION ACTIVITIES
Analysis and Conclusions

1. Why is variety in the job an important factor in work satisfaction?
   Can there ever be too much variety?

2. Do you agree with the author that riveting aircraft wings is a
   more significant job than riveting trash containers? What makes
   one job more significant than another?

3. The author states that piecework tends to interfere with friend-
   ships on the job. Do you think this is true? Have you ever had any
   experiences or have you known anyone who has had experiences
   doing piecework? Did they have a similar experience to the one
   the author describes?

Writing and Point of View

1. Compare the style of writing in this excerpt with the style in "How Different Are the Sexes?" on page 157. Which did you prefer? Why?

2. What do the names and dates in parentheses mean? Why does the author include them?

3. What does the author do to help the reader understand new words and phrases? What examples of this can you find?

Personal Response and Evaluation

1. Of all the factors that the author mentions as contributing to job satisfaction, which is the most important to you?

2. What is the most satisfying job you have ever had? Discuss why this job was so satisfying. Do your reasons for liking the job correspond to the excerpt's analysis of job satisfaction?

3. Have you ever had a job that you did not like? If you have, describe the job to the class or to your group and explain in detail why this job was not satisfactory to you.

4. The author states that "success can generally be judged by workers themselves." If workers know they are doing a good job, why is external recognition so important?

QUESTIONNAIRE

This textbook article is based on the findings of many different researchers (the names in parentheses). The researchers named attempted to find out what factors were most important in determining job satisfaction. It is important for you as students to examine and question such research. Most of us have had jobs or know people who have jobs. If we were to develop our own questionnaire dealing with job satisfaction, some of us might give responses similar to those given by the people surveyed for this article. Some of us, however, might have different expectations. Working is a very individual experience.

As a group, make a list of questions that you would ask in order to determine what factors people think are important for job satisfaction. Then make enough copies of the questionnaire to distribute at least five copies to everyone in the class.

To indicate which respondents are members of the class, each student should put a *C* in the top right-hand corner of his or her questionnaire. Each student should then fill out the questionnaire and ask four other people outside of class to answer the questionnaire.

As a class, add up the responses and compare the results of your survey with the findings in the excerpt. Did you find that most people thought mental challenge was the most important factor in job satisfaction? Did most people favour straight salaries? Were the responses from the class members, the *C* group, different from the other responses to the questionnaire? If so, what might explain this?

You will learn many things from doing this activity. You will learn how to create a questionnaire. You will learn how research is conducted, and you will be able to compare your results with the results of the other researchers. You may then realize how interesting and often unpredictable research is.

JOURNAL WRITING

A student once wrote that the worst job she ever had was stuffing feathers into pillows in an un-air-conditioned factory in the summertime. The feathers got stuck in her mouth and her lungs, and she coughed all the time. The workers couldn't turn on a fan because the feathers would blow all over the factory. The student couldn't quit the job because she spoke very little English and needed the money. So she stayed and coughed.

The story is unforgettable. Every detail of it — the feathers, the pillows, the heat, and the coughing — remain in the mind of the reader. In your journal entry, think about the best or worst job experience you have ever had. (If you have never worked, write about an imaginary experience.) Close your eyes and recall every detail — the smells, tastes, colours, voices. When you can see a picture of the job clearly in your mind, start to write. Write everything down, not stopping to worry about grammar, spelling, or organization. Concentrate on making the experience vivid and alive.

EXTRA READING

Alison Kennedy, a Canadian college student from Vancouver, describes the demands of her job in the following essay.

A Career Choice

I have seen people through weddings, anniversaries, divorces, and funerals. I know the names of their children and am told when they are sick or are having trouble in school. I am there with tissue for their tears when their husbands leave them for someone else. They have learned to confide in me as a trusting, unbiased sounding board. Since I don't mix with their circle of friends or visit their homes, they know their secrets are safe with me.

It is my duty to understand the bitter women and work-weary men who demand my attention. When they are angry, I cannot take it to heart for they don't mean to hurt me. It is important that I realize their needs and look beyond their icy exteriors. I am expected to be sensitive to each and every one and show an interest in their lives. Their children come to me when they are small, with fear in their eyes, needing to be reassured with soothing words and toys. I know they will eventually learn to trust me. I watch them grow older and see them start school; and with each passing birthday party, I am compelled to notice how quickly time slips away.

I have been introduced to people from all segments of society and have learned that, although the rich and the poor lead different lives, they all suffer pain and experience joy. How many times have I heard the over-privileged teenager complain about the loneliness of boarding school, or the doctor's wife complain that she never sees her husband? Yet in the same afternoon I have seen men and women struggle with life's hardships, knowing that they must think about last night's dinner, which they never had. I have cried with the woman who slowly died of cancer. Each month, I watched her as she dried up like a crisp leaf in the fall. I listened to her and was humbled by her pain.

I must laugh at the jokes they tell and listen with an enthusiastic ear to tales of voyages and adventures. Yet with some I am silent and allow them a time of tranquil relaxation as they gather their thoughts and escape the burdens of the outside world for a while. However, I must not burden them with my troubles or let them see my fears. I must not get sick and must never look tired. I am expected to be strong and happy, for they depend on me. They know I will be there for them when they call.

I am a hairdresser.

ALISON KENNEDY

WRITING STRATEGIES

ESSAY STRATEGIES
The Conclusion

There are several ways to conclude an essay. The most basic conclusion is a summary of the essay that restates the thesis statement and the main supporting points of the essay. The concluding paragraph in this case is about three or four sentences long. For this type of conclusion, it may help to picture the essay as a clock with the introduction starting at 12 o'clock, the body of the essay moving through the hours of the day, and the conclusion arriving back at 12 o'clock to form a complete circle.

The conclusion often begins with the thesis sentence. Then some of the main points of the essay are restated in different words. All the ideas of the essay are brought together in one final summary sentence. The easiest technique for writing this type of conclusion is to reread the essay and look for the thesis sentence and the main points of the essay. Then reword them.

Another type of conclusion is one sentence long. This type of conclusion makes a strong point; it may be humorous, and it should be memorable.

"Falling from Eden was enough to teach Adam; the same is true for me."

This is Marty Chan's conclusion in Chapter One, page 6. It is effective because it corresponds so well to the introduction, in which Chan presents the problem of being expelled from university. The body of the essay talks about his irresponsible behaviour while at university. The end of the essay returns to the original problem: he fails and is expelled. This is an example of how a conclusion can take the reader full circle.

"I'm the best hockey player in the neighbourhood," he says. "So, I must be Canadian now."

This is the conclusion to the article in Chapter Four by Carolyn Parrish about the problems faced by immigrants to Canada. The conclusion is effective because it leaves the reader with a quote from one of the difficulties immigrants face and the conclusion leaves readers with a ray of hope. The message is that it is possible to feel part of one's adopted home.

EXERCISES

1. There is no true conclusion to the Oskamp selection in this chapter. Write a conclusion, using the thesis statement, as just described.

2. Reread the conclusions to the selections that we have read so far. Rewrite the conclusions in one of the formats described here. Read the original and your revision. Which do you prefer? Why?

3. Look through newspapers and newsmagazines to find articles that you find interesting. Examine the conclusions. Bring the articles to class, and discuss them with your fellow students. What other types of conclusions do you find?

ESSAY FORM

Summary Writing

The summary condenses a piece of writing into its essential points. A summary can be used to include another writer's ideas in your own writing. A summary can be used to take notes from library material when doing research for term papers. The techniques for summary writing can be helpful when you take notes in class, by training you to listen for the essential points in a lecture.

What are the techniques for writing a summary? First, use your own words. Occasionally you may want to copy a few words or phrases from the original piece of writing, but in general, the most effective summary is written in your own words. Look for the main ideas in the writing and include them in your summary. Then look for the important supporting or explanatory details.

Second, you do not have to follow the exact organizational pattern of the original author. The summary is yours, and it should reflect your way of thinking and writing.

Third, even though the summary is organized by you and is written in your own words, it should not contain your ideas. You are summarizing another writer's ideas for your own use.

Finally, use your own style of writing. Do not copy the original author's writing style.

Reread the excerpt at the beginning of this chapter; then read the following summaries. Although their styles are quite different, each is a good summary. Summary writing is individual.

The author presents many work attributes that relate to job satisfaction. The main factors about the work are that it should (1) offer a mental challenge, (2) be interesting and meaningful, (3) seem significant, and (4) offer variety and autonomy. There should be little physical strain, and external recognition should be available. Pay is a factor, especially if there are not many other satisfactions from the job. In relation to pay, most people prefer a straight salary to hourly pay or piecework systems.

What makes people like their jobs? This article asks this question. People like jobs where they have some challenge but not too much. They want variety, yet they don't want to feel overtaxed. People like to feel that they have a say in their jobs and, at the same time, have the ability to see a job from start to finish. They don't want to have to work too hard; if they do, they want some recognition for what they have done. Higher pay helps, and most people would rather get a straight salary than hourly pay.

Which summary do you prefer? One is more informal and uses fewer of the author's original words. Which would you find it easier to study from? Just as in any other form of writing, you have to begin to develop your own style.

EXERCISES

1. Write a summary of the text selection in Chapter Two (page 22), Chapter Eight (page 157), or Chapter Nine (page 179).

2. In a small group, read your summary or make a copy for each member of the group. Compare your summary with those of your classmates. Discuss what makes a good summary. Which summary in your group do you like best? Why?

3. Choose an article from a newspaper or a newsmagazine, and write a summary of its contents.

SUGGESTIONS FOR WRITING

Before you begin to write on the topic of your choosing, try writing an outline as described in the "Getting Started" section below. Many writers create outlines before doing any formal writing.

1. In essay form, write about your experiences creating the questionnaire, and discuss the results you obtained from it. How did your results compare with the findings in the article? What were the differences? How do you explain these differences?

2. Choose the three factors that are most important to you in determining job satisfaction, and write an essay explaining your choices. Support your choices with details of your own experiences and your observations.

3. Describe in detail the worst job you have ever had. Close your eyes and try to imagine how it felt to work in that place. When you begin to write, concentrate on trying to make your reader really feel what it was like to work there. Use descriptive words and dialogue, if appropriate.

4. Following the same procedure as in suggestion 3, write about the best job you have ever had.

5. Use your imagination to write an essay describing your dream job. Begin your essay with the sentence "If I could have any job in the world, I would work as a _____." Make your writing rich with details.

6. Imagine that you run a small company and have only enough money to offer your workers three of the benefits listed here. Which would you choose? In essay form, explain the reasons for your choices.

comprehensive retirement plan

good health plan

bright, cheerful cafeteria with nutritious and inexpensive food

day-care centre for children of employees

end-of-year bonuses based on work output

stock in the company

employee social events such as parties on important holidays and summer picnics

7. "People should be forced to change jobs every ten years. If they work at the same place for any longer than that, they begin to fall into dull routines, and their work is no longer as good as it was when the job was new and exciting." Do you agree or disagree? Write an essay supporting your point of view with your own experiences or your observations of others.

GETTING STARTED
Outlining

Many writers find outlining helpful in their prewriting organization, and some books teach very formal outlining techniques. However, writers can spend so much time outlining that they don't have enough time to write. The outlining technique presented here is simple and effective; it will help you to think your essay through before you actually begin to write.

The outline is a guide that you will refer to as you are writing. It can be changed as you go along. Its purpose is only to help you organize and to give you the confidence that you will have something to say throughout your essay.

An outline does not have to be written in complete sentences. It is a list of ideas that you will develop more fully. The basic shape of an outline is as follows:

I. *Main idea or topic sentence*

    A.   *First supporting detail*

        1. *Development 1*

        2. *Development 2*

    B.   *Second supporting detail, etc.*

To see how the outline works in the Oskamp selection, let's examine the second paragraph more closely.

I. *Work must be interesting and meaningful to the individual.*

     A.   *Individual variables influence what makes work satisfying.*

          1. Values

          2. Abilities

          3. Background

     B.   *Task significance also determines work satisfaction.*

          1. Impact of work on other people

          2. Importance of work to other people

This outline may be very different from the author's actual outline. You have the option of making your outline more detailed or very brief, with just a few key words to help you remember what you wanted to write about. Keep in mind that all writers are different. Some writers find outlines essential to orderly writing; others say they do all their outlining in their head. In the following exercises, you will have the opportunity to try outlining to see if it works for you.

EXERCISES

1. Prepare an outline for one of the other paragraphs in the article.
2. Prepare a brief outline for the entire article.
3. Before you write your next essay, prepare a brief outline using the techniques you have just learned. See if the outline helps you to organize your essay.

REVISING

Choose a partner and make a copy of your essay for that person. Each of you will have a turn being interviewer and interviewee. The interviewer will ask the interviewee the following questions about the essay, writing down the answers as they are spoken. Practice this first with the student essay that follows.

1. What is the main idea of the essay? What is the author really trying to say?
2. If you had to leave out one line or one part, what would it be?
3. If you had to add something to one part of the essay, where would you add it and what would you add?
4. What part(s) of the essay do you like best?
5. What part(s) would you like to rewrite completely?
6. Do you think the essay says what the author wanted it to say? How could you have said it better?

When both interviews are finished, read your own interview and make any changes in your essay that you feel are necessary to improve your writing. Share your revised writing with your classmate.

A Student Essay

This student wrote this essay about her first job in Canada.

Factory Worker

You can imagine that anyone who comes to a foreign country knowing nothing, not even its language, finds it hard to live there! You are always classified as a stupid person because you cannot speak. How can I describe my feelings when I arrived in Canada. How cold and hopeless I felt at that time! Immigrating to Canada was the end of my innocent childhood and the beginning of my grown-up life. There were so many pressures: language problems, family problems, and personal problems. Because I was forced to solve these, I became more mature.

In order to help my family pay a heavy debt, I had to work. Working in a factory! I had never thought of it before in my life, but I had to do it. The day my uncle brought me to see the boss, I was so frightened. After passing through a huge and noisy room, we arrived in the boss's office. A tall, fat man greeted us. From his expression I knew he must be the boss. While he was talking to my uncle, I saw his sharp, cold eyes judging me as if they asked, "Is she really able to work here?" To my surprise, my uncle told me that I was hired. Convincing a boss must not have been so difficult for my sharp-tongued uncle. Now I was a worker, not a child anymore, I thought.

Although I had been taught a hundred times that working people were different from children and well-educated people, when I really understood this was the day I started working in the factory in Montreal. My master builder was a kind, cultured, and gentle person who knew that I could not speak French; therefore, she always showed me slowly and clearly each step of the work. I appreciated her because she was the first kind Canadian I had met since arriving in Canada about two weeks before. But when some non-educated workers learned that I could not speak French, they were very nasty to me. They picked on me and laughed at me as if I were born more stupid than they. When I considered those kind of people, I thought of a proverb: "Big fish eats small fish. Small fish eats shrimp!" Sometimes I tried to be friendly to them. The only way I could show it was by smiling, but they seemed to find my smiling stupid and unkind.

"No hard time can stay forever." This is my philosophy of life. Although immigrating to Canada has made my life very hard, I have learned quite a lot from working people and the world of work. Because I have gone through difficult experiences, I appreciate my studies now and I am glad to be at school.

Li Yuin Tam, China

EDITING STRATEGIES

WORD DEVELOPMENT
Using Context Clues

When people speak to us, we have clues to help us understand what they are saying. We can watch their faces, listen to their tone of voice, notice their body language. In a similar way, written material often contains useful clues to help the reader understand words and special phrases. These are called *context clues*, clues that provide the meanings of words used in the piece of writing. The following sentences from the Oskamp article contain examples of such context clues.

1. A more objective aspect of meaningfulness is task significance — the impact of the work on the lives of other people. (paragraph 2)

   According to this sentence, what does "task significance" mean?

   _____

2. Another job aspect related to skill is job autonomy — the worker having a say in when and how to perform the job. (paragraph 4)

   According to this sentence, what does "job autonomy" mean?

   _____

3. A somewhat similar work attribute is task identity — doing a "whole" job, or at least a portion where one's personal contribution is clear and visible. (paragraph 4)

   According to this sentence, what does "task identity" mean?

   _____

   As you read other texts, look for context clues to help you determine the meanings of difficult words without having to use the dictionary.

Collective Nouns

Certain nouns are collective nouns. A collective noun stands for a group of people, animals, or objects considered as a single unit. The following are examples of collective nouns: *family, class, committee, factory, government, group, majority, minority, nation, public, team.*

A collective noun used as a subject usually takes a singular verb in Canadian English.

The public is ruled by a system of laws.

The committee is meeting on Thursday.

However, to emphasize the individual members of the unit, the plural verb can be used.

The team have argued among themselves about who should be considered the best player.

In British English, the plural verb is used with collective nouns. Collective nouns are countable nouns; they can be used in the plural.

In each of the following sentences, choose the correct form of an appropriate present tense verb.

1. The class _____ to know when a test will be given.

2. That group _____ to go out together on the weekends.

3. The family that _____ together _____ together.

4. The audience _____ the performers to concentrate on the play each night.

5. The crowd _____ among themselves about who should get in the crowded train first.

COMMONLY CONFUSED WORDS

who's/whose

Read the following paragraph, noticing the use of *who's* and *whose*.

> *The man* whose *wife returned to work only to find herself receiving many promotions is an interesting case.* Who's *to say that she would have responded the same way if he had started to get promotions and had to begin travelling?* Whose *problem is worse, hers or his?*

Going by what you observed in the paragraph, complete the following definitions.

_____ means "who is" or "who has."

_____ means "belongs to whom."

Now use *who's* and *whose* in sentences of your own.

_____

_____

MECHANICS

Dashes and Hyphens

the dash

The dash (—) is used for several purposes:

1. To set off a definition of a difficult or unfamiliar word or phrase.
2. To indicate a pause that is longer than a comma but not as long as a period.
3. To emphasize or dramatize a point.

The following sentences are taken from the Oskamp selection. Decide for what purpose each dash is being used.

1. A more objective aspect of meaningfulness is task significance — the impact of the work on the lives of other people.
2. Another job aspect related to skill is job autonomy — the worker having a say in when and how to perform the job.
3. A somewhat similar work attribute is task identity — doing a "whole" job, or at least a portion where one's personal contribution is clear and visible.

the hyphen

The hyphen (-) is used for several purposes:

1. To make a compound word:

   worker-in-training, five-year-old, mother-in-law
2. To form new words beginning with the prefixes *half, self, pro, great,* and *ex:*

   half-cooked, self-confidence, pro-students, great-grandfather, ex-president
3. To join compound numbers from *twenty-one* to *ninety-nine* when you write them out.

4. To break a word at the end of a line of writing. Find two examples of words that are broken with a hyphen in the Oskamp selection. When you break a word, break it at the end of a syllable. You cannot divide a one-syllable word such as *through*. Avoid dividing short words of five letters or under. Do not divide contractions. *Always check your dictionary for the correct place to divide a word.*

EXERCISE

Reread some of your earlier writing, looking to see how and when you used dashes and hyphens. When you edit your first draft, make sure you have used dashes and hyphens correctly.

Substitution Words

Writers do not want to repeat the same words over and over. They often substitute words such as *one, this, that, these,* and *those.* In order for these words to be effective, the reader must know what they are replacing.

The following paragraphs from the excerpt illustrate the use of substitution words. In each paragraph, circle the substitution and underline the word or words to which it refers. The first one has been done for you.

Probably the most basic attitude here is that the work must be personally interesting and meaningful to the individual in question. Obviously, this specification makes work satisfaction subject to a wide range of individual differences ...

"Utility workers" and others who rotate from job to job usually show higher satisfaction than workers who perform only one operation all day long, and this finding has been the basis of many "job enrichment" schemes.

Thus success or achievement in reaching an accepted standard of competence on the job is an important factor in satisfaction, though again individual differences make this a less important factor for individuals with a low need of achievement ...

A final task attribute that contributes to satisfaction is the relative absence of physical strain. This is one major advantage of automation in heavy industrial jobs. …

EDITING PRACTICE

The following paragraph is a first draft that contains many surface errors: one pronoun agreement error, two run-ons, one subject—verb agreement error, four *there/their* errors, and one *though/through* error. Find and correct the mistakes. Answers are on page 328.

According to Oskamp, there are many factors involved in job satisfaction. People have to feel there jobs are meaningful and interesting it has to offer the workers a mental challenge. Even through their is individual differences in what people think is important, most people agree that there jobs should offer some challenge. Pay has greater importance for individuals who cannot gain other satisfactions from there jobs. Jobs that offer external recognition, good pay, and a mental challenge are sought by most people, each person wants a feeling of fulfilment.

GRAMMAR STRATEGIES

RELATIVE PRONOUNS

The most common relative pronouns are *who, whom, whose, that,* and *which. When, where,* and *why* are also sometimes used as relative pronouns. Relative pronouns are used to form adjective clauses that describe or explain a noun or noun phrase in another part of the sentence. Here are some examples of adjective clauses that Oskamp used:

1. <u>On assembly lines and other jobs</u> *that* involve much repetitive work, the amount of variety in the job has frequently been found to be related to job satisfaction.

2. "Utility workers" and others *who* rotate from job to job usually show higher satisfaction than workers *who* perform only one operation all day long, and this finding has been the basis of many "job enrichment" schemes.

3. However, so much challenge *that* the worker cannot cope with it may lead to failure and frustration, also an unsatisfying state of affairs.

4. A final task attribute *that* contributes to satisfaction is the relative absence of physical strain.

5. One reason for this is that piecework systems tend to disrupt social relationships on the job, *which* are another major source of worker satisfaction.

Who is used to refer to people. *Who* is used as the subject of an adjective clause. (sentence 2)

Whom is also used when referring to people, but *whom* is used as the object of the adjective clause:

The employer, whom *you prefer to work for, is aware of employee abilities and needs.*

Whose is used to show possession:

The workers, whose *needs are met, are likely to remain on the job and to work hard.*

Which is used to refer to things other than people. *Which* can function as the subject or object of an adjective clause. How does *which* function in sentence 5?

That can be used to refer to people, animals, or things. *That* can function as a subject or as the object of an adjective clause.

The jobs that *students can get are often uninteresting and offer few benefits.*

When is used to mean "at which time":

My boss still reminds me of the day when *I arrived late for my interview.*

Where is used to mean "at which place":

In the 1990s computers and fax machines have enabled more people to work where *they live.*

Why means "for which":

Oskamp suggests many reasons why *people prefer to work at particular types of jobs.*

EXERCISES

1. Simple sentences can be combined with the relative pronouns just described. Fill in the blanks in the following sentences. The first one is done for you. Keep in mind that there may be more than one correct answer.

a. Hélène preferred a certain type of job.

The job allowed her to be creative and intelligent.

Hélène preferred a job that allowed her to be creative and intelligent.

b. Hélène sent out many letters to big companies.
The big companies had room for advancement.

_____

_____

c. She received one reply to her letters.
Her letters told about her background and requested an employment interview.

_____

_____

d. The letter was sent to her home.
The letter told her the time and place of the interview.

_____

_____

e. Hélène discussed her interview with a friend.
The friend worked in the same company.

_____

_____

f. The office building occupied a whole city block.
The building was 100 stories high.

_____

_____

2. Finish the story about Hélène. What was her experience at the interview? What was the job? Did she get the job?

FINDING AND CORRECTING FRAGMENTS

Sentence fragments (incomplete sentences) sometimes pose a big problem for writers. During editing, it may be hard to find and correct these errors. In the following paragraph, there are several fragments. Read the paragraph, and underline the fragments.

In each of our lives. There are certain important passages or steps. Such as graduating from high school, graduating from college or university, getting a job, and getting married. People mature. When it is the right time for them. They cannot just follow their friends. Because it is not right for them. Growing into adulthood. Is not an easy process.

The paragraph contains six fragments. If you missed any of them, study the information presented next.

A complete sentence must have a subject, have a verb, and express a complete thought. We will examine several sentences to determine how we can know when a sentence is complete and how we can repair a problem sentence. The following table can serve as a guide. If an entry has an X in each column, it is a complete sentence. If it is missing an X in any column, it is a fragment.

	Subject	Verb	Complete Thought	
The baby. (This is a fragment. It has a subject, but it has no verb and it does not express a complete thought. The baby what?)	X			Fragment
The baby laughed. (This is a complete sentence.)	X	X	X	Sentence
Jumped. (This is a fragment. It has a verb, but it has no subject and it does not express a complete thought. Who or what jumped?)		X		Fragment
The horse jumped. (This is a complete sentence.)	X	X	X	Sentence
When the horse jumped. (This is a fragment. It has a subject and a verb, but it does not express a complete thought.)	X	X		Fragment

	Subject	Verb	Complete Thought	
What happened when the horse jumped?) When the horse jumped, the baby laughed. (This is a complete sentence.)	X	X	X	Sentence
Driving a car. (This is a fragment. It does not have a subject, it has only part of a verb, and it does not express a complete thought.)				Fragment
The teenager was driving a car. (This is a complete sentence.)	X	X	X	Sentence
To travel to Montreal. (This is a fragment. It does not have a subject, it does not have a complete conjugated verb, and it does not express a complete thought.)				Fragment
I want to travel to Montreal. (This is a complete sentence.)	X	X	X	Sentence
If I want to travel to Montreal. (This is not a complete sentence because it does not express a complete thought. What do I do if I want to travel to Montreal?)	X	X		Fragment
If I want to travel to Montreal, I will have to take a plane. (This is a complete sentence.)	X	X	X	Sentence
Such as chairs, tables, and sofas. (This is a fragment. It does not have a subject or a verb, and it does not express a complete thought.)				Fragment
A furniture store has many things, such as chairs, tables, and sofas. (This is a complete sentence.)	X	X	X	Sentence

EXERCISE

Using the criteria of subject, verb, and complete thought, decide whether each of the following is a complete sentence or a fragment. Then correct each fragment by making it into a complete sentence.

1. When I finish school.
2. I will look for a job.
3. Got married and moved to Halifax.
4. Because he wanted to try engineering.
5. Cooking in the kitchen.
6. He cried.
7. Such as going to the movies, singing at karaoke bars, giving parties, and eating out with friends.

12 GETTING A JOB

PREREADING ACTIVITIES

1. In a group, discuss the steps one should take to find a job.

2. Discuss your experiences on job interviews.

3. As a group, discuss and write the advice you would give to someone who has never gone on a job interview.

A Mortal Flower

Han Suyin was born and raised in Beijing. She is a pediatric physician and the author of many novels, including the well-known A Many Splendored Thing, *which was made into a movie.* A Mortal Flower *is the second of five volumes of history, biography, and autobiography, interweaving Chinese history of the past century with the experiences of the author and her family, both in and out of China. This excerpt describes the author's experience of looking for her first job.*

The day after meeting Hilda I wrote a letter to the Rockefeller Foundation, applying for a job.

Neither Father nor Mother thought I would get in. "You have to have pull. It's an American thing, Rockefeller Foundation. You must have pull."   5

°important people

Mother said: "That's where they do all those experiments on dogs and people. All the Big Shots° of the Nanking government also came here to have medical treatment, and sometimes took away a nurse to become 'a new wife.' "

It made sense to me, typing in a hospital; I would learn about   10
medicine, since I wanted to study medicine. And as there was no money at home for me to study, I would earn money, and prepare myself to enter medical school. I had already discovered that a convent-school education was not at all adequate, and that it would

take me at least three more years of hard study before being able to 15
enter any college at all. Science, mathematics, Chinese literature and
the classics ... with the poor schooling given to me, it would take me
years to get ready for a university.

°lower intestines

"I will do it." But clenched teeth, decision tearing my bowels,°
not enough; there was no money, no money, my mother said it, said 20
it until I felt as if every morsel of food I ate was wrenched off my
father's body.

"No one is going to feed you doing nothing at home." Of course,
one who does not work must not eat unless one can get married,
which is called: "being settled at last." But with my looks I would 25
never get married; I was too thin, too sharp, too ugly. Mother said it,
Elder Brother had said it. Everyone agreed that I should work,
because marriage would be difficult for me.

Within a week a reply came. The morning postman brought it,
and I choked over my milk and coffee. "I'm to go for an interview. 30

°chief accountant's

At the Peking Union Medical College. To the Comptroller's° office."

Father and Mother were pleased. Mother put the coffee pot
down and took the letter. "What good paper, so thick." But how
could we disguise the fact that I was not [even] fifteen years old? I
had claimed to be sixteen in the letter. In fact, said Papa, it was not a 35
lie since Chinese are a year old when born, and if one added the New
Year as an extra year, as do the Cantonese and the Hakkas, who
became two years old when they reach their first New Year (so that

°calculated

a baby born on December 31st would be reckoned° two years old on
the following January 2nd), I could claim to being sixteen. 40

"You look sixteen," said Mama; "all you have to do is to stop
hopping and picking your pimples. And lengthen your skirt."

What dress should I wear? I had two school uniforms, a green

°ruffles

dress, a brown dress, and one dress with three rows of frills° for
Sunday, too dressy for an interview. I had no shoes except flat-heeled 45
school shoes, and tennis shoes. There was no time to make a dress
and in those years no ready-made clothes existed. Mother length-

°sheer fabric

ened the green dress, and added her voile° scarf. I squeezed two
pimples on my forehead, then went to the East market and bought
some face powder, Butterfly brand, pink, made in Shanghai by a 50
Japanese firm.

The next morning, straw-hatted, with powder on my nose, I
went with my father to the gates of the hospital.

"It's not this gate, this is for the sick. It's the other gate, round the
corner," said the porter. 55

The Yu Wang Fu Palace occupied a whole city block. We walked
along its high grey outer wall, hearing the dogs scream in the kennels, and came to its other gate, which was the Administration

Building gate. It had two large stone lions, one male, one female. We crossed the marble courtyard, walked up the steps with their carved   60
dragons coiling in the middle, into an entrance hall, with painted beams and intricate° painted ceiling, red lacquered° pillars, huge lamps. There was cork matting° on the stone floor.

°complicated
°shinily painted
°woven floor covering

"I'll leave you," said Papa. "Try to make a good impression."
And he was gone.   65

I found the Comptroller's office easily; there was a messenger in the hall directing visitors. An open door, a room, two typewriters clattering and two women making them clatter.

I stood at the door and one of the women came to me. She had the new style of hair, all upstanding curls, which I admired, a dress   70
with a print round the hem; she was very pregnant, so that her belly seemed to be coming at me first. She smiled. "Hello, what can I do for you?"

"I have an interview."

She took the letter from my hand. "Glad you could come. Now,   75
just sit you down. No, sit down there. I'll tell Mr. Harned you've come."

The office had two other doors besides the one to the corridor, on one was "Comptroller." That was the one she went through and returned from.   80

"Mr. Harned will see you now."

Mr. Harned was very tall, thin, [with] a small bald head, a long chin, enormous glasses. I immediately began to quiver with fright. His head was like a temple on top of a mountain, like the white pagoda° on the hill in the North Sea Park. I could not hear a word of   85

°sacred temple

what he said. A paper and a pencil were in my hand, however, and Mr. Harned was dictating to me, giving me a speed test in short-hand.

I went out of his office and the pregnant secretary sat me in front of her own typewriter. I turned a stricken face to her, "I couldn't   90
hear. I couldn't hear what he said…."

"Wait, I'll tell him." She bustled off. At the other desk was a blonde, thin girl, who had thrown one look at me and then gone back to clattering. The pregnant one reappeared, a pink sheet in hand: "Now just copy this on the typewriter, best you can."   95

I hit the keys, swiftly; the typewriter was the same make as mine, a Royal.

"My, you are fast. I'll tell Mr. Harned."

And Mr. Harned came out, benign° behind those enormous goggle glasses.° "Well, Miss Chou, we've decided to take you on as   100
a typist, at thirty-five local dollars a month. To start Monday. Is that all right?"

°kindly, gentle
°large glasses that make the eyes bulge

I nodded, unable to speak. Had he said ten dollars I would have accepted.

The kind secretary said: "Now take your time, and wipe your ~~105~~ face. How old are you, by the way"

"Sixteen, nearly."

"Is that all? Why my eldest is bigger than you, and she isn't through school yet. I told Mr. Harned you were shy and upset, and that's why you couldn't take dictation. He's all right, just takes get- 110 ting used to, that's all."

"I couldn't understand his English."

"Oh, you'll get used to it. Now, I won't be around on Monday, I'm going to have a baby. It's your letter that got them interested in you, you wrote such good English, better than all the other letters 115 we've had. Mr. Harned will give you a try." She whispered, "I put in a good word for you."

"Thanks, thanks a lot. I need the money, I. ..."

"Yes, dear, we know." Obviously she wanted her typewriter °good-bye back, and her chair. I was still sitting on it. "Well, toodle-doo° for 120 now; hope you enjoy yourself in this job. I've been here six months and I've enjoyed every minute. Don't let Mr. Harned worry you; he's really great, once you get used to him." *excited, joyful, delighted*

I had a job, had a job, had a job. *her excitement and happiness.*

READING AND THINKING STRATEGIES

DISCUSSION ACTIVITIES

Analysis and Conclusions

1. What happens during the interview with Mr. Harned? Why does she get the job after all?

2. Why isn't the girl's family more helpful and supportive? Is there anything in the story that makes you believe they care for her despite their behaviour?

3. Do you think the young girl has confidence in herself when she goes for the interview? Support your point of view with evidence from the story.

Writing and Point of View

1. Why do you think Han Suyin titled her story "A Mortal Flower"? How does the title relate to the story?

Homework

① *Find a job advertisement in the newspaper, cut it out & write a covering letter to go with your resume*

Chief Executive officer principle employee

2. Using evidence from "A Mortal Flower," show how Han Suyin made you aware of how she felt during the job interview. What descriptive words did she use?

3. "A Mortal Flower" is excerpted from an autobiography, as is "Age and Youth" by Pablo Casals (page 179). What is similar about these two pieces of writing? What is different about the two styles? Which did you prefer? Why?

Personal Response and Evaluation

1. If you were going on a job interview, what would you do that was similar to what the girl in this story did? What would you do that was different? Why?

2. What should you do on an interview so that you make a good impression? What shouldn't you do?

3. What steps should a person take in order to find a job?

ROLE PLAYING

In a small group, write the dialogue of an interview. It can be a job interview, a school interview, an interview with a landlord, or an interview with a loan official. Two people should be talking. Read the dialogue out loud in your group to make sure that it sounds natural. Each group should act out its dialogue in front of the class.

JOURNAL WRITING

Han Suyin's story is about success. A young girl many had seen as a failure goes off on her own to a strange place, meets a kind, supportive person, and has a successful experience. She gets a job. In your journal, write about your experience with success. Have you ever had an experience like this nervous young girl's in which you were afraid of failure but, in the end, succeeded? If you have had this kind of experience, write about it.

The following quotation is taken from an article in *Self* magazine titled "Five Ways to Cash In on Your Mistakes":

Failure intimidates most people, but to the successful it is a challenge to try again. Look behind most successes and you'll find a solid foundation of failures they have learned from. Success is not something we are born to — we achieve it.

Think about this quote. What is failure? Can we learn from it? Has a failure ever led to a success in your life? For this journal entry, think about failure and success. What is the relationship between the two?

WRITING STRATEGIES

ESSAY STRATEGIES
Résumé Writing

Write your résumé as though you were preparing to go for a job interview. What should employers know about you that will make them want to hire you? What special talents do you have? What education do you have? What job experience have you had? Your résumé may take the following form, or your teacher may suggest another style to you.

Name Address City, Province, Postal Code

Telephone Number

Date of Birth (This is optional.)

Educational Background:
(List the schools you have attended, in reverse chronological order, the most recent one first. If you majored in something special or have any unique educational experience, mention it here.)

Work Experience:
(List the jobs you have had, in reverse chronological order, the most recent one first. You may want to explain the duties of your jobs if you think it will help you get the job you are applying for.)

Special Abilities:
(List the languages you speak and any other unique abilities you have that may help you get the job.)

References:
(List the names and addresses of two or three people who know you well enough to recommend you for a job. You should contact these people before using their names. A former employer and a teacher would be good choices.)

Type your résumé, single-spaced, making sure there are no typing or spelling errors. Use 8 1/2-by-11-inch white or off-white typing paper. Make sure your original is neat and clean; make photocopies, keeping your original for future reference. See the sample résumé.

RÉSUMÉ

Carmen Perozo
114 Huron Street, Apt 4A
Vancouver, B.C.
V8S 3A6
(604) 377-7802

Date of birth: 10/15/70

EDUCATIONAL BACKGROUND

September 1989–present	Capilano College, third year Major undecided; probably accounting or business Grade point average: 2.8
April–July 1989	Camosun College, Victoria, B.C. — studied English as a Second Language
1984–1988	San Sebastian High School, Bogota, Colombia Average: B +

WORK EXPERIENCE

August 1989–May 1991	Part-time bookkeeper and salesclerk Chime Gift Shop, Vancouver, B.C.
June 1988–August 1989	Waitress, Three Sisters Restaurant, Victoria, B.C.

SPECIAL ABILITIES

I speak fluent Spanish and French. I have studied English for six years
(three in Colombia and three in Canada). I type 60 words a minute on an
electric typewriter, and I can operate a word processor and a calculator.

REFERENCES

Kay Winston, owner Chime Gift Shop 331 Main Street Vancouver, B.C. V9A 4H2	Professor James Manley Accounting Department Capilano College Vancouver, BC. V9A 2Z4

TRANSITION WORDS

The following paragraphs, which describe how to prepare yourself for a job interview, contain many transition words. There are transitions that indicate importance or emphasis as well as transitions that indicate time. Underline all the transition words in the paragraphs.

The first thing you have to do to prepare for a job interview is to write your résumé. Most of all, the résumé should emphasize all the related experience you have had. The résumé should be clear and should be written with an awareness that the person reading it will probably be reading many other résumés. The best thing you can do is to make it obvious why you can do the job better than anybody else. Your résumé should be neatly typed.

Once you have organized your résumé, check your closet. Pay special attention to what you will wear for the interview. You don't want to be dressed up as if you were going to a party, but you also don't want to be underdressed. Consider getting your hair trimmed before the interview. Remember that neatness counts. You should be neat in your appearance as well as in your résumé.

Finally, you must keep in mind that employers do not like people to smoke or chew gum during an interview. The basic reason for this may be that you appear too relaxed. Remember, you are not visiting a friend; you are trying to get a job. If you follow all of the advice given here, you have a better chance of getting the job you desire.

Check your answers on page 328. If you had any difficulty, refer to the following lists. Transition words add a flow to your writing.

Time transitions: *first, next, then, before, after, during, now, while, finally*

Emphasis transitions: *keep in mind, remember, most of all, the most important, the best thing, the basic reason, the chief reason, the chief factor, special attention should be paid to*

EXERCISE

Rewrite the paragraphs, changing them from the second person (*you*) to the third person (*he* or *she*). The first sentence should read "The first thing a person has to do to prepare for a job interview is to write his [or her] résumé."

EXERCISES

1. After looking at the sample business letter and rereading the directions for writing a business letter, write the answers to the following questions on the blank lines.

   a. What are the parts of a business letter?

   _____

   b. What is the purpose of the introduction?

   _____

   c. What is contained in the body of the letter?

   _____

   d. What goes in the upper right corner of the page?

   _____

   e. Where is the date found in a business letter?

   _____

   f. What is at the upper left-hand side of the page?

   _____

   g. What punctuation mark is used after the salutation?

   _____

   h. How do you conclude a business letter?

   _____

2. With a partner or in a small group, write a formal letter applying for a job, requesting information, or complaining about a product you have bought.

3. Write a business letter applying for a job and introducing your résumé to a prospective employer.

ESSAY FORM
Writing a Business or Formal Letter

People write business letters to request information, to complain about a product they have bought, to explain why they haven't paid a bill on time. They write to request job interviews, to introduce their résumés. Business letters generally consist of an introduction, a body, and a conclusion. Formal essays consist of these same parts. The introduction to a business letter is usually found in the first paragraph. It is what makes the reader want to read more. It introduces the main idea that the letter will be about. The body of the letter offers specific details or examples to support the main idea that has been presented in the introduction. The letter ends with the conclusion, in which the ideas from the rest of the letter are summarized or restated.

The form of a business letter is important. At the upper right-hand side of the page goes the writer's full address. Under the address is the date when the letter is being written. One line below this, at the left-hand side of the page, is the address to which the letter is being sent. The writer skips a line and types "Dear _____:" and skips another line, indents five spaces, and begins the introductory paragraph. The entire letter is typed, indenting for each new paragraph. After the conclusion, the writer skips a line and types "Sincerely," or "Yours truly," aligned with the address and date at the right-hand side of the page, skips five lines, and types his or her name. The writer then signs the letter, folds it into thirds, and places it in a long, rectangular envelope on which the address has been typed. The writer finally places a stamp on the envelope and mails it.

A sample letter appears on page 249.

SUGGESTIONS FOR WRITING

Before you begin to write, try making a brainstorming list, as described on page 250 in "Getting Started," or try one of the techniques discussed throughout, the book. You also may want to refer to your journal for ideas.

114 Broadway, Apt. 4A
Vancouver, B.C.
V8S 3A6
May 15, 1994

Mr. Henry Walsh, Personnel Manager
Caldicott Publishing Company
177 West Vernon Boulevard
Vancouver, BC
V6S 3H7

inside address

Dear Mr. Walsh:

I am interested in applying for a weekend job as a word processor in your company. I saw your advertisement in the Vancouver Sun this past Sunday, and I feel that I am qualified for this job. I have studied computers for two years at Capilano College. I am familiar with the Windows system, which you mention in your ad. I type about 60 words a minute, and I am very accurate. I enclose my résumé, and I will be glad to send you reference letters if you so desire.

I hope that you will consider me for this job. I can be reached at the above address or at 377-7802 in the evenings after school. I look forward to hearing from you. ~~Thank you~~ for considering me for this job.

Yours truly / sincerely

~~Very~~ truly yours,

Carmen Perozo

Carmen Perozo

Enc. (enclosure)

4 cm

1. Describe a job interview you have been on. Create a mood that lets your reader can feel what your experience was like. Use descriptive words.

2. First impressions do not always reveal the total person. Have you ever had an experience in which a first impression of a person turned out to be wrong? Describe what happened and what you learned from it.

3. Write a letter of recommendation to Mr. Harned telling him why he should hire Miss Chou.

4. Write a dialogue that takes place between the girl and her parents when she returns home to tell them that she has gotten the job. (You may want to act out your dialogue in front of the class with two other classmates.)

5. Looking for a job can be very difficult. Use this as your thesis; then give examples and experiences to support your point of view.

6. "Success is not something we are born to — we achieve it." Explain the steps that you think someone has to go through in order to achieve success. What does success mean to you?

7. Many people learn more from their failures than they do from their successes. Give examples from your own life or from your observations of others to support this point of view.

8. Imagine that you are an employer who is interviewing someone for a job. In a well-developed essay, describe what you would expect in an employee. What are the characteristics you value, and why are they important?

GETTING STARTED
Making a Brainstorming List

Before you start to write, take out a piece of blank paper and at the top of your page, write in five words or less your main idea or thesis — what you want to write about. As soon as you finish writing this, look at it again and start to make a list of any words or ideas that come to your mind. Your list should not contain sentences or fully developed ideas. It should be fragmentary and loose, recording ideas that will lead to your future essay development. Write the list for at least five minutes. Then spend five more minutes examining the list. Star the words or ideas that seem to relate to your main idea. Cross out words or ideas that do not seem to be related. As you are doing this, other words or ideas may occur to you; put them on your list. Use this list when you get ready to start writing your essay or story.

REVISING

One great aim of revision is to cut out. In the exuberance of composition it is natural to throw in — as one does in speaking — a number of small words that add nothing to meaning but keep up the flow and rhythm of thought. In writing, not only does this surplusage not add to meaning, it subtracts from it. Read and revise, reread and revise, keeping reading and revising until your text seems adequate to your thought.

JACQUES BARZUN

Jacques Barzun's advice may seem surprising after our emphasis on adding detail to your writing to make your descriptions come alive. However, there is a difference between rich, exciting language and repetitive or wordy writing. Look critically at what you have written. Every time you see the words *in my opinion,* cross them out. It is obvious that your writing expresses your opinion because you have written it. Every time you see the words *you know,* cross them out. If your reader knows, why bother to say it again? Every time you find yourself repeating something you have already said a few sentences before, cross it out. In place of those excess bits of writing, add some new and exciting ideas. Keep reading and revising until "your text seems adequate to your thought."

A Student Essay

This student is responding to writing suggestion 7. Read her essay; then discuss it using one of the revising exercises from the book that has been helpful for you.

Success Comes after Failure

When I first arrived in Canada, I could not understand a single word and I did not know what was going on in classes at all. I never asked questions nor answered questions in classes. The only thing I did was copy the notes from the board. When I studied at night, I did not understand 90 percent of the vocabulary; therefore, my notebooks were almost covered with Chinese. Besides, everything made me confused — the grammar, verb tenses, spelling, and pronunciation.

I always complained to my father when I got upset after failing tests. I told him that I did not want to go to school and I could find a job in Chinatown. It would not be difficult. My father always said: "You will never succeed if you are afraid of difficulties, but if you are not afraid of them, they will be afraid of you, and at last you will win; Success comes after failures. You fail this test; you will pass the next one. But do not give up whenever you have difficulties."

He also said to me and my brother, "I want you to finish high school, go to university, and gain as much knowledge as possible. This is the main reason we have come to Canada."

My parents influence me a lot. They give me willpower and courage. They expect a great deal from me. I cannot let them be disappointed; therefore, I face the challenge. I study hard, I do my best in everything, and I feel I am getting better and better.

Nora Chao, China

EDITING STRATEGIES

WORD DEVELOPMENT

idiomatic expressions

Each of the following paragraphs contains a context clue that will help you understand one of the idiomatic expressions used in "A Mortal Flower." Underline these context clues; the first one has been done for you. Then use the expressions when you answer the questions that follow each paragraph.

1. ***to have pull*** (lines 4 and 5)

   The girl's family thinks she has to have pull before her letter of application will be considered. They think she has <u>to have influence from someone who is important</u> in order to get a job.

   Have you ever needed to have pull in order to do something in your life?

2. ***ready-made clothes*** (line 47)

   At the time Han Suyin writes of, no ready-made clothes existed.

   People could not just walk into a department store and buy clothes off the racks. All clothes were made by hand, usually at home.

   In today's world it is rarer to find homemade clothes than ready-made clothes. Have you or has anyone in your family ever made your clothes, or are all of your clothes ready-made?

3. ***make a good impression on*** (someone) (line 64)

The girl's father hopes that she will make a good impression on her future boss. He wants the comptroller to think good things about her when he meets her.

It is also possible to make a bad impression on someone. Often our first impression of someone remains with us. Has anyone ever made one type of impression on you, and you later found that person to be very different from what you had first thought?

4. ***to get used to*** (someone/something) (line 123)

The secretary promises the girl that she will like Mr. Harned once she gets used to him. She has to grow accustomed to the kind of person he is.

When we meet someone for the first time, we do not know how to behave. We have to get used to the person. Can you think of any person in your life that it took you a long time to get used to? Can you think of anything else in your life that took you a long time to get used to (speaking English, perhaps)?

the

The word *the* has been omitted throughout the following paragraph. Rewrite the paragraph, adding *the* where it is necessary.

> *Trying to get a job at Rockefeller Foundation is difficult for a girl who does not have pull. Finally morning postman brings letter. She is to go for an interview at Peking Medical College, to Comptroller's office. She prepares her clothes and goes to East market to buy face powder to cover her pimples. Next morning, she goes with her father to Yu Wang Fu Palace to Administration building. They cross marble courtyard and go into entrance hall. Her father leaves. She finds office and meets her future employer, Mr. Harned. His bald head reminds her of white pagoda on hill in North Sea Park. She takes required typing test and gets job.*

Check your answers on page 329.

ADJECTIVE WORD ORDER

Bass Ē

In Chapter Six, we examined the typical order of adjectives used in English. As a review of this, the following sentences have been taken from "A Mortal Flower," but the order of the adjectives has been mixed up. In the blanks, arrange the adjectives in the correct order. If you have difficulty, refer to the chart on page 131.

1. I had *two school uniforms*, a green dress, a brown dress, and one
   (two, uniforms, school)

   dress with three rows of frills for Sunday, too dressy for an interview.

2. I had no shoes except *flat-heeled school shoes* and tennis shoes.
   (shoes, flat-heeled, school)

3. We walked along its *high grey outer wall*, hearing the dogs scream
   (outer, high, wall, grey)

   in the kennels, and came to its other gate, which was the
   Administration building gate.
   (gate, Administration, building)

4. It had *two large stone lions*, one male, one female.
   (two, stone, large, lions)

5. Mr. Harned was tall, thin, [with] *a small bald head*, a long chin,
   (bald, small, head, a)

   and enormous glasses.

COMMONLY CONFUSED WORDS

past/passed

Read the following paragraph, observing the use of *past* and *passed*.

> In the past, men passed up being with their families so they could succeed in their jobs. Often their children grew up and their childhoods had passed their fathers by. A man once told me, "I got off the bus and a boy drove past me on his bicycle. He waved and I didn't recognize him. He was my son." Those days have passed for most men, and they will stay in the past. Nowadays fathers are as involved as mothers in their children's lives, and they are enjoying it too.

On the basis of what you observed in the paragraph, complete the following definitions.

passed is a verb that means "went by," "handed to," or "succeeded in."

past is a noun or adjective that means "a time before the present."

past is a preposition that means "by."

Now write sentences of your own using *past* and *passed*.

MECHANICS

Using Numbers in Your Writing

1. Numbers from one to nine or ten are usually written out as words. Higher numbers are usually written in numerals. However, if you use numbers very infrequently in your writing, you may choose to write out the numbers when you can do so in two or three words.

   five   seven   17   178   5,891

2. When you use the following abbreviations, use numerals.

   3.5 m   2 tsp.   10° C   99%   3 cm

3. When numbers begin a sentence, write them out.

   One hundred students waited on line to get the new book.

4. Numbers that are being compared or contrasted should be kept in the same style. Look at the following excerpt from the text to see when Han Suyin wrote out the numbers and when she used numerals.

   But how could we disguise the fact that I was not [even] *fifteen* years old? I had claimed to be *sixteen* in the letter. In fact, said Papa, it was not a lie since Chinese are a year old when born, and if one added the New Year as an extra year, as do the Cantonese and the Hakkas, who became *two* years old when they reach their first New Year (so that a baby born on December *31st* would be reckoned *two* years old on the following January *2nd*), I could claim to be *sixteen*.

   What patterns do you find in Han Suyin's use of numbers in this paragraph? *She writes number in word form*

EDITING PRACTICE

The following paragraph is a first draft that contains many surface errors: two fragments, one *their/there/they're* error, one *advice/advise* error, two run-ons, and inconsistent pronoun use. Find and correct the errors. Answers are on page 329.

Looking for a job can be difficult, ~~their~~ there are many different types of problems. For one thing, the interviewee is never sure what to bring on the first interview. I usually bring too much ~~this~~ which can be confusing to the interviewer. From now on, I will bring only the necessary documents, ~~Such~~ such as ~~your~~ my résumé, ~~your~~ my birth certificate, and ~~your~~ my high school diploma. In addition, I try to impress the interviewer by dressing very neatly and never chewing gum. I always look directly into the interviewer's eyes. I want the interviewer to believe that I can be trusted. If I remember to follow my own ~~advise~~ advice, I believe I will get a job soon.

GRAMMAR STRATEGIES

USE OF PARTICIPLE FORMS

A *participle* is a verb form that can function as an adjective or as a verb. The present participle ends in *-ing;* the past participle ends in *-ed* or *-en.* (Past participles are listed in Appendix A.)

Watching a *boring* movie always puts me to sleep.

The *-ing* participle functions as an adjective describing the noun *movie.*

The *bored* student drew pictures in his notebook.

The *-ed* participle functions as an adjective describing the noun *student.*

The letter *describing* her abilities arrived at the right time.

The *-ing* participle functions as a verb because it has an object, *letter*.

EXERCISES

1. In the following sentences, tell whether the participle is functioning as an adjective or a verb, and explain why.
   a. The *stolen* car had been taken from 117 Main Street.
   b. A witness said he had seen a man *stealing* the car.
   c. The *confused* witness could not remember anything about the thief.
   d. The *confusing* story did not help the police very much.
   e. The victims *appealing* for help offered a reward of $50.
   f. Two weeks later, the *worried* victims found their undamaged *stolen* car *parked* in front of their building.

2. Reread Han Suyin's story, looking for participles. Notice how they are used in the story.

   The day after meeting Hilda, I wrote a letter to the Rockefeller Foundation, *applying* for a job. (*Applying* is used as a verb in this sentence.)

CONTRAST TRANSITIONS

Contrast transitions guide the reader to expect a change of direction or something unexpected to happen. These are some common contrast transitions:

instead of	still
but	otherwise
however	in contrast with / to
yet	~~on the contrary~~
even though	on the other hand
although	

In the following paragraph, underline all the contrast transition words or phrases.

John accepted a job working as a bus driver <u>even though</u> he often got carsick. The first few days of training were difficult, <u>but</u> finally he passed his road test. That first Monday morning he was beginning to feel ~~queasy~~ *readily to vomit*. *Still,* he started up the engine and backed out of the garage. A senior bus driver sat near the front of the bus and said, "Step on it, John. We have to make time. *Otherwise,* we'll be late." John wanted to drive slowly; *however,* he wanted to keep his job, *so* he stepped on the accelerator, *and* the bus *lurched* for- ~~ward~~. *Instead of* thinking about how sick he felt, John stared out the front window and counted to ten, then twenty. When he was up to one hundred, he told the older bus driver that he had a prob- lem with car sickness. "I used to have it too. Just relax. You're doing fine," the experienced driver responded. John believed the reassuring words; *on the other hand,* he worried that he wouldn't make it through the next hour, *although* he was trying to forget about his stomach. *Yet* he made it through the day, and through the next two weeks. *In contrast to* his early fears, five years later John found himself sitting near the front of a big old bus telling a new bus driver to "just relax."

[handwritten margin note: the bus suddenly accelerated, and your body fell to the back]

[handwritten note: turching → lurched]

Compare your answers with the list on page 329.

EXERCISE

Write a paragraph in which you use three contrast transitions. Possible topics are the first day on a new job, learning how to do something new, and problems with first impressions.

HOME AND FINDING ONE'S PLACE

FINDING ONE'S HOME

PREREADING ACTIVITIES

1. This essay is about a person who came to Canada from Korea at a young age. In a small group, discuss Korea. Where is it? What is its history?

2. As a class, find out what Korea is like today.

3. What do you think the title of the essay "An Immigrant's Split Personality" means? In a group, discuss what you consider to be home — the country in which you were born or another country? Why? When does a country become "home"?

An Immigrant's Split Personality

Sun-Kyung Yi is a freelance author. Among the many subjects she writes about are the experiences of Korean immigrants in Canada. The article below first appeared in The Globe and Mail.

I am Korean-Canadian. But the hyphen often snaps in two, obliging me to choose to act as either a Korean or a Canadian, depending on where I am and who I'm with. After sixteen years of living in Canada, I discovered that it's very difficult to be both at any given time or place. 5

When I was younger, toying with the idea of entertaining two separate identities was a real treat, like a secret game for which no one knew the rules but me.

I was known as Angela to the outside world, and as Sun-Kyung at home. I ate bologna sandwiches in the school lunch room and rice 10 and kimchee for dinner. I chatted about teen idols and giggled with my girlfriends during my classes, and ambitiously practiced piano and studied in the evenings, planning to become a doctor when I grew up. I waved hellos and goodbyes to my teachers, but bowed to my parents' friends visiting our home. 15

I could also look straight in the eyes of my teachers and friends and talk frankly with them instead of staring at my feet with my mouth shut when Koreans talked to me.

Going outside the home meant I was able to relax from the constraints of my cultural conditioning, until I walked back in the door and had to return to being an obedient and submissive daughter.

The game soon ended when I realized that it had become a way of life, that I couldn't change the rules without disappointing my parents and questioning all the cultural implications and consequences that came with being a hyphenated Canadian.

Many have tried to convince me that I am a Canadian, like all other immigrants in the country, but those same people also ask me which country I came from with great curiosity, following with questions about the type of food I ate and the language I spoke. It's difficult to feel a sense of belonging and acceptance when you are regarded as "one of them." "Those Koreans, they work hard… You must be fantastic at math and science." (No.) "Do your parents own a corner store?" (No.)

Koreans and Canadians just can't seem to merge into "us" and "we."

Some people advised me that I should just take the best of both worlds and disregard the rest. That's ideal, but unrealistic when my old culture demands a complete conformity with very little room to manoeuvre for new and different ideas.

After a lifetime of practice, I thought I could change faces and become Korean on demand with grace and perfection. But working with a small Korean company in Toronto proved me wrong. I quickly became estranged from my own people.

My parents were ecstatic at the thought of their daughter finally finding her roots and having a working opportunity to speak my native tongue and absorb the culture. For me, it was the most painful and frustrating 2 1/2 months of my life.

When the president of the company boasted that he "operated little Korea," he meant it literally. A Canadianized Korean was not tolerated. I looked like a Korean, therefore I had to talk, act, and think like one, too. Being accepted meant a total surrender to ancient codes of behaviour rooted in Confucian thought, while leaving the "Canadian" part of me out in the parking lot with my '86 Buick.

In the first few days at work, I was bombarded with inquiries about my marital status. When I told them I was single, they spent the following days trying to match me up with available bachelors in the company and the community.

I was expected to accept my inferior position as a woman and had to behave accordingly. It was not a place to practice my feminist

views, or be an individual without being condemned. Little Korea is 60
a place for men (who filled all the senior positions) and women don't
dare speak up or disagree with their male counterparts.

The president (all employees bow to him and call him Mr.
President) asked me to act more like a lady and smile. I was openly
scorned by a senior employee because I spoke more fluent English 65
than Korean. The cook in the kitchen shook her head in disbelief
upon discovering that my cooking skills were limited to boiling a
package of instant noodles. "You want a good husband, learn to
cook," she advised me.

In less than a week I became an outsider because I refused to 70
conform and blindly nod my head in agreement to what my elders
(which happened to be everybody else in the company) said. A
month later, I was demoted because "members of the workplace and
the Korean community" had complained that I just wasn't "Korean
enough," and I had "too much power for a single woman." My 75
father suggested that "when in Rome do as the Romans." But that's
exactly what I was doing. I am in Canada so I was freely acting like
a Canadian, and it cost me my job.

My father also said, "It doesn't matter how Canadian you think
you are, just look in the mirror and it'll tell you who you *really* are." 80
But what he didn't realize is that an immigrant has to embrace the
new culture to enjoy and benefit from what it has to offer. Of course,
I will always be Korean by virtue of my appearance and early conditioning, but I am also happily Canadian and want to take full
advantage of all that such citizenship confers. 85

But for now I remain slightly distant from both cultures,
accepted fully by neither. The hyphenated Canadian personifies the
ideal of multiculturalism, but unless the host culture and the immigrant cultures can find ways to merge their distinct identities, sharing the best of both, this cultural schizophrenia will continue. 90

READING AND THINKING STRATEGIES

DISCUSSION ACTIVITIES

Analysis and Conclusions

1. Sun-Kyung Yi feels frustrated because, although she takes part in
   both Canadian and Korean cultures, she is fully accepted by neither. This leads, as she expresses it, to "cultural schizophrenia."
   Define the term and tell how it applies to Sun-Kyung Yi's life.

2. What is meant by a "hyphenated Canadian"? What are the difficulties involved in trying to live in two cultures at once? Could this situation also be advantageous? Explain your answer.

3. Why is Sun-Kyung Yi's boss intolerant of Canadianized Koreans? How is this reflected in his treatment of her?

Writing and Point of View

1. What is this essay about? What is Sun-Kyung Yi trying to make you aware of? Does she make you feel what she has been through? If so, how does she do this? Are there enough examples to convince you of her situation?

2. In what person is this essay written? Rewrite the first three paragraphs in the third person. ("She is Korean-Canadian," etc.) Does the meaning of the essay change when it is written in the third person? Which version do you prefer? Why?

3. Compare the personal writing styles of Marty Chan (Chapter One) and Sun-Kyung Yi with the article "Between Two Worlds" in Chapter Four. What makes a piece of writing personal or impersonal? How do you decide when your writing should be more personal or more impersonal?

Personal Response and Evaluation

1. Compare Sun-Kyung Yi's experience in Canada to your own experiences.

2. What kind of experience do you think the author would have in Korea? Have you ever returned to a place that you left years before? What was your experience?

3. Is it important to hold on to the customs and cultural patterns of your native country? Is it important to maintain your first language when you are living in a new country?

COLLABORATIVE STORY WRITING

In a group of no more than five students, work together to write a story beginning with one of the following lines.

1. Sun-Kyung Yi talked to a cousin who had just moved to Canada from Korea. She told her cousin …

2. Sun-Kyung Yi visited Korea. When she arrived, the first thing she did was …

3. Sun-Kyung Yi receives a letter from a Canadian friend who is living in Korea. The letter says …

After your group has agreed on which story to write, one student writes the first line of the story and then passes it to another student, who writes the next line. Pass the story around, each person adding a line, until you reach a satisfying ending. Each group then shares its story with the class.

JOURNAL WRITING

The theme of this chapter is adaptation to a new home, combining elements from one's past to one's present circumstances. The upheaval of confronting a new country, a new language, and a new way of life is probably one of the most emotionally charged experiences a person can have in life. By this time, you have made many adjustments to your new life; there is probably a part of you, however, that thinks of the past with sadness, joy, or a bit of both.

In this journal entry, you may want to think about home. A famous writer, Thomas Wolfe, wrote a book titled *You Can't Go Home Again*. Do you agree with the title? Do you ever think about returning to your home country? Do you still have friends and family in your country? Where do you feel your real home is?

If you have difficulty writing about this, you might want to try the clustering technique, using *home* as the nucleus word.

WRITING STRATEGIES

ESSAY STRATEGIES

Time Transitions

In the essay in this chapter, Sun-Kyung Yi includes a narrative about her experiences at work. She makes transitions using phrases that signify time, including these:

In the first few days at work

In less than a week

A month later

Using time phrases to make transitions is an effective way of connecting ideas. Time transitions are particularly useful for telling a story in which the sequence of events is important.

Time indicators help the audience to follow the story from the beginning to the present ("but for now") or even into the future. Here are some useful time indicators:

first	when	at last	whenever
second	during	after that	while
third	until	as soon as	now
afterwards	as early as	after	meanwhile
later	finally	early	to begin with
next	soon	prior	in the first place
then	eventually	before	tomorrow
last	in due time	thereafter	next year

You can use these time phrases to create your own paragraph, for example:

> *I came to Canada when I was almost nine years old. I began to remember how during my childhood I had to try extra hard to do well in school. During the fourth grade I was shy and my English was not good. In due time, however, I began to do better in school than many of the students who had been born in this country. Now, I feel proud of my accomplishments. When I try to review my life, I realize that there were, at first, many difficult moments, but eventually there were also many great times.*

Use these time phrases to create a paragraph about yourself or someone you know.

Details make stories rich, and a sense of time, a chronology that we can follow, makes a story easier to understand.

Look back at the Marty Chan essay in Chapter One, observing his use of transitions of time. Notice how they make the story easy to follow. In the writing exercises for this chapter, keep in mind the elements that make a story work for you. You may want to go back to the stories you wrote in the previous chapters and revise them, keeping in mind detail and chronology.

EXERCISE

Read the following poem and then read it again, thinking about Sun-Kyung Yi's essay.

These Days

whatever you have to say, leave
the roots on, let them
dangle

And the dirt
just to make clear
where they have come from.

CHARLES OLSON

1. Why do you think this poem has been included in this chapter? What is this poem about?

2. Poems are condensations of emotional feelings into a short, tight form. In a few words, they can say many things. Therefore, each word must be selected very carefully. The words resonate — like the sun, their meaning beams out in many directions. Poems are often symbolic. What might *roots* refer to other than roots of plants in the soil? What might *dirt* symbolize?

3. Do Charles Olson and Sun-Kyung Yi have similar ideas? If so, what are these ideas?

ESSAY FORM

Writing a Process Essay

On page 265, we discussed the importance of a sense of time or chronology in a narrative. Another type of writing in which order is important is the process or step-by-step ordering of a task, an event, or a realization.

When you write about a process, you are making clear to your readers the steps that are involved in doing something, in coming to a decision, or in experiencing something. Try some of the writing strategies described in the following five steps as you organize your process writing.

1. *Look around* and carefully observe the specific details of the way you or other people behave while going through the process you are writing about. If you are writing in the classroom, use your memory. Think about the step-by-step details of the process before you begin to write.

2. *Define* or narrow your subject. Some writers use the dictionary or other source book to help them define the process they wish to describe. Others narrow the process down after step 1, once they have recognized the detail that will be needed in the final essay.

3. *Describe* in detail the steps that are needed to understand the process or pattern. Readers see the picture through your words, so make them clear and direct. How do specific details add to the overall effectiveness of an essay?

4. *Analyze* the parts or steps of the pattern or process you are explaining. Then tell how these steps work together. Tell the reader about the history and the future of your subject.

5. *Evaluate* the reasons why the pattern or process you are explaining is important to the reader.

You will not need to use all five steps in every process essay that you write, but keeping them in mind can help you write a clear and effective essay.

EXERCISES

1. In Marty Chan's essay on pages 3 to 6, he explains the step-by-step process leading to his failure at university. Reread his essay, listing the steps that end in his expulsion. Are the steps in any particular order?

2. In the story on page 239, Han Suyin tells the steps that Rosalie Chou takes to get her first job. Reread that story, listing the steps leading to her job. How does she order these steps?

Process writing enables the reader to understand us better or to do something that we have done before. When we look at Casals' "Age and Youth" (page 179), we learn something about him from the step-by-step outline of his day-to-day routine:

> Casals gets up each morning and goes to the piano. He plays two preludes and fugues of Bach. Then he takes a walk along the beach. He observes the nature that surrounds him.

What do we learn about Casals from this?

There are many uses for the process type of writing, but the most common example is the recipe. The writer attempts to tell the reader, with sufficient detail and in the right order, the way to prepare a dish. The following is a recipe for "Grandma Robbins's Potato Latkes (Pancakes)":

To make 18 to 20 potato latkes or pancakes, first peel 6 large potatoes and then grate them into a colander. With your hands, squeeze some of the liquid out and put the potatoes in a bowl. Then grate 1 medium-sized onion into the same bowl and add two beaten eggs, 1/2 cup flour, and 1/2 teaspoon of salt. Mix this together well. Next heat oil in a skillet and drop the potato batter by spoonfuls into the hot oil, forming small pancake shapes. Let the latkes fry until they are crisp at the edge and brown. Then turn and cook the other side in the same way. Drain the pancakes on brown paper or paper towels. Then keep them warm in the oven while you cook the others. Finally, serve them to your hungry guests. These are delicious served with sour cream or applesauce.

If a recipe is well written, the reader should be able to follow each step and make the dish. Reread the recipe, underlining all the transition words.

We also use process writing when we want to explain to someone how to do something. If someone asks us how to register for a class or get a passport, for example, we will give the steps that are required to do the activity. In the following example, a student describes the way to eat a slice of pizza:

First, you order the pizza by walking up and looking the counterperson straight in the eye and saying, "A slice, please." The slice comes on a thin, waxy piece of paper. Next you grab a napkin and quickly slip it under the paper, so you don't spill hot oil all over. Then you put your index finger in the middle of the crust and try to bend it in half. This way you can hold the slice in one hand without dropping it. At this point, you have to be careful because you can burn your finger on the hot cheese. Slowly bring the slice close to your mouth. Breathe in as you do this. Then your mouth begins to water in anticipation of the taste. Take a bite at the tip of the triangle and chew carefully because the first taste, believe it or not, is always the best. Eat slowly and enjoy. Always remember to save a little of the cheese and sauce at the end so the crust will not be too dry. Finally, finish it all, even though it is probably cold.

Reread this description, underlining the transition words.

EXERCISES

1. Write a step-by-step explanation of how to get from school to the front door of your home.
2. Write a step-by-step recipe.
3. Write a step-by-step explanation of your decision to attend your college/university.
4. Write a step-by-step explanation of your realization of the importance of a certain subject.

SUGGESTIONS FOR WRITING

Take some time to think about your ideas before you start to write. You may want to look at your journal for ideas, or you may want to try reminiscing, as described in the "Getting Started" section that follows.

Choose one of the following topics to write about.

1. What does Sun-Kyung Yi mean by her description of herself as a "hyphenated Canadian"? Have you ever felt this way in relation to your country? If you have, describe your feelings and experiences.

2. Write a letter to Sun-Kyung Yi telling her how her essay affected you.

3. "... unless the host culture and the immigrant cultures can find ways to merge their distinct identities, sharing the best of both, this cultural schizophrenia will continue." Sun-Kyung Yi struggles against the stereotypes imposed on her by both the Canadian and Korean cultures, in order to find meaning and a sense of belonging in her life. Many people believe that such struggle makes us stronger. How can struggle make someone strong? Write about yourself or about someone you know or have heard of who has grown stronger through struggle.

4. Many people feel confused about how much of their cultural heritage they should keep in Canada and how much they should give up in order to become more "Canadianized." How have you resolved this question? Tell a story describing how you or someone you have heard of dealt with this issue.

5. Do you think that we all have a responsibility to be political? Should we be familiar with what is going on in other countries of the world? Or do you believe that our responsibility should be only to ourselves, our families, and our neighbourhoods? Explain and give examples supporting your point of view.

GETTING STARTED
Reminiscing

In Sun-Kyung Yi's essay, she wrote about her past and the heritage of her family. In doing this, she reminisced about her family background. This helped to make her writing more powerful and real to her readers.

As you prepare to write one of the essays from the "Suggestions for Writing" above, think about your past and your family history. Focus on the personal experiences or observations that relate to the question you will answer. Jot down a few words that will help you recall these events. Write down as many events or memories as you can recall in five to ten minutes. Then, before you write your essay, look through these reminiscences or memories and choose the ones that, developed more fully, will enrich your writing.

A Student Essay

The following student essay was written in response to the suggested topics.

Who Am I?

When I was in China, my mother told me that Canada was so far away it would take us more than fourteen hours to get there. Now I am living in Canada, but sometimes I still feel that Canada is so far from me.

Language is my major problem. Although I am able to deal with the assignments and the tests, I feel that I simply can't communicate with other students. Actually, I should say that I am really nervous about misunderstanding others so that I become more and more reticent.

Also, it seems that there is a demarcation line between students who speak English as a first language and students who speak English as a second language. There is even a barrier between the students who speak Mandarin and the students who speak Cantonese. Those Cantonese students stick together and always appear to have a little prejudice against the students who speak Mandarin. You can see many Chinese at school, but most of them go past you like strangers. You wouldn't believe it! Sometimes I feel so depressed and lonely. I don't blame anybody. I just feel it is so hard to really be a member of Canadian society.

Anyway, I don't regret coming to Canada. I should not always think about the negative side. Actually I have learned much during the eight months. For instance, I feel that my English is much better than those days when I was first here.

Also, I have changed a lot during the eight months. I have begun to accept many Canadian values and beliefs that my parents don't understand. For example, I think that it is very important for teenagers to be independent. But my parents say, "What's wrong with you! Remember we are Chinese. We have our own traditions. It is not necessary to learn those ideas from Canadians. We are going to look after you and fix up everything for you until you get married!"

Yesterday, I received a letter from my Chinese friend. After I finished reading it, I had a strange feeling that my friends were so unfamiliar. No, they hadn't changed. They were still the people I used to know. It is I who have changed so much that I am not the person they used to know. All of a sudden, I just felt that my friends were so far from me and China was so far from me.

I repeated, "Who am I?" Of course, I am not Canadian. But it seems I am no longer Chinese either. Then, who am I? Who will I be? I feel so confused.

Xuan Cen, China

When you finish reading Xuan Cen's essay, review some of the other student essays in this book. What have you learned from reading these essays and doing revision exercises on them? How has their writing influenced your writing? What are you more careful about when you write now that you were not aware of earlier in the term?

REVISING

After discussing Xuan Cen's essay with your classmates, review the draft of the essay you wrote as you prepare to revise it. Put away the pen you used to write the essay; use a different pen or pencil now. Read your essay aloud, and ask yourself questions about it; you may want to write these questions on a separate piece of paper. Some possible questions are these:

1. What is the writer trying to say in this essay?

2. Does it make sense?

3. Are there enough examples, and are they clear?

4. Are there enough details?

5. Is the essay interesting to read?

Use these questions to help you during the rewriting process. Try to be a helpful critic. Focus on the organization of the essay. Does one idea lead to the next? Are there enough details so that you can form pictures in your mind? How can this piece of writing be made to come alive to its readers?

EDITING STRATEGIES

WORD DEVELOPMENT

word forms

A useful way to increase vocabulary is to learn new forms of words that you already know. In this way you more than triple the number of words that you can understand and use.

The underlined forms of the following words appear in "An Immigrant's Split Personality."

They are all words that are commonly used in college-level material.

adjective	*adverb*	*noun*	*verb*
acceptable	acceptably	acceptance	accept
agreeable	agreeably	agreement	agree
identifiable	identifiably	identity	identify
submissive	submissively	submission	submit
		submissiveness	

EXERCISE

Use the correct word form in each of the following sentences. If the word form is a verb, be sure to use the appropriate ending.

acceptable   acceptably   acceptance   accept

1. Did the children behave _____ at the concert?

2. She did not _____ her boss' guidelines about how to behave.

agreeable   agreeably   agreement   agree

3. This room is _____ warm.

4. She told me that her last job was _____.

identifiable   identifiably   identity   identify   identification

5. Her _____ is both Korean and Canadian.

6. Can you _____ the author simply by looking at a single writing sample?

submissive   submissively   submission   submit   submissiveness

7. The author does not believe women should be _____.

8. I will _____ my research essay tomorrow.

These words will become part of your active vocabulary if you use them. Write sentences using these words in each of their forms. In addition, try to use some of them in your next essay.

COMMONLY CONFUSED WORDS

where/were

Read the following paragraph, observing the use of *where* and *were*.

> *Sometimes our response to bad news is affected by* where *we hear it. If we* were *at home, we might allow ourselves to cry and feel grief. If we* were *out on the street, we might find ourselves trying to hold back our tears and deep feelings until we got to a place* where *we felt safe.*

On the basis of what you observed in the paragraph, complete the following definitions.

_____ is the plural past tense of the verb *be*.

_____ asks in what place something is.

> *Wear* and *ware* are also sometimes confused with *where* and *were*. *Wear* means "to have on," as clothing. (She *wears* a suit to work every day.) *Ware* means "piece of goods to be sold." (A peddler was selling his *wares*.)
>
> Fill in the blanks in the following sentences with *where, were, wear,* or *ware(s)*.

1. She didn't know what to _____ because she didn't know

   _____ they _____ going on their date.

2. The peddler sold his _____ on the street corner.

3. They _____ not sure _____ to go after they heard the news.

> Now write your own sentences using *where, were, wear,* and *ware*.

MECHANICS

Parentheses

The first rule to remember about using parentheses is to avoid using them as much as possible. They are distracting to the reader. However, writers do use parentheses to separate explanatory or supplementary material from the body of the main text when necessary.

Parentheses are also used in research papers when a writer reports or rephrases what another writer has written. In that case, the parentheses enclose the name and date of the source of research.

Look at the Oskamp selection on page 217 to see how writers use parentheses to credit the source of research findings being discussed.

When quoting someone's exact words, a writer uses quotation marks around the words and follows them, in parentheses, with the original author's name, the date of the publication, and the page number; for example, "Quotation" (Rose, 1989, p. 17).

This is a general description of the use of parentheses. The exact format for documenting research and other writing can vary, depending on your teacher's style requirements. Check this with your teacher before writing a research paper.

EDITING PRACTICE

The following paragraph is an unedited first draft. Read it and edit the paragraph, looking for errors of any kind. If you have difficulty, discuss it with a classmate. To check your answers, turn to page 329.

The essay "An Immigrant's Split Personality" by Sun-Kyung Yi made me think about returning to my country. I grown up thinking that their was no reason to go back, but now I am not sure. Its interesting for me to think about the world that I left behind, I feel mixed emotions. Such as happiness, sadness, and regret. My aunts and uncles still lives in my country. They still live in the same town; in the same house. I have never seen most of my cousins, the youngest one is five month old and I would like to know him to. My brother visited my family last year, and he told me all the news. Its strange hearing about my best girlfriends which are getting married and one even has a baby. The essay, my brother's visit, and my dreams makes me: want to return to my country for a visit.

GRAMMAR STRATEGIES

PARALLELISM

Words in a pair or in series should have a balanced or parallel structure. The following examples of parallel structure are taken from

Sun-Kyung Yi's essay.

> I waved *hellos and goodbyes to my teachers, but* bowed *to my parents' friends visiting our home. (Both are past tense verbs.)*

> I looked *like a Korean, therefore I had to* talk, act, *and* think *like one, too. (These are all infinitive forms of the verb; the initial* to *modifies them all.)*

The following examples of parallel structure are taken from the Han Suyin story on page 239.

> *But with my looks I would never get married; I was* too thin, too sharp, too ugly. *(These adjectives are all modified by* too.*)*

> *"You look sixteen," said Mama; "all you have to do is to stop* hopping *and* picking *your pimples." (both words end in* -ing.*)*

EXERCISES

1. Fill in the blanks with appropriate words in parallel structure.

   Sun-Kyung Yi explained that she felt both _____ and

   _____. She was _____ Angela to the outside world and

   _____ Sun-Kyung Yi at home. At night she ambitiously

   _____ the piano and _____. She was an _____ and

   _____ daughter. It was difficult to play both roles, but she real-

   ized that she couldn't change the rules without her parents and

   _____ all the cultural implications and consequences that came

   with being a hyphenated Canadian.

2. Combine the following sentences, making sure to use parallel constructions and commas between the items in a series. The first one is done for you.

   a. She came to Canada.
      She moved to Whitehorse.
      She entered school.

      She came to Canada, moved to Whitehorse, and entered school.

   b. She learned English by talking.
      She learned English by listening.

She learned English by thinking.

_____

_____

c. Her grandmother remained in Korea.
   Her aunts remained in Korea.
   Her uncles remained in Korea.

_____

_____

d. She wanted to speak English.
   She wanted to fit in.
   She wanted to be accepted.

_____

_____

ESTABLISHING AN IDENTITY

PREREADING ACTIVITIES

1. In a small group, discuss the influences that have made you the person you are today. How have you been influenced by your family, peers, and the larger society you grew up in?

2. In a small group, decide on the ten historical events that have most influenced the world we live in today. Then decide on the ten historical events that have occurred during your lifetime that have most influenced the world we live in today. Share your lists with the rest of the class. Discuss in what ways your first list differs from your second. Now make a personal list of three important historical influences in your country. Explain these events to the rest of your small group.

3. Many people say that it is important to study sociology because it helps us understand our world better. Find a definition for "sociology" in the library, and share your definition with the others in your group. Discuss the ways in which studying sociology can help you understand society.

Socialization

This excerpt from the introductory textbook Sociology *(fourth edition), edited by Robert Hagedorn, explains the socialization process by which human beings adopt the behavioural norms of their society, and establish a social identity that allows them to conform to the other members of the larger societal group. It was written by Marlene Mackie, Professor of Sociology at the University of Calgary.*

Human beings must eat to stay alive. For babies, the matter is quite straightforward. They experience abdominal discomfort; they cry; a parent responds; they suck. Adult satisfaction of this basic physiological° need is more complicated. Canadians consider some things proper food (steak, hamburgers), but gag° at the thought of eating equally nutritious alternatives (caterpillars, horsemeat). Food preferences also mark ethnic° group boundaries (Anderson and Alleyne, 1979). Italian Canadians are often partial to pasta, German

°physical
°choke

°cultural

5

°starving
°stuff (verb)

°realized

°sudden urge to act without thinking

°standards

Canadians to sauerkraut, and Jewish Canadians to bagels and lox. Eating is surrounded by rules (Goffman, 1963a). Even when people are ravenous°, they are not supposed to attack the apple pie before the spinach. Adults who jam° food into their mouths until their cheeks bulge seem disgusting, especially if they try to talk while they stuff. Plucking an interesting item from a neighbour's plate will result in raised eyebrows. So will scratching one's tonsils with a fork. [15]

How, then, does the carefree infant become transformed into the disciplined adult? There is a one-word answer to this question — socialization. The whole story, of course in not quite that simple.

Socialization is the complex learning process through which individuals develop selfhood and acquire the knowledge, skills, and [20] motivations required for participation in social life. This process is the link between individual and society and may be viewed from each of these two perspectives.

From the point of view of the individual, interaction with other people is the means by which human potentialities are actualized.° [25] The newborn infant is almost completely helpless. Although more is happening in infant heads than scientists previously guessed, the newborn's abilities are limited to crying, sucking, eliminating wastes, yawning, and a few other reflexes. It has no self-awareness. Though it has the potential for becoming human, it is not yet human. [30] The physical care, emotional response, and training provided by the family transform this noisy, wet, demanding bundle of matter into a functioning member of society. It learns language, impulse° control, and skills. It develops a self. Knowledge is acquired of both the physical world and the social world. The child becomes capable of [35] taking on social roles with some commitment. It learns whether it is female or male. It internalizes, or accepts as its own, the norms° and values of, first, the family and, later, the wider society.

Effective socialization is as essential for the society as it is for the individual. Untrained members disturb the social order. For [40] example, physically handicapped people report that children often stare and ask blunt questions about their conditions (Goffman, 1963b). Furthermore, Canadian society could not continue to exist unless the thousands of new members born each year eventually learned to think, believe, and behave as Canadians. Each new gen- [45] eration must learn the society's culture. Social order demands self-discipline and impulse control. The continuity of our society requires that children come to embrace societal values as their own. Citizens must adhere to cultural norms because they themselves view those norms as right and proper. Cultural breakdown occurs [50] when the socialization process no longer provides the new generation with valid reasons to be enthusiastic about becoming members

°varied in composition made up of many different peoples

°continuation

°the Depression era of the 1930s

°difference in moral or social standards from what is considered normal

of that society (Flacks, 1979). However, individuals may redefine social roles and obligations, as well as accepting them as they stand. Social change thus occurs over time (Bush and Simmons, 1981). 55

The heterogeneous° nature of Canadian society complicates the socialization process. Although many values and norms are shared by all Canadians, differences are found by language, by region, by ethnicity, by religion, by social class, by urban/rural residence. These variations in social environment bring with them variations in 60
the content of socialization. The perpetuation° of these distinctive Canadian groups depends on children learning the relevant subcultural norms and values. For example, the Danish-Canadian community cannot continue in any meaningful fashion unless children of this ethnic background learn to view themselves as Danish 65
Canadians, and learn the traditions and perhaps the language of that group. Similarly, the continuation of the unique features of the Maritime region requires that Canadians who live there acquire, by means of specialized socialization, the identity of Maritimers and the special norms, values, and history of that region. 70

Historical events — such as the Great Depression, World War II, and the protest era of the late 1960s — mean the successive generations of Canadians have different socialization experiences (Mannheim, 1953). For example, people who grew up during the "Dirty Thirties"° often learned what it meant to go hungry, to give 75
up career plans, to delay marriage. We would expect their perspective on life to contrast sharply with that of earlier and later generations (Elder, 1974).

The socialization process explains how commitment to the social order is maintained. Paradoxically, most people find their own ful- 80
fillment as individuals while simultaneously becoming social beings. However, it is important to note that socialization for deviance° also occurs. Some folks learn to forge cheques, to crack safes, and to snort cocaine.

READING AND THINKING STRATEGIES

DISCUSSION ACTIVITIES

Analysis and Conclusions

1. In your own words, define *socialization*. Why is it viewed by sociologists as "the link between individual and society"?

2. Why are newborns "not yet human"? How do they become "functioning members of society"? Why is this behavioural change essential?

3. How is the heterogenous nature of Canadian society preserved by socialization practices?

Writing and Point of View

1. The author tries to show by examples some of the social forces that shape societies and affect individuals within them. List some of the evidence she uses to illustrate her position. Does she give sufficient evidence to clearly explain the sociological perspective on identify formation?

2. Reread the excerpt, paying special attention to the way in which Mackie incorporates material from expert sources to support her perspective. How does her use of research materials strengthen her essay?

3. Compare the writing style of this excerpt with Parrish's description of immigrant cultural adaptation on page 69. How do the styles of the two pieces differ? Which piece did you prefer reading and why?

Personal Response and Evaluation

1. Gail Sheehy in her book *Passages* writes, "The work of adult life is not easy." In what ways is adulthood more difficult than childhood?

2. Discuss with your group a major historic event that has affected you or someone you know. What was learned from the experience?

3. Share your memories of a person who has influenced you, and, in some way, made you the person you are today. What important lessons about life did this person teach you?

WRITING THE SURVEY

Sociologists base much of their research on surveys of large groups of people, to find out how social forces affect their lives. Much of the information given by experts used by Mackie in her study was probably based on surveys in which questions were asked of individual members of specific groups to determine group response.

As a class, prepare a survey containing ten questions that will provide information about your class members. Decide on the questions, and then conduct the survey. As a follow-up, you might want to conduct this survey at one-month intervals throughout the semester. If you decide to conduct follow-up surveys, you may want to consider questions whose answers might vary, such as "What is your biggest problem adjusting to life in Canada?" or "What is the easiest part about learning English?" (Answers to questions such as "How tall are you?" would probably not change in the follow-up surveys.)

JOURNAL WRITING

A student wrote in her journal, "I may look different in five years, and I may be living a very different life. I expect I will be married by then, or at least I will have found someone to love. But deep down inside I will be the same person. Deep down inside people really don't change very much at all." This journal entry would seem to be in agreement with the article we have read. On the basis of your own experience, do you agree or disagree?

What event in your life has had the greatest influence on you? Is there any event that has made a change in where you live or how you live? Do you feel that you are a very different person today from the person you were five years ago?

WRITING STRATEGIES

ESSAY STRATEGIES

Getting Information from Your Textbook

One important skill for college students is being able to get information from various sources. One source is your textbook. When you read a textbook, you cannot expect to remember every detail. However, the text itself is constructed in a way that can help you find and remember the most important ideas. Some students highlight these important ideas with specially coloured pens; other students copy them into their notebooks or onto index cards. Copying the main ideas and supporting details is a good idea because most people find it easier to remember material that they have written down than material that they have simply read and underlined.

In your classes, when you read textbook material, you should make notes that you will refer to later. One way to break down the notes into a usable form is to label them with the authors' names, the title, and the page number. If you write down the authors' exact words, put them in quotation marks, and record the page number. This will help you if you need to find this information again. It will also help if you are writing a research paper and want to quote or paraphrase the material.

The following exercises will help you break down and analyze the selection at the start of this chapter. Although you will not go through all of these steps when you read your textbooks, these exercises will give you experience in analyzing the structure of textbook writing. When you take notes for your classes or research papers, you should concentrate on finding the main idea or theme and the most important supporting details.

EXERCISES

1. In the first three paragraphs, what is the sociological term the author defines? What examples does she use to explain the term?

   _____

   _____

   _____

2. The author developed the first three paragraphs with facts that lead to a general conclusion. This is deductive reasoning (see page 97 for an explanation of this). Did you find this method of explanation effective?

   _____

   _____

   _____

3. What is the main idea in paragraph four? What details support the main idea?

   _____

   _____

   _____

4. What is the main idea in paragraph five? What details support the main idea?

   _____

   _____

   _____

5. How is socialization achieved within the heterogeneous Canadian social system?

_____

_____

_____

6. How do historical events affect socialization?

_____

_____

_____

7. Summarize the conclusion in a single sentence.

_____

_____

_____

8. Reread the selection. Put an *F* next to the details that are based on fact and an *O* next to the details that are based on opinion. In what types of writing would you expect to find more facts? In what types of writing would you expect to find more opinions?

_____

_____

_____

Summary Writing

Students often write short summaries of textbook material. These summaries include the names of the writers, the title of the piece, and the pages on which it occurs. The summary should contain the most important ideas from the original piece of writing, expressed in your own words. Your summary should be no longer than one-third or one-quarter of the original piece of writing. You may include a quotation from the original selection, but if you do this, put it in quotation marks so that you will remember that this is not your own writing.

When you write your summary, look for key words or phrases. Be sure to include important names, places, dates, and facts. Answer the *who, what, where, when, why,* and *how* questions as clearly and concisely as possible.

EXERCISES

1. Write a summary of "Socialization."
2. Write a summary of another selection from the book, and share it with a classmate.

ESSAY FORM

Writing a Cause-and-Effect Essay

The author of the textbook excerpt focuses on the effects of socialization on individual behaviour. In Chapter One, Chan used cause-and-effect reasoning to explain the causes of his failure at university. When you organize your writing using cause and effect, you are clarifying the connections between events for your reader. The following steps are useful in establishing cause and effect:

1. *Define* the cause. Put the event or occurrence in a historical context — tell what happened immediately before, and briefly outline the steps that led to the major event. Tell your readers why it is important for them to know about and understand this event.

2. *Describe* in detail what followed the event or occurrence you define in step 1. Readers follow your reasoning through your words, so make them clear and direct.

3. *Analyze* the details you are explaining. Tell in what ways these details are direct responses to the cause you have defined in step 1. Explain the history and the future of your subject to your readers.

4. *Evaluate* why the cause led to the effect you describe. Generalize about what this can mean to others or to the future. Convince your reader that your subject is important for them to know.

SUGGESTIONS FOR WRITING

Before you begin to write, choose one of the topics that follow. Discuss some of your ideas about this subject with a classmate, or use the "Getting Started" suggestions on page 286 (or others found in this book) to help you find ideas. You may also decide to look at your journal for ideas. Always spend some time thinking before you start to write.

1. The historical events that occur in a country can have profound effects on the lives of the people of that country. Describe a situation in which a historical event markedly changed someone's life. Write about the cause and the effects that followed it. Explain to your readers how the person coped with the changes. Generalize about what this meant to the person or what it might mean to society at large.

2. Write an essay in which you analyze the effect of a tuition increase at your college or university. Imagine that students are faced with double the tuition they are now paying. Describe the effects that such an event might have on students. Generalize about how this could affect students' educational experiences and educational future.

3. Some people believe that everyone in Canada should be required to become fluent in both English and French. Write an essay in which you explore the possibility of this occurrence and analyze its effect. Generalize about how this could affect life in your community and in Canada as a whole.

4. People want to be individual and unique. At the same time, however, they want to be accepted by their peers, so they conform in many ways. Explain how you or someone you know has resolved this conflict.

5. A student writes, "The best part of growing up is freedom. And the worst part of growing up is freedom." What do you think this student means? How can one deal with the responsibilities and freedoms of adult life? Use your experiences and observations to support your point of view.

6. "Young people should move away from home as soon as they are able to support themselves because it is important for them to be independent and self-sufficient before making a commitment to anyone else." Do you agree or disagree? Support your point of view with your own experience or your observations of others.

GETTING STARTED

Freewriting with a Purpose: Creating Your Own Context

It has been said that "any great cultural or social changes — in fact, all broad influences — are experienced by individuals through what happens in their daily life." According to this, all of us live in the context of what happens around us that affects our lives. For the next ten minutes, write about the context in which you live. To do this, think about the place you live in, the people you see on the street, the newspaper you read, the television programs you watch, the music you listen to, and the school you attend. Describe as many of these and any other influences that occur to you. Look at the world that surrounds you, and write about how it has affected your values, ambitions, and daily life.

A Student Essay

This student responded to writing suggestion 6.

Sooner or later all teenagers grow up. And usually, when the crucial moment comes, the moment to take the big step from being a teen to being an adult, the majority of teenagers make a lot of mistakes. These kinds of mistakes cannot be caused by anyone around them, but by life itself. In order to be prepared for the "adult life," meaning all the difficulties and problems that are usually for an adult, but might be extremely difficult for a teenager, teenagers should learn to make their own decisions.

Young people should move away from home as soon as they are able to support themselves. It is important for them to be independent and self-sufficient before making a commitment to anyone and anything else in life.

Making the right decision is the first and most important step for teenagers to learn. As soon as teenagers move out, they learn that now they have to make decisions by themselves. There are no parents and brothers or sisters around to make decisions for them. No, they are on their own. By making their own decisions, they grow more mature and intelligent.

By living separately from their parents, young people learn about the problems they never had at home. Household problems were always taken care of by their parents. On their own, they have to face the problems. At that time, young people realize the difficulties their parents had but they never noticed before.

All these new experiences that young people will face as soon as they become independent are excellent lessons in life. Before young people make the commitment to someone else, they should necessarily experience the task of life. This way they will have more chances that their future life and family will work out for the best.

Margaret Nesterovskya, Poland

REVISING

Here are some questions to ask yourself about Margaret Nesterovskya's essay. After you have reviewed her essay, meet with a classmate to discuss the essay you have written. Write out the following questions, and ask your classmate to write out answers for you about your draft.

1. What is the purpose of this essay? What was the writer trying to say?

2. Which ideas or examples best support the main point of the writing?

3. In which part of the essay would you have liked more information? Where did you have trouble following the writing?

4. Is there anything else that you would like to know about this topic that is not included? Is there anything that would make the essay more interesting to you as a reader?

Revise what you have written, and share this with the same classmate.

EDITING STRATEGIES

WORD DEVELOPMENT

Academic Terms

As you continue your studies and as you read in specialized areas, you will have to learn many forms related to specific fields of study. These words will be useful to you throughout your college or university career.

EXERCISES

1. List six vocabulary words that a student needs to know to understand the meaning of the Mackie selection.

_____   _____

_____   _____

_____   _____

How did you choose those words?

2. Explain the following concepts.

Socialization _____

_____

Social roles _____

_____

Cultural norms _____

_____

Ethnicity _____

_____

Social class _____

_____

Subcultural norms _____

_____

Review the difference between a word and a concept on page 33.

3. Draw a line from each word in column A to the word or words in column B that are opposite in meaning. The first one has been done for you.

A	**B**
1. impulsive	a. troubled
2. discomfort	b. psychological
3. physiological	c. society
4. ravenous	d. disciplined
5. individual	e. compliance
6. urban	f. rural
7. deviance	g. comfort
8. carefree	h. satiated

Fill in each of the following blanks with a word from the exercise above (in its appropriate form).

1. Part of growing up is learning to control one's _____ behaviour.

2. Would you rather spend your holiday in an _____ or _____ setting?

3. Smoking marijuana and snorting cocaine are presently seen as acts of _____ in our society.

4. I couldn't wait to eat; I was _____.

5. One must learn to balance one's _____.

   Now use eight words from list A or B in sentences of your own.

COMMONLY CONFUSED WORDS

affect/effect

> Marlene Mackie explained how socialization affects *individual identity formation.*

Is *affect* used as a verb or as a noun? Does it mean "influence" or "bring about"?

> The responses made by parents to the cries of their babies have a later effect *on the behaviour of these children.*

> The effects *of subcultural socialization in Canada support the heterogeneous nature of our society.*

> The historical context of growing up has effected *changes in socialization patterns.*

> Socialization for deviance also occurs, having a negative effect *on some people within Canada.*

Is *effect* used as a verb or as a noun in each of the preceding sentences? If you had to use a synonym for *effect* in these sentences, what would it be?

Examine how *affect* and *effect* are used in the following paragraph. Then complete the definitions.

> The effects *of becoming an adult are varied. Your younger brothers and sisters can be* affected *because they can see the positive things you are doing with your life. The* effect *may be that they will grow up and try to be like you. You can* effect *real changes in their lives.*

_____ is a noun that means "result."

_____ is a verb that means "to influence."

_____ is a verb that means "to bring about."

Fill in the blanks in the following sentences with either *affect* or *effect.*

1. The birth of her first child had a big _____ on her life.

2. It _____ed the way she related to her own mother.

3. The _____ was very positive. She was able to _____ some changes in her family relationships.

Now write your own sentences using *affect* and *effect.*

MECHANICS
Abbreviations

An abbreviation is a shortened form of a word. In general, most writers avoid most abbreviations in the formal writing that is required of college students. However, some abbreviations are acceptable in college writing.

Acceptable abbreviations followed by a period: Mr., Mrs., Ms., Dr., Jr., Sr., a.m., p.m., B.C., A.D.

Acceptable abbreviations that do not need a period: FM, AM, CBC, BBC, NFB, PPS, CIA.

Do *not* abbreviate the names of months, days, countries, provinces, units of time, or names of courses in your writing. Do not abbreviate the words, *street, road, avenue, company*, or *association* or other words that are part of a proper name. Do not use signs such @, #, or & in your writing. The $ sign is acceptable when you are writing a number that contains both dollars and cents.

EXERCISES

1. As part of your editing process, review essays that you have written earlier in the semester, noting how you handled the words and abbreviations described above.

2. When you write, check this list to make sure that you have used abbreviations appropriately.

EDITING PRACTICE

The paragraph below is an unedited first draft that contains many errors. Find and correct as many as you can. If you have difficulty, discuss the paragraph with a classmate. The answers are on page 329.

Although getting engaged has changed Samia's life. But she doesn't want to marry now. Ahmed, her boyfriend, want to get married right away, but she disagree. For now, she like showing her girlfriends her diamond ring. She also enjoy discussing her future wedding with them. When she is in school. Even through she is knowing that she make her friends jealous, but she enjoys showing off. The other day her best friends did a real effort not to review there homeworks with her in the cafeteria as they usually did every afternoon after class. She is realizing they envied her, yet she is continuing the same behaviour. Samia claim that she is liking being engaged, but she doesn't want to get married right away. Being housewives doesn't sound like to much fun to her.

GRAMMAR STRATEGIES

MODAL AUXILIARIES WITH *HAVE* + PAST PARTICIPLE

In Chapter Seven on page 149 we discussed modal auxiliaries (*can/could, have to, may/might, must, shall, will/would, should, ought to*). These words are followed by the simple form of the verb (*I can swim* or *He can swim*). Modal auxiliaries are not usually indicators of time and tense, although most users of English agree that "I can swim" has a different time meaning than "I could swim."

When we combine the modal auxiliary with *have* and the past participle (a list of past participles appears in Appendix A), the meaning of the modal auxiliary is altered. The modal with *have* and the past participle can be used in the following ways.

1. To indicate that the action referred to was not accomplished:

   He could have gotten a better job by now (but he hasn't).
   They should have graduated from college by now (but they haven't). You would have been rich if you had taken the opportunity (but you didn't).
   You would have been rich if you had taken the opportunity (but you didn't).

2. To infer something:

   He must have missed the train (because he isn't here yet).
   She might have decided to go by bus (because she wasn't on the train).

3. To show advisability or a social obligation:

   They should have visited her when she was in the hospital.
   She must have called her mother to tell her about the baby.
   He could have paid for half the taxi ride.

4. To show possibility:

   Thuy might have lived in Hong Kong when she first left Vietnam.

Jaime could have studied English in his country.
Who can that have been?
What could have caused that much noise?

5. To predict (*will* and *shall* only):

In the year 2000, she will have lived in Winnipeg for ten years.
She will have been living in Winnipeg for ten years in the year 2000.
By 2000, I shall have repaid my school loan.
By the year 2000, we shall have lived in Canada longer than we lived in Ecuador.

EXERCISE

Write your response to the following situations using the modal auxiliary with *have* and the past participle of the verb that you think makes the most sense. Because there is more than one correct answer for each, discuss your answers in a small group in class.

1. A student fails a course that she thinks she should have passed. She sees her teacher in the hall, and she turns away to avoid talking to her teacher. Later, she feels angry and upset. What could this student have done so she wouldn't have felt angry and upset about this situation?

2. Two good friends had an argument about who should have paid for dinner at an expensive restaurant. One person thinks that he should have paid because it was his friend's birthday. The other person thinks that he should have paid because he invited his friend to join him. Who should have paid? Why?

3. A student moves her desk and finds a book that she borrowed from the library one year ago. She doesn't say anything and just puts it in the return book slot. When the library sends her a letter telling her that she cannot get her grades, she goes there and claims that she doesn't know anything about the book. Afterward, she feels guilty and goes back to tell the truth. What might she have done in the beginning that would have saved her embarrassment?

4. Two cars are parked at a red light. A third driver suddenly appears and smashes into one of the cars. The driver is not hurt, but his car is badly damaged. When the police arrive at the scene, they question the driver of the other car waiting at the light. The driver is in a hurry, and he doesn't want to get involved. The police say that he must have seen what happened, and they insist on taking his name. Although he saw everything, he tells them that he was looking the other way. Did he make the right decision? Why? What could he have done to help the other driver but still not lose time?

RESPONDING TO CHANGE

PREREADING ACTIVITIES

1. This story is about a person who left Iran to come to North America. In a small group, discuss Iran. Where is it? What is its history? What do you know about the relationship between the West and Iran?

2. The main character in the story is returning to Iran after being away for 14 years. What do you expect her to feel when she returns to her country, home, and family?

3. What do you think the title of the story "Foreigner" means? In a group, discuss the feeling of being a foreigner in a country. Do you think you might feel like a foreigner if you returned to your home country? Have you ever felt like a foreigner in Canada?

Foreigner

This excerpt is from the novel Foreigner *by Nahid Rachlin, an Iranian woman who now lives and writes in North America. It is about a woman returning home to Iran after 14 years. She has to learn to deal with changes in herself, her family, and her country.*

°dazed, half awake
°confused
°suitcase
°Iranian women's clothing

In the Teheran airport I was groggy° and disoriented.° I found my valise° and set it on a table, where two customs officers searched it. Behind a large window people waited. The women, mostly hidden under dark chadors,° formed a single fluid shape. I kept looking towards the window trying to spot my father, stepmother, or stepbrother, but I did not see any of them. Perhaps they were there and we could not immediately recognize each other. It had been fourteen years since I had seen them.

A young man sat on a bench beside the table, his task there not clear. He wore his shirt open and I could see bristles of dark hair on his chest. He was making shadow pictures on the floor — a rabbit, a

5

10

°flowed

bird — and then dissolving the shapes between his feet. Energy emanated° from his hands, a crude, confused energy. Suddenly he looked at me, staring into my eyes. I turned away.

I entered the waiting room and looked around. Most people had left. There was still no one for me. What could possibly have happened? Normally someone would be there — a definite effort would be made. I fought to shake off my groggy state. 15

°handmade wares

A row of phones stood in the corner next to a handicraft° shop. I tried to call my father. There were no phone books and the information line rang busy, on and on. 20

I went outside and approached a collection of taxis. The drivers stood around, talking.

"Can I take one of these?" I asked.

The men turned to me but no one spoke. 25

"I need a taxi," I said.

"Where do you want to go?" one of the men asked. He was old with stooped shoulders and a thin, unfriendly face. I gave him my father's address.

"That's all the way on the other side of the city." He did not move from his spot. 30

"Please … I have to get there somehow."

The driver looked at the other men as if this were a group project.

"Take her," one of them said. "I would take her myself but I have to get home." He smiled at me. 35

"All right, get in," the older man said, pointing to a taxi.

In the taxi, he turned off the meter almost immediately. "You have to pay me 100 tomans° for this."

°Iranian money

"That much?" 40

"It would cost you more if I left the meter on."

°yellowish
°trees

There was no point arguing with him. I sat stiffly and looked out. We seemed to be floating in the sallow° light cast by the street lamps. Thin old sycamores° lined the sidewalks. Water flowed in the gutters. The smoky mountains surrounding the city, now barely visible, were like a dark ring. The streets were more crowded and there were many more tall western buildings than I had remembered. Cars sped by bouncing over holes, passing each other recklessly, honking. My taxi driver also drove badly and I had visions of an accident, of being maimed.° 45

°physically harmed

50

°Moslem place of worship
°dirty and neglected

We passed through quieter, older sections. The driver slowed down on a narrow street with a mosque° at its centre, then stopped in front of a large, squalid° house. This was the street I had lived on for so many years; here I had played hide-and-seek in alleys and

hallways. I had a fleeting sensation that I had never left this street, 55
that my other life with Tony had never existed.

I paid the driver, picked up my valise, and got out. On the
cracked blue tile above the door, "Akbar Mehri," my father's name,
was written.

I banged the iron knocker several times and waited. In the 60
light of the street lamps I could see a beggar with his jaw twisted
sitting against the wall of the mosque. Even though it was rather
late, a hum of prayers, like a moan, rose from the mosque. A
Moslem priest came out, looked past the beggar and spat on the
ground. The doors of the house across the street were open. I had 65
played with two little girls, sisters, who had lived there. I could
almost hear their voices, laughter. The April air was mild and velvety against my skin but I shivered at the proximity° to my childhood.

°nearness

A pebble suddenly hit me on the back. I turned but could not see 70
anyone. A moment later another pebble hit my leg and another
behind my knee. More hit the ground. I turned again and saw a
small boy running and hiding in the arched hallway of a house
nearby.

I knocked again. 75

There was a thud from the inside, shuffling, and then soft footsteps. The door opened and a man — my father — stood before me.
His cheeks were hollower than I had recalled, the circles under his
eyes deeper, and his hair more evenly grey. We stared at each other.

"It's you!" He was grimacing,° as though in pain. 80

°making a twisted facial
expression

"Didn't you get my telegram?"

He nodded. "We waited for you for two hours this morning at
the airport. What happened to you?"

I was not sure if he was angry or in a daze. "You must have gotten the time mixed up. I meant nine in the evening." 85

My father stretched his hands forward, about to embrace me
but, as though struck by shyness, he let them drop at his sides.
"Come in now."

I followed him inside. I too was in the grip of shyness, or something like it. 90

"I thought you'd never come back," he said.

"I know, I know."

"You aren't even happy to see me."

"That's not true. I'm just . . ."

"You're shocked. Of course you are." 95

He went towards the rooms arranged in a semicircle, on the
other side of the courtyard. A veranda° with columns extended

°porch

along several of the rooms. Crocuses, unpruned rosebushes, and pomegranate trees filled the flower beds. The place seemed cramped, untended. But still it was the same house. Roses would   100
blossom, sparrows would chirp at the edge of the pool. At dawn and dusk the voice of the muezzin would mix with the noise of people coming from and going to the nearby bazaars.

We went up the steps onto the veranda and my father opened the door to one of the rooms. He stepped inside and turned on the   105
light. I paused for a moment, afraid to cross the threshold. I could smell it: must, jasmin, rosewater, garlic, vinegar, recalling my childhood. Shut doors with confused noises behind them, slippery foot-

°lazy

steps, black, golden-eyed cats staring from every corner, indolent°
afternoons when people reclined on mattresses, forbidden subjects   110
occasionally reaching me — talk about a heavy flow of menstrual blood, sex inflicted by force, the last dark words of a woman on her death bed.

My father disappeared into another room. I heard voices whispering and then someone said loudly, "She's here?" Footsteps   115
approached. In the semidarkness of a doorway at the far end of the room two faces appeared and then another face, like three moons, staring at me.

"Feri, what happened?" a woman's voice asked, and a figure stepped forward. I recognized my stepmother, Ziba. She wore a   120
long, plain cotton nightgown.

"The time got mixed up, I guess." My voice sounded feeble and hesitant.

A man laughed and walked into the light too. It was my stepbrother, Darius. He grinned at me, a smile disconnected from his eyes.   125

"Let's go to the kitchen," my father said. "So that Feri can eat something."

They went back through the same doorway and I followed them. We walked through the dim, intersecting rooms in tan-

°one in front of another

dem.° In one room all the walls were covered with black cloth,   130
and a throne, also covered with a black cloth, was set in a corner — for monthly prayers when neighborhood women would come in and a Moslem priest was invited to give sermons. The women would wail and beat their chests in these sessions as the priest talked about man's guilt or the sacrifices the leaders of Islam had   135

°unchangeable

made. They would cry as if at their own irrevocable° guilt and sorrow.

We were together in the kitchen. Darius, Ziba, my father — they seemed at once familiar and remote like figures in dreams.   140

READING AND THINKING STRATEGIES

DISCUSSION ACTIVITIES

Analysis and Conclusions

1. Do you think Feri is wearing a chador, or is she dressed in Western style? Do you think this affects the way she is treated by the men at the airport and the little boy throwing the pebbles?

2. What are some of the details from the story that suggest that Feri feels like a foreigner in her own country?

3. Her father stretches his hands forward as though to embrace her, and then he drops his hands. Why does he drop his hands? How does this make her feel?

Writing and Point of View

1. Writers try to create moods by their choices of words and images. This story is dreamlike. What words and images does Rachlin use to make this story dreamlike?

2. Like Callaghan and Buckler, Rachlin uses dialogue throughout the story. Do you enjoy stories in which there is dialogue? Why or why not?

3. "A Mortal Flower" in Chapter Twelve is excerpted from an autobiography; "Foreigner" is excerpted from a novel. Are there differences in the styles of writing? Are there any indications that "Foreigner" is fictional? If so, what are they?

Personal Response and Evaluation

1. Rachlin says that the veranda seems "cramped and untended." Sometimes when we return to a place that we knew as children, it seems cramped and smaller than we remember it. Have you ever had that experience? Why do you think this occurs?

2. Do you think Feri will remain in Iran or return to her life in the West? What in the story helps you to decide?

3. Have you ever had an experience similar to Feri's? How did it make you feel?

RESPONSE PARAGRAPH

After you have read "Foreigner," write a paragraph about how this story made you feel and what you thought about as you read it.

Share your paragraphs with your classmates.

One student wrote the following paragraph:

> After I read "Foreigner," it made me think about me visiting my country after I had been gone for four and a half years. I'd been gone only four and a half years, but I understand her feeling that she thought she hadn't gone anywhere. Everyone was strange, even my friends, but the places and streets were the same. I talked about our past with my friends. After a few hours, I could feel that they were my friends and they still are. Then I felt I really had come to my hometown. It was hard to catch up to the distance made by four and a half years that we'd been apart, but I believe it was more difficult for Feri. It will take time for her to fit in her family as she was before.
>
> *Sohyung Kim, South Korea*

Did you feel any of the same feelings as Sohyung felt when she read "Foreigner"?

JOURNAL WRITING

> *What is writing, if it is not the countenance of our daily experience: sensuous, contemplative, imaginary, what we see and hear, dream of, how it strikes us, how it comes into us, travels through us, and emerges in some language hopefully useful to others.*

M. C. RICHARDS, *CENTERING: POETRY, POTTERY AND THE PERSON*

Journals let us record our impressions of the world and make sense of them with our words. Sometimes we record dreams and sometimes real events; regardless, we try to use our journal entries to deepen our understanding of ourselves and, at the same time, to improve our writing.

When you write this time, think of dreams, of returning to places that you have thought about and had mixed feelings about. Before you write, you might want to cluster around the word *foreigner* or *dream*. You may want to write a story, a poem, or prose (writing that is not a poem). A short poem by the Russian poet Olga Berggolts may help you to reflect on these ideas and stimulate your mind and pen.

To My Sister

I dreamt of the old house
where I spent my childhood years,
and the heart, as before, finds
comfort, and love, and warmth.

I dreamt of Christmas, the tree,
and my sister laughing out loud,
from morning, the rosy windows
sparkle tenderly.

And in the evening gifts are given
and the pine needles smell of stories,
And golden stars risen
are scattered like cinder above the rooftop.

I know that our old house is falling into disrepair
Bare, despondent branches
knock against darkening panes.

And in the room with its old furniture,
a resentful captive, cooped up,
lives our father, lonely and weary — he feels abandoned by us.

Why, oh why do I dream of the country
where the love all consumed, all?
Maria, my friend, my sister,
speak my name, call to me, call ...

WRITING STRATEGIES

ESSAY STRATEGIES

Setting the Mood in Your Writing

Images

To understand how images can create a feeling or understanding on the part of the reader, let's examine some of the images Rachlin uses.

In the Teheran airport, Rachlin tells us about the relationships between men and women.

The women, mostly hidden under dark chadors, formed a single fluid shape.

What does this sentence tell us about the women in the airport?

Do you think Feri is wearing a chador? Why would Rachlin want the reader to know if Feri were wearing a chador?

A young man sat on a bench beside the table, his task there not clear. He wore his shirt open and I could see bristles of dark hair on his chest

Contrast these two descriptions. What is Rachlin telling us about the differences between men and women in Teheran?

The April air was mild and velvety against my skin but I shivered at the proximity to my childhood.

There is an interesting contrast of images in this sentence. What does it tell the reader about Feri's childhood?

Mood

Rachlin creates a dreamlike mood with her choice of descriptive words.

We seemed to be floating in the sallow light cast by the street lamps.

"Floating" creates a very dreamy feeling. "Sallow light" is a shadowy light, as contrasted with bright, sunny light.

The smoky mountains surrounding the city, now barely visible, were like a dark ring.

"Smoky mountains" conveys an image that is vague, cloudy, and dreamy. "Barely visible" gives the reader the same feeling.

Read through the story, looking for other images that suggest dreams.

Rachlin has used many delicate poetic images to convey strong feelings. What do you think Rachlin wants the reader to think about Feri?

What do you think Rachlin wants the reader to think about Feri's family?

What do you think Rachlin wants the reader to think about Teheran?

Similes and Metaphors

Writers use comparisons to enrich their writing. One type of comparison is the *simile* — a comparison of unlike things, usually using the word *like* or *as:*

In the semidarkness of a doorway at the far end of the room two faces appeared and then another face, like three moons staring at me. (Moons are known to us yet they are remote and mysterious.)

Writers also use *metaphors* to describe feelings and events. A metaphor uses a word or term that usually stands for one thing to stand for another:

The women, mostly hidden under dark chadors, formed a single fluid shape. (This suggests that the women look the same and seem to melt into each other, to form a liquid mass.)

The April air was mild and velvety against my skin ... (This implies a softness in the air.)

Poets use words very carefully. They are always looking for exactly the right word to convey meaning. Poets work with fewer words than prose writers do; however, prose writers must also be concerned with finding the right word. The examples illustrate some of the ways in which Rachlin was able to influence the reader's view of her characters and the city she describes. When you write, keep in mind the power of words. Search for the right word to help your reader understand what you have written.

ESSAY FORM

Describing a Person

In "Foreigner," Nahid Rachlin describes a young man at the airport.

A young man sat on a bench beside the table, his task there not clear. He wore his shirt open and I could see bristles of dark hair on his chest. He was making shadow pictures on the floor — a rabbit, a bird — and then dissolving the shapes between his feet. Energy emanated from his hands, a crude, confused energy. Suddenly he looked at me, staring into my eyes. I turned away.

This choice of the young man as the first person described in Iran helps the reader to share the main character's feelings about arriving as a foreigner in her own country. Later, Rachlin describes Feri's father, whom the woman has not seen for fourteen years:

The door opened and a man — my father — stood before me. His cheeks were hollower than I had recalled, the circles under his eyes deeper, and his hair more evenly grey. We stared at each other.

Rachlin could have just written that the father had gotten older, but instead she describes his cheeks, his eyes, and his hair. How does this description make you feel as a reader?

In "A Mortal Flower"' in Chapter Twelve, Han Suyin describes Mr. Harned:

Mr. Harned was very tall, thin, [with] a small bald head, a long chin, enormous glasses. I immediately began to quiver with fright. His head was like a temple on top of a mountain, like the white pagoda on the hill in the North Sea Park. I could not hear a word of what he said. A paper and a pencil were in my hand, however, and Mr. Harned was dictating to me, giving me a speed test in shorthand.

This description helps the reader to see Mr. Harned and to feel the terror the young girl feels during her job interview. We picture a person who is cold and unfriendly. If she had wanted him to appear warm and cuddly, she could have described him as "short and chubby." We read that he wears "enormous glasses." His glasses probably magnify his eyes and make him seem even more frightening and forbidding. She continues, "His head was like a temple on top of a mountain, like the white pagoda on the hill in the North Sea Park." A temple on top of a mountain is something far away and not easily approached, and a pagoda is a holy temple that in some cases women are not even allowed to visit. Han Suyin uses similes, comparisons that use the word *like* or *as*, to create a mood of distance and fear.

"I could not hear a word of what he said." Once again, the girl is removed from Mr. Harned. They cannot communicate. "A paper and a pencil were in my hand, however, and Mr. Harned was dictating to me, giving me a speed test in shorthand." Han Suyin does not tell us that Mr. Harned handed her the paper. He does not even smile at her. There is no connection between the two of them. He dictates to her; he does not speak to her or talk with her. Throughout the paragraph, Han Suyin creates a mood of aloofness on the part of Mr. Harned and perceived isolation on the part of the girl. She is alone and frightened during the interview. In fact, we find out later in the story that Mr. Harned is benign (kindly or gentle), but we do not get this feeling in our first impression of him. Han Suyin has used description to create a mood and a feeling about a character.

The following excerpt from *Meneseteung* by Alice Munro illustrates how description can make us feel about a character.

> *The poetess has a long face; a rather long nose; full, sombre dark eyes, which seem ready to roll down her cheeks like giant tears; a lot of dark hair gathered around her face in droopy rolls and curtains. A streak of grey hair plain to see, although she is, in this picture, only twenty-five. Not a pretty girl but the sort of woman who may age well, who probably won't get fat. She wears a tucked and braid-trimmed dark dress or jacket, with a lacy, floppy arrangement of white material — frills or a bow — filling the deep V at the neck. She also wears a hat, something like a soft beret, that makes me see artistic intentions, or at least a shy and stubborn eccentricity, in this young woman, whose long neck and forward-inclining head indicate as well that she is tall and slender and somewhat awkward. From the waist up, she looks like a young nobleman of another century. But perhaps it was the fashion.*

The poetess, as Munro describes her, exudes an air of eccentricity, and grief. Her physical features express her mood: "long face," "sombre dark eyes" like "giant tears," "drooping" hair tinged with grey, and a tall, angular figure. Her creativity, which sets her apart from others, is exemplified by her "unusual, untrimmed, shapeless hat." Overall Munro has written a short description that creates a somewhat somber mood and that make us feel that the poetess is a striking woman with a romantic nature.

In one of her letters, Katherine Mansfield says:

The old woman who looks after me is about 106, nimble and small, with the loveliest skin — pink rubbed over cream — and she has blue eyes and white hair and one tooth, a sort of family monument to all the 31 departed ones.

The images are soft and gentle. Words like *nimble* and *small* begin to suggest a picture of a child. Mansfield describes the woman's skin as "pink rubbed over cream," a very poetic but also lovely image. The one tooth, which could have made the woman frightening and witchlike, is described in a humorous way. The reader likes the old woman and feels she is beautiful in a very special way.

Description makes us feel something about a person or a place. By our choice of words, we can make a person or a place seem inviting or forbidding, kindly or hostile. It is up to us as writers to choose the words that best convey what we are trying to express.

Writing about a Person

When you write about a person, the following four steps will help you think about and organize your writing.

1. *Observe* and reflect on the person before you start to write. Make notes about the stories that tell you something about the person's character and behaviour patterns.

2. *Describe* the person so that your reader can visualize him or her clearly. Use picture words that are specific and vivid. Avoid words like *nice, cute, sweet,* and *great.* Show your reader how the person looks, sounds, moves, and smells.

3. *Analyze* the person's weaknesses and strengths, and explain how they make the person unique and interesting to know.

4. *Evaluate* why you have chosen to write about this person and why a reader should want to read about the person. Why is this person important to you and to others?

Keep these steps in mind when you describe a person in your next piece of writing.

EXERCISES

1. Write a description in which you make the person being described seem frightening and forbidding. Use similes (comparisons that use *like* or *as*).

2. Write a description in which you make the person being described seem friendly and gentle. Use similes to create your image.

3. Rewrite Han Suyin's description of Mr. Harned so that he seems to be a warm and friendly man.

4. Write a description of someone in your class, and read it aloud to the class. See if anyone can recognize the individual you have written about.

SUGGESTIONS FOR WRITING

Before you begin to write, choose one of the following topics listed here. Discuss some of your ideas about this subject with a classmate, or use one of the "Getting Started" exercises in this book to help you find ideas. You may also decide to review your journal for ideas. Always spend some time thinking before you start to write.

1. Feri is a foreigner in her own land. Have you ever felt this way? Have you ever felt foreign and strange anywhere? Write an essay in which you analyze what people did that made you feel this way. What effect did your feeling have on your behaviour and your self-image? What would you do to help someone who feels like a foreigner in your neighbourhood or school?

2. Write a description of a person that will help your reader to imagine the person, your feelings about the person, and your relationship with each other.

3. Feri describes the feeling of going home. In Chapter Thirteen, Sun Kyung Yi writes of her dual identity. If she were to go to Korea, do you think Sun's experience would be similar to Feri's? Imagine that you are Sun returning to Korea. What will your experience be like? Compare it to Feri's. (If you prefer, you can visualize yourself returning to your own country.)

4. Imagine that you are Feri and it is your first night home in Teheran. Write a letter to your North American husband telling him about your experiences. Describe in detail the people and events that you experience.

5. "Childhood is not always the happy, peaceful time it is usually pictured to be." Do you agree or disagree? Support your point of view with your experiences or observations.

6. In the poem by Olga Berggolts on page 299 to 300, the poet describes dreaming of Christmas in the old house where she spent her childhood years. Visualize returning to your childhood house at holiday time. Describe in detail what you see, smell, hear, and taste. What about it seems different now that you are no longer a child?

GETTING STARTED
Visualization

In this chapter, we will examine another way to stimulate interesting and creative writing. Using this technique, the writer visualizes or sees what is going to be written about. The writer totally enters the life or the world of the piece of writing.

New Zealand writer Katherine Mansfield describes her writing process:

> *When I write about ducks, I swear that I am a white duck with a round eye floating on a pond fringed with yellow-blobs and taking an occasional dart at the other duck with the round eye, which floats beneath me.... In fact the whole process of becoming the duck ... is so thrilling that I can hardly breathe, only to think about it....*
> *I don't see how art is going to make that divine spring into the bounding outline of things if it hasn't passed through the process of trying to become these things before recreating them.*

> LETTERS OF KATHERINE MANSFIELD

Mansfield describes a process similar to the one you will use. Once you have decided on the topic you will write about, close your eyes and try to enter the world of that topic. You can use experiences that you have had in your life to help you see more clearly. Mansfield wrote about the duck because when she was a little girl, she witnessed the killing of a duck that she had loved. The duck was to be made into dinner, but young Mansfield was unaware of this as she went down to the water's edge with some other children. The duck's head was chopped off in front of the impressionable child, and the duck ran around headless until it died. Mansfield never forgot this moment, and she was able to use her feelings for the duck to make her writing come alive.

When you visualize, use any experience or observation you have had, and try to bring it alive inside your head. By the time you actually begin to write, you should have the sights, sounds, smells, and feelings inside your head. If you are writing a comparison-and-contrast essay, visualize the ideas until they come alive inside you. If you are writing a persuasive essay, persuade yourself first by totally immersing yourself in the topic.

If you have trouble getting started, use the clustering technique. Begin to cluster around a word, and when an image starts to come to you, close your eyes and try to make the image as vivid as possible.

EXERCISES

1. Visualize someone or something else's world. Mansfield visualizes being a duck. You can visualize yourself as your sister, your father, a dog, a cat, or a tree on the street. Try to re-create in its entirety the world of that person, creature, or thing.

2. Visualize as completely as possible your first day in this country or any other important day in your life. Re-create your experience, and then write down as much of it as you can in the next 20 minutes. Don't worry about spelling or grammar for this exercise.

3. By yourself or with a classmate, create your own visualization exercise.

REVISING

Using the questions in this section to guide you, discuss the essay that follows, by Wan Ping Wu. Then, using the same questions, reread your writing and have a classmate read it. Keep in mind that your writing is not in its final form. As you read now, you may want to make changes. You may add or delete ideas. You may want to move or remove sentences or paragraphs. You may decide that other words express your meaning better.

Ask your partner the following questions about your writing, and write your answers on a separate piece of paper that you will refer to when you revise.

1. Does the paper have a clear beginning that makes the reader want to read more?

2. What is the main idea that the entire piece of writing holds together?

3. What are the supporting details — facts, observations, and experiences that support the main points?

4. Are the details specific — can the reader understand, see, hear, smell, and feel what this piece of writing is about?

5. Does the draft have a clear ending so that the reader knows the piece is completed?

After revising your essay, share it with your partner.

A Student Essay

A student wrote this description of a woman she would never meet

One day I saw an old wooden trunk on the street. I went over to it and when I opened it, a beautiful woman's eyes looked into my eyes. The picture was old and dusty. And the woman was dressed in a long, low-cut dress. She looked very rich because she wore a necklace, a ring, and a tiny hair clip shaped like a butterfly in her upswept hair. But I didn't know the colour of her hair because the picture was colourless.

I forgot the other things in the trunk, but I think there was an old comb, old clothes, and many old letters. They seemed to have belonged to a man, maybe an old man. But there was a little box in the corner of the trunk. Inside, there was a tiny elaborate hair clip; it looked like it was made from the yellow gold of a butterfly. I wanted to keep it.

I thought this trunk had been dumped by an old man at least eighty years old, and the things inside had been very important to him. Maybe the woman in the picture had been the old man's lover when they were young. I closed the trunk and I knew I had to leave it because I could feel the old man looking at me from a long time ago. When I saw him, I felt guilty, so I hurried home.

When I got home, I told my mother all these things. I told her I wanted to keep the tiny yellow gold butterfly hair clip. But my mother told me it was an unlucky thing, and she didn't let me keep it. So now the tiny yellow gold hair clip will be in my memory forever.

WAN PING WU, PEOPLE'S REPUBLIC OF CHINA

EDITING STRATEGIES

WORD DEVELOPMENT

Words relating to Iran and Islam

"Foreigner" introduces us to the special vocabulary of the country of Iran and the religion of Islam. As you read about different countries and peoples, you will be exposed to such new vocabulary.

chador: a dress that Iranian women wear, which is draped around the body, across the shoulders, over the head, and across the lower part of the face

tomans: Iranian money

mosque: a Moslem place for the worship of God

muezzin: a crier who calls faithful Moslems to prayer

Islam: the religion taught by the Prophet Mohammed in the 600s (Mohammed, who was born in Mecca in 570, taught the worship of one God, Allah, and proclaimed that he, Mohammed, was Allah's messenger. Islam is an Arabic word that means "submission." Islam is the faith of approximately one-fifth of the world's population.)

Moslems (Muslims): Believers in Allah who accept Mohammed as God's messenger (In Arabic, Moslem means "one who submits to God.")

EXERCISES

1. If there is a Moslem student in the class, that student might inform the other class members about the Islamic religion and traditions.

2. You might want to consult your library to find out more about Islam or about other religions. Write a short paper to hand in to your teacher or present to the class.

COMMONLY CONFUSED WORDS

cloth/clothes

Read the following paragraph, noticing the use of *cloth* and *clothes*.

Cloth *is a piece of fabric. You make* clothes *out of* cloth. Cloth *is not singular for* clothes. Clothes *are the items that we put on our bodies when we dress. Men's and women's* clothes *are very different in some parts of the world. In Iran, for example, women wear very different* clothes *from those that men wear. In Canada, by contrast, some* clothes *that men and women wear are very similar.*

Fill in each of the following blanks with *cloth or clothes*.

1. I bought some _____ to make some _____.

2. A designer buys beautiful _____ to put together a new line of

   _____.

3. Because there was no door, the heavy dark _____ hung in

   front of the _____ closet.

   Write two more sentences using these words.

SENTENCE SKILLS: TENSE REVIEW

Simple Past Tense

In the following sentences from "Foreigner," the past tense verbs have been removed. Fill in the correct form of the verb. If you have difficulty, see Appendix A for a list of irregular verbs. Refer to the story to check your answers.

1. I _____ my valise and _____ it on a table where two custom
       (find)   *(set)*

   officers _____ it.
         (search)

2. I _____ looking towards the window trying to spot my father,
     (keep)

   stepmother, or stepbrother, but I _____ not see any of them.
                           (do)

3. A row of phones _____ in the corner next to a handicraft shop.
            (stand)

4. I _____ outside and _____ a collection of taxis.
     (go)   *(approach)*

5. I _____ the driver, _____ up my valise, and _____ out.
     (pay)   *(pick)*   *(get)*

6. A pebble suddenly _____ me on the back.
           (hit)

7. I _____ nine in the evening.
     (mean)

8. My father _____ his hands forward, about to embrace me but, as
        (stretch)

   though _____ by shyness, _____ he them drop at his sides.
       (strike)   *(let)*

Past Perfect Tense

Fill in the following blanks. If you have any difficulty, see Chapter Three, page 62.

The past perfect tense is used when we want to write about more than one event that occurred in the _____. We use the _____ tense to describe the event that happened first and we use the _____ tense to describe the event that happened next.

The past perfect tense is formed with _____ plus the past.

Examine the following examples from the story.

I entered the waiting room and looked around. Most people had left.

Which happened first — Feri entered the room or people left?

_____

Why did Rachlin use the past perfect tense for the second sentence?

_____

The streets were more crowded and there were many more tall western buildings than I had remembered.

Why does Rachlin use "had remembered" in this sentence?

_____

His cheeks were hollower than I had recalled ...

When had Feri last seen her father?

_____

Why does Rachlin use "had recalled" in this sentence?

_____

COMBINING SENTENCES

Using some of the techniques from earlier chapters, combine these short sentences into longer ones. Keep in mind that there are many correct ways to create new sentences. Try several combinations, and share them with a classmate.

1. I found my valise.
   I set it on the table.
   Two customs officers searched it.

2. I kept looking towards the window.
   I was trying to spot my father, stepmother, or stepbrother.
   I did not see any of them.

3. We went up the steps.
   The steps led to the veranda.
   My father opened the door.
   The door led to one of the rooms.

4. A man laughed.
   He walked into the light.
   He was my stepbrother.
   His name was Darius.

INDIRECT SPEECH

In Chapter Ten, on page 210, we examined indirect speech — expressing what someone has said or written without using quotation marks or the exact words. This is also called reported speech.

"I need a taxi," she said. (line 26)	Direct quotation
She said that she needed a taxi.	Indirect speech

Notice the pronoun change from direct quotation to indirect speech. *I*, the person speaking, changes to *she*.

"Where do you want to go?" one of the men asked. (line 27)	Direct quotation
One of the men asked where she wanted to go.	Indirect speech

Notice the pronoun change from *you* to *she*.

Her father said, "We waited for you for two hours this morning at the airport." (lines 82 and 83)	Direct quotation
Her father said that they had waited for two hours that morning at the airport.	Indirect speech

Notice the change from *this* in the direct quotation to *that* in indirect speech.

"Feri, what happened?" a woman's voice asked. (line 119)	Direct quotation
A woman's voice asked her _____.	Indirect speech

Notice that the speaker is identified before the reported speech begins.

"You have to pay me 100 tomans for this," said the taxi driver. (lines 38 and 39)	Direct quotation

The taxi driver said that

_____ had to pay

_____ 100 tomans.	Indirect speech

Feri asked, "Didn't you get my telegram?" (line 81)	Direct quotation
Feri asked if they had _____ telegram.	Indirect speech

Notice how the question form changes in reported speech.

EXERCISES

1. For more practice, change the following direct quotations to indirect or reported speech.
   a. "I am happy to see you," she said to her father.
   b. "Things have really changed here," he told her.
   c. "Do you have a phone?" Feri asked her brother.
2. For extra practice, change other direct quotations in the story to indirect speech.

TRANSITIONS OF PLACE

Rachlin moves her reader by using transitions of place, which she locates at the beginnings of the paragraphs. To illustrate, we will examine the first lines of several of the paragraphs. As we examine the words of transition, think about why Rachlin might want to make the reader very conscious of place.

A young man sat on a bench beside the table. ...

I entered the waiting room and looked around.

A row of phones stood in the corner next to a handicraft shop.

I went outside and approached a collection of taxis.

Where has Rachlin taken us in these paragraphs? _____

_____

What do we know about Teheran at this point?_____

_____

How do you think Feri feels about Teheran? What does Rachlin say

that makes you think that way? _____

_____

We passed through quieter, older sections.

I followed him [her father] inside.

He went towards the rooms …

We went up the steps onto the veranda …

My father disappeared into another room.

They went back through the same doorway and I followed them.

We were together in the kitchen.

Is Feri happy to be home? How does the reader know? _____

_____

Did Feri have a happy childhood? How does Rachlin use words

about place to let the reader know the answer to this question?_____

_____

Rachlin has taken us on a tour of Feri's life using the transitions of place. We have followed her through the confusing airport to the expensive taxi that drove her through streets familiar yet strange. We have arrived at her street and seen the mosque, the house of old playmates, and finally her old home, which looks frighteningly similar to the way it had looked when she left fourteen years before. Once in the house, Rachlin leads us through a maze of a veranda, into the rooms. Finally we end up the kitchen.

Why do you think the author used these transitions of place? How does reading them make you feel? _____

_____

According to the story, how does Feri see her world?_____

_____

Look back at the other stories we have read. Do any of them use place in the way that Rachlin does? _____

_____

MECHANICS
Underlining

When you are putting an essay on your computer or writing an essay by hand and you do not have *italics* (the slightly slanted print in which the word *italics* appears), you underline. How do you know which words need to be underlined? Follow these guidelines:

1. Underline the names of books, plays, movies, magazines, newspapers, pamphlets, radio and television programs, recordings and videos, legal cases, and ships and aircraft.
2. Underline foreign words that are not commonly used in English.
3. Do not underline or put in quotation marks sacred writing (including books from the Bible, the Koran, the Talmud, or the Torah).

EXERCISES

1. Reread or review any of your earlier writing assignments this semester to make sure that you used underlining correctly.
2. When you edit your next draft, check to make sure that you have used underlining correctly.

EDITING PRACTICE

The following paragraph is a first draft. It contains many surface errors. Edit and rewrite the paragraph, correcting the errors.

Returning home can be very difficult. As we see in Nahid Rachlin's story foreigner. People return to their home countries they often find many changes. The streets may not look the same. People they remember may not recognized them. If they go back to there own childhood house. The house may look very different. It may appear small and cramped. One women wrote that she returned to her neighbourhood and their house was gone. In it's place was a little store. No one remembers her. She is extremely depressed. It is also possible to return to a place where everyone remember you. That makes a person happy inside; on least you where not forgotten.

For the answers, turn to page 330.

GRAMMAR STRATEGIES

CONDITIONALS USING *if*

Conditionals are used in English for a number of reasons and in a number of forms:

1. To express relationships that are true and unchanging:

   If you lower the temperature of water to 0°C, it freezes.
   If you boil water, it vaporizes. (Notice the present tense is used in both clauses. This kind of conditional is often used in scientific writing.)

2. To express relationships that are habitual:

   If I wash the car, it rains.
   If I had washed the car, it would have rained.

Note: In 1 and 2, it is possible to substitute *when* or *whenever* for *if* without changing the meaning of the sentence:

When (whenever) you lower the temperature of water to 0°C, it freezes.
Try using *when* or *whenever* with the other examples.

3. To express inferences:

   If the police can't solve that crime, no one can solve it.
   If you'll go to Pierre's party, I'll go too.
   If you act happy, the baby will stop crying.

4. To express a condition in the future:

   If it snows, I'll wear my boots.
   If you do your homework, you'll pass the course.
   If you call me tonight, I'll call you tomorrow. (The first clause uses the present tense and the second clause uses the future tense.)

5. To express unlikely but possible events:

   If I had the energy, I would jog tonight.
   If he had left work early, he would be home by now. (Notice that the first clause uses *had* and the second clause uses *would*.)

6. To express impossible events:

   If I had your face, I would become a model.
   If Gandhi were alive today, he would make peace in the world.

Using *were* in Conditionals

English uses *were* to indicate unlikely or impossible circumstances. "If I were a genius" means that the writer is not a genius. *Were* is used with all subjects *(I, you, we, he, she, it, they)* to indicate an unlikely or untrue situation:

If he were to win the lottery, he would buy his parents a new house. (He does not expect to win the lottery.)

If they were to quit their jobs, they would go to Victoria. (They do not expect to quit their jobs.)

If I were you, I would study harder. (I am not and could never be you.)

Notice that the independent clause that follows the *were* part of the sentence uses *would* and no ending on the verb that follows. You can also use *should, could, ought to,* and *might* in this structure.

EXERCISE

Complete the following sentences using the structure just described.

1. If he were to win the contest, he ought to _____.

2. If I were you, I might _____.

3. If a student were to fail a course, she might _____.

4. If schools were to give automatic passing grades to all students, students could _____.

5. If I were to win the lottery, I would _____.

PRINCIPAL PARTS OF IRREGULAR VERBS

Base	Past	Past Participle
awake	awoke, awaked	awoken, awaked
be	was, were	been
bear	bore	borne
beat	beat	beat, beaten
become	became	become
begin	began	begun
bend	bent	bent
bet	bet	bet
bind	bound	bound
bite	bit	bit, bitten
bleed	bled	bled
blow	blew	blown
break	broke	broken
breed	bred	bred
bring	brought	brought
build	built	built
burst	burst	burst
buy	bought	bought
catch	caught	caught
choose	chose	chosen
come	came	come
cost	cost	cost
creep	crept	crept
cut	cut	cut
deal	dealt	dealt
dig	dug	dug
dive	dived, dove	dived
do	did	done
draw	drew	drawn
dream	dreamed, dreamt	dreamed, dreamt
drink	drank	drunk
drive	drove	driven
eat	ate	eaten
fall	fell	fallen
feed	fed	fed

Base	Past	Past Participle
feel	felt	felt
fight	fought	fought
find	found	found
fit	fit, fitted	fit, fitted
flee	fled	fled
fly	flew	flown
forbid	forbade	forbidden
forget	forgot	forgotten, forgot
freeze	froze	frozen
get	got	gotten, got
give	gave	given
go	went	gone
grind	ground	ground
grow	grew	grown
hang (an object)	hung	hung
hang (a person)	hanged	hanged
have	had	had
hear	heard	heard
hide	hid	hidden, hid
hit	hit	hit
hold	held	held
hurt	hurt	hurt
keep	kept	kept
kneel	knelt, kneeled	knelt, kneeled
knit	knitted, knit	knitted, knit
know	knew	known
lay (put)	laid	laid
lead	led	led
lean	leaned, leant	leaned, leant
leave	left	left
lend	lent	lent
let (allow)	let	let
lie (recline)	lay	lain
light	lighted, lit	lighted, lit
lose	lost	lost
make	made	made
mean	meant	meant
pay	paid	paid
prove	proved	proved, proven
quit	quit, quitted	quit, quitted
read	read	read
rid	rid, ridded	rid, ridded
ride	rode	ridden
ring	rang	rung
rise	rose	risen
run	ran	run

Base	Past	Past Participle
say	said	said
see	saw	seen
seek	sought	sought
sell	sold	sold
send	sent	sent
set	set	set
shake	shook	shaken
shine	shone, shined	shone, shined
shoot	shot	shot
show	showed	shown, showed
shrink	shrank	shrunk
shut	shut	shut
sing	sang	sung
sink	sank	sunk
sit	sat	sat
sleep	slept	slept
slide	slid	slid, slidden
speak	spoke	spoken
speed	sped, speeded	sped, speeded
spend	spent	spent
spin	spun	spun
split	split	split
spread	spread	spread
spring	sprang	sprung
stand	stood	stood
steal	stole	stolen
stick	stuck	stuck
sting	stung	stung
strike	struck	struck, stricken
swear	swore	sworn
swim	swam	swum
swing	swung	swung
take	took	taken
teach	taught	taught
tear	tore	torn
tell	told	told
think	thought	thought
throw	threw	thrown
wake	woke, waked	woken, waked
wear	wore	worn
weave	wove	woven
weep	wept	wept
win	won	won
wring	wrung	wrung
write	wrote	written

MODELS FOR TENSES

Active Voice

Singular	Plural	Singular	Plural
Simple Present Tense		*Present Continuous Tense*	
I go	we go	I am helping	we are helping
you go	you go	you are helping	you are helping
he goes		he is helping	
she goes	they go	she is helping	they are helping
it goes		it is helping	
Simple Past Tense		*Past Continuous Tense*	
I lived	we lived	I was sleeping	we were sleeping
you lived	you lived	you were sleeping	you were sleeping
he lived		he was sleeping	
she lived	they lived	she was sleeping	they were sleeping
it lived		it was sleeping	
Simple Future Tense		*Future Continuous Tense*	
I will learn	we will learn	I will be playing	we will be playing
you will learn	you will learn	you will be playing	you will be playing
he will learn		he will be playing	
she will learn	they will learn	she will be playing	they will be playing
it will learn		it will be playing	
Present Perfect Tense		*Present Perfect Continuous Tense*	
I have seen	we have seen	I have been trying	we have been trying
you have seen	you have seen	you have been trying	you have been trying
he has seen		he has been trying	
she has seen	they have seen	she has been trying	they have been trying
it has seen		it has been trying	

Active Voice

Past Perfect Tense

I had jumped	we had jumped
you had jumped	you had jumped
he had jumped	
she had jumped	they had jumped
it had jumped	

Past Perfect Continuous Tense

I had been running	we had been running
you had been running	you had been running
he had been running	
she had been running	
it had been running	they had been running

Future Perfect Tense

I will have left	we will have left
you will have left	you will have left
he will have left	
she will have left	they will have left
it will have left	

Future Perfect Continuous Tense

I will have been getting	we will have been getting
you will have been getting	you will have been getting
he will have been getting	
she will have been getting	they will have been getting
it will have been getting	

Passive Voice

Singular	Plural	Singular	Plural

Simple Present

		Present Continuous	
I am given	we are given	I am being taken	we are being taken
you are given	you are given	you are being taken	you are being taken
he is given		he is being taken	
she is given	they are given	she is being taken	they are being taken
it is given		it is being taken	

Simple Past

		Past Continuous	
I was brought	we were brought	I was being carried	we were being carried
you were brought	you were brought	you were being carried	you were being carried
he was brought		he was being carried	
she was brought	they were brought	she was being carried	they were being carried
it was brought		it was being carried	

Simple Future

I will be found	we will be found
you will be found	you will be found
he will be found	
she will be found	they will be found
it will be found	

Passive Voice

Present Perfect

I have been offered

you have been offered

he has been offered

she has been offered ⎫

it has been offered ⎭

we have been offered

you have been offered

they have been offered

Past Perfect

I had been loved

you had been loved

he had been loved

she had been loved ⎫

it had been loved ⎭

we had been loved

you had been loved

they had been loved

Future Perfect

I will have been seen

you will have been seen

he will have been seen

she will have been seen ⎫

it will have been seen ⎭

we will have been seen

you will have been seen

they will have been seen

ANSWERS TO EXERCISES

page 18

My Poor Study Habits

I have been a college student in Canada for two years. Last semester, I failed two courses, and, as a result, realized I was spending too much time on social activities. My friends and I watch videos together five times a week and we go to the local mall every day. When we want to chat, we go to our favourite restaurant, where we stay until late at night. I rarely get to bed before two. I know I should study more, but I am having too much fun to really care.

page 35

Eugen Lupri is writing about the family from a sociological point of view. He mentions three types of families: nuclear, extended, and polygamous. Nuclear families are the most common family type in Canada. The term can refer to any two related persons, and their offspring, sharing a common household. If the couple are married, they form a conjugal nuclear family. Extended families, composed of two or more nuclear families related by blood and sharing a residence, are less common in Canada than nuclear families, although they are advantageous for many reasons. Polygamy is less common than either of the above-mentioned family structures, but it does still exist.

page 59

"The Snob" describes the mixed emotions of a young man, John Harcourt. When he sees his father in the department store, he decides to leave and go to a restaurant. He feels disappointed with the way his father lives. His girlfriend, Grace, wants to know why John wants to leave so suddenly. She doesn't seem to understand John's sudden anger. Although the father and son seem to love each other, they have some problems to resolve.

page 83

Many men, women, and children have left their homeland to come to Canada. They have had to leave their parents, friends, and families behind. When these people arrived, they suffered many crises; often they found their lives were difficult. They had to attend classes to learn the new language, and they usually had to move to overcrowded cities in order to get job opportunities. Traditionally, people have come to Canada from countries all over the world. Despite the many difficulties of adjusting, these immigrants give a vitality to the country, and the country offers many possibilities to these newcomers.

page 87

One part of learning a new language involves learning to use the language with others. Recently, a researcher in the way people learn languages wrote that if people want to learn how to talk in a second language, they should not be afraid to make mistakes. They should make contact with speakers of the new language. They should ask for corrections, and they should memorize dialogues. If students want to learn to read, they should read something every day. They should read things that are familiar. They should look for meaning from the context without always looking at the dictionary. To gain confidence, they should start by reading books at the beginner's level.

page 105

Sung Hee moved to Toronto from Korea. She attended York University and lived in a dorm with her cousin. She began to work on Saturday nights at Eaton's, a big department store, and she practiced English with her customers. On Sundays Sung Hee usually rented a little Chevrolet from Avis. Carrying a tourist book called *Inside Toronto*, she visited such famous sites as the C. N. Tower and the Royal Ontario Museum. She spent hours at the Toronto Public Library looking at the Emily Carr paintings. She met Tony at a midnight showing of *Casablanca*, and last New Year's they said "I do." Now she is teaching Tony Korean and planning to travel home to introduce him to her family.

pages 106–7

When Mikhail and Fatima volunteered to work one afternoon in the Western College Post Office, they were in for a surprise. In one corner, there were many boxes piled high. They found three heavy cartons of French language tapes addressed to Professor Maude Cousteau, now of the Canada Council. She had left the school back in February and had moved to New Brunswick. Fatima accidentally opened a box filled with the Lotus 1-2-3 programs needed for the college IBM computers. "Mr. Smith, this post office is a mess," Mikhail told the postmaster. "I know it, son. We just have to get a little more organized. The mail has to go through, and we will do it. Soon." Mikhail and Fatima left wondering if the college mail would ever get through.

page 107

Marie learns languages very easily. She was born in Haiti and has spoken French and Creole all her life. Now Marie also knows English, Spanish, and Italian. She has a special technique that always works for her. At night she goes to sleep by hypnotizing herself as she stares at a poster of the stained glass window of Notre Dame Cathedral in Paris. Her Sony Walkman tape deck is on her head, and she listens to a different tape each night.

page 113

Once upon a time there was a smart young man who decided to trick a wise old man. He caught a little bird and held it in one hand behind his back. The boy approached the wise man and said, "Sir, I have a question for you. I want to see how wise you are. I am holding a bird in my hand. Is it alive, or is it dead?" The boy thought that if the man said the bird was dead, he would open his hand to reveal the live bird, but if the man said the bird was alive, he would crush the bird, killing it. The old man stared into the boy's eyes for a long time. Then he said, "The answer, my friend, is in your hands."

page 130

Ernest Buckler's story "A Penny in the Dust" tells about a young boy who loses a prized penny. "I'd better hide," he thinks, and crawls under the covers of his bed. From there, he doesn't hear his parents' voices as they call: "Pete, where are you?" While playing with the shiny penny, Pete had been dreaming of telling his father: "I'm going to buy you a new mowing machine and a car." When he finds Pete, the boy's father is still upset. "What's the matter, Pete?" he asks. "I wouldn't have beat you." The next day Pete's father easily finds his son's penny in the dust.

pages 130–31

My sister, Hilda, lives in an apartment on the top of a high hill in West Vancouver. She works as a computer operator in a big bank there, and when she looks out her window, she sees the Granville Street Bridge. She loves heights. She even flew in a private airplane over the Rocky Mountains. Once she said to me, "I saw both the Pacific and the Atlantic Oceans in one day." She would like to travel around the world someday.

pages 146–47

March 14, 1995

3778 Hudson Street
Victoria, BC
V8S 3H8

Dear Aunt Millie,

I think you should sit down before you read this letter, and I think you should have your handkerchief handy. I am sitting here in Santo Domingo with Luis, your favourite nephew. He was happy to see me, and he wants you to know how much he misses seeing you and the rest of the family. Luis said to give you 10,000 kisses when I get home, so I know I will be busy. I am sure you want to know how everyone else is, but I have not travelled out to see the rest of the family yet. Well, Luis says they are all fine. By the way, he is married, and he has a little girl. Just like that, you are a great aunt. Even though you have never seen her, her name is Millie. Standing there with her short curly hair, she looks just like you. Millie, your new 4-year-old niece says, "Hi!" I will bring you a picture of her, some homemade candy, and a crocheted scarf. I guess I will see you soon, won't I?

Always,

Carmen

Carmen

pages 148–49

Travelling to a different country, whether it is returning home or going to a new destination, is exciting. When the airplane arrives in the airport safely, even people who travel often are glad. Suddenly, they are in a new, exciting world. Feeling tired, they get off the plane, and they head for their destination. They convert their money, wait in line for taxis, and spend too much money on foolish things. On the way home, they feel mixed emotions, but, overall, most of them are glad they took the chance and travelled.

pages 170–71
Sociologists examine how people live in groups. They examine phenomena such as people's behavioural patterns in relation to love and marriage. They want to know if people in Italy celebrate marriage in the same way as people in the Philippines. Their studies show some customs and traditions are similar from place to place. For example, people usually get married with some kind of ceremony. They usually get dressed up for their wedding. However, there are some differences. In some places, marriages are arranged. In other places, people meet and fall in love. In general, everyone hopes that the marriage will be happy and long-lasting.

page 191
Like Pablo Casals, Marc Chagall was a remarkable man who lived a long and productive life. He was born in 1887, and he died in 1985. Chagall lived for almost a century. His paintings make people feel happy. They usually show dancing figures such as flying cows and pigs, playful lovers, and bright coloured flowers. Chagall was born in Russia in the Jewish quarter of the town of Vitebsk. He had eight brothers and sisters. Chagall knew he wanted to be an artist when he was a little boy. However, he did not become famous until he was in his fifties.

page 209
Reading about the differences between men and women can help people learn a lot that will help them in their everyday lives. Many scientists are conflicted about whether these differences are caused by nature or nurture. No one knows for sure how much in-born genetic characteristics determine people's lives. Men and women may be influenced by their environment as much as by their genetics. According to research, the brain changes. It can change because of many things, such as diet, the air, handedness, etc. It makes sense that one should take good care of oneself by eating right, exercising, and trying to live a healthy life. However, despite everything people do, there will always be some differences between the sexes.

page 233
According to Oskamp, there are many factors involved in job satisfaction. People have to feel their jobs are meaningful and interesting. They have to offer the workers a mental challenge. Even though there are individual differences in what people think is important, most people agree that their jobs should offer some challenge. Pay has greater importance for individuals who cannot gain other satisfactions from their jobs. Jobs that offer external recognition, good pay, and a mental challenge are sought by most people. Each person wants a feeling of fulfillment.

page 246
The first thing, Most of all, the best thing, Finally, The basic reason

page 253

Trying to get a job at the Rockefeller Foundation is difficult for a girl who does not have pull. Finally, the morning postman brings the letter. She is to go for an interview at Peking Medical College, to the Comptroller's office. She prepares her clothes and goes to the East market to buy face powder to cover her pimples. The next morning, she goes with her father to Yu Wang Fu Palace to the Administration building. They cross the marble courtyard and go into the entrance hall. Her father leaves. She finds the office and meets her future employer, Mr. Harned. His bald head reminds her of the white pagoda on the hill in North Sea Park. She takes the required typing test and gets the job.

page 256

Looking for a job can be difficult. There are many different types of problems. For one thing, the interviewee is never sure what to bring on the first interview. I usually bring too much. This can be confusing to the interviewer. From now on, I will bring only the necessary documents such as my résumé, my birth certificate, and my high school diploma. In addition, I try to impress the interviewer by dressing very neatly and never chewing gum. I always look directly into the interviewer's eyes. I want the interviewer to believe that I can be trusted. If I remember to follow my own advice, I believe I will get a job soon.

page 258

even though, but, Still, Otherwise, however, Instead of, on the other hand. although, Yet, In contrast to

page 275

The essay "An Immigrant's Split Personality," by Sun Kyung Yi, made me think about returning to my country. I grew up thinking that there was no reason to go back, but now I am not sure. It's interesting for me to think about the world that I left behind. I feel mixed emotions such as happiness, sadness, and regret. My aunts and uncles still live in my country. They still live in the same town, in the same house. I have never seen most of my cousins; the youngest one is five months old, and I would like to know him, too. My brother visited my family last year, and he told me all the news. It's strange hearing about my best girlfriends who are getting married, and one even has a baby. The essay, my brother's visit, and my dreams make me want to return to my country for a visit.

pages 291–92

Although getting engaged has changed Samia's life, she doesn't want to marry now. Ahmed, her boyfriend, wants to get married right away, but she disagrees. For now, she likes showing her girlfriends her diamond ring. She also enjoys discussing her future wedding with them when she is in school. Even though she knows that she makes her friends jealous, she enjoys showing off. The other day her best friends made a real effort not to review their homework with her in the cafeteria as they usually do every afternoon after class. She realizes they envy her, yet she continues the same behaviour. Samia claims that she likes being engaged, but she doesn't want to get married right away. Being a housewife doesn't sound like too much fun to her.

page 316   Returning home can be very difficult, as we see in Nahid Rachlin's story "Foreigner." When people return to their home countries, they often find many changes. The streets may not look the same. People they remember may not recognize them. If they go back to their own childhood house, the house may look very different. It may appear small and cramped. One woman wrote that she returned to her neighbourhood and her house was gone. In its place was a little store. No one remembered her. She was extremely depressed. It is also possible to return to a place where everyone remembers you. That makes a person feel happy inside; at least you were not forgotten.

COPYRIGHT ACKNOWLEDGMENTS (continued from page ii)

Diagram from Robert B. Kaplan, "Cultural Thought Patterns in Inter-Cultural Education," *Language Learning* 16 (1966): 1–20. Reprinted by permission of the author and publisher.

Eugen Lupri, "The Family," in *Sociology: An Introduction*, edited by K. Ishwaran (Toronto: Addison-Wesley, 1986), pp. 256–57. Reprinted by permission of the author.

Morley Callaghan, "The Snob," reprinted in *Best Canadian Short Stories*, edited by John Stevens (Toronto: McClelland & Stewart [Bantam], 1986). Reprinted by permission of the author's estate.

Garry Engkent, "Why My Mother Can't Speak English," in *Pens of Many Colours: A Canadian Reader*, by Eva C. Korpenskit and Ian Lea (Toronto: Harcourt Brace & Company Canada, 1993). Reprinted by permission of the author and publisher.

Carolyn Parrish, "Between Two Worlds," in *Canada and the World* 52, no. 4 (December 1986). Reprinted with the permission of *Canada and the World* magazine, Waterloo, Ontario.

Hwan Lee, "Leadership in a Multi-Cultural School," in *New Canadian Voices*, edited by Jessie Porter (Toronto: Wall & Emerson, 1991), pp. 45–46. Reprinted by permission of the publisher.

Ernest Buckler, "Penny in the Dust," in *Oxbells and Fireflies* (Toronto: McClelland & Stewart, 1968). Reprinted by permission of Curtis Brown. Copyright 1968 by the author.

Emily Carr, *Growing Pains* (Toronto: Clark, Irwin and Company, 1946, first paperback edition, 1966). Reprinted by permission of Stoddart Publishing Co., Don Mills, Ont.

Barbara J. MacKay, "Who Pays the Cheque When You're Dating?" in *Chatelaine* 60, no. 9 (Toronto: Maclean Hunter 1987), p. 24. Reprinted by permission of the author.

Ian Robertson, "How Different Are the Sexes?" from *Society: A Brief Introduction* (New York: Worth Publishers, 1989). Reprinted by permission of the publisher.

Pablo Casals, "Age and Youth," in *Joys and Sorrows*. Copyright 1970 by Albert E. Kahn. Reprinted by permission of Simon and Schuster, Inc.

Facts & Figures from Canada and the World, 1987. Reprinted with permission of *Canada and the World* magazine, Waterloo, Ontario.

Randy Boswell, "Toss Out the Hard Sell, It's Time to Get Intimate with Customers," in *The Ottawa Citizen*, February 17, 1994.

John Wong, "Two Managers," in *New Canadian Voices*, edited by Jessie Porter (Toronto: Wall & Emerson, 1991). Reprinted by permission of the publisher.

Lois Chan, "Not a Princess," in *New Canadian Voices*, edited by Jessie Porter (Toronto: Wall & Emerson, 1991). Reprinted by permission of the publisher.

Stuart Oskamp, *Applied Social Psychology*, 1984, pp. 180–81. Reprinted by permission of Prentice Hall, Englewood Cliffs, New Jersey.

Alison Kennedy, "A Career Choice" in *Contest Essays by Canadian Students*, first edition, edited by Robert Hookey and Joan Pilz (Toronto: Holt Rinehart and Winston of Canada, 1991). Copyright © 1991 Holt Rinehart and Winston of Canada Limited. Reprinted by permission of Harcourt Brace & Company Canada, Inc. All rights reserved.

Li Yuin Tam, "Factory Worker," in *New Canadian Voices*, edited by Jessie Porter (Toronto: Wall & Emerson, 1991). Reprinted by permission of the publisher.

Han Suyin, "A Mortal Flower." Reprinted by permission of Han Suyin. Han Suyin, born and raised in Peking (Beijing), is a medical physician (pediatrics) and author of many novels (two of them made into movies), of which one is the well-known *A Many Splendored Thing*. *A Mortal Flower* is the second of five volumes of history, biography, and autobiography linking the history of China for the past century to the author's family and to the author's own life and experiences in and out of China.

Nora Chao, "Success Comes After Failure," in *New Canadian Voices*, edited by Jessie Porter (Toronto: Wall & Emerson, 1991). Reprinted by permission of the publisher.

Xuan Cen, "Who Am I?" in *New Canadian Voices*, edited by Jessie Porter (Toronto: Wall & Emerson, 1991), pp. 22–23. Reprinted by permission of the publisher.

Excerpt from Robert Hagedorn, *Sociology*, fourth edition. Copyright © 1990 Holt Rinehart and Winston of Canada Limited. All rights reserved. Reprinted by permission of Harcourt Brace & Company Canada, Inc.

Reprinted from *Foreigner*, by Nahid Rachlin, by permission of W.W. Norton & Company, Inc. Copyright © 1978 by Nahid Rachlin. Reprinted by permission of the publisher.

"To My Sister," by Olga Berggolts, translated by Daniel Weissbort, from *A Book of Women Poets from Antiquity to Now* by Aliki and Willis Barnstone, © 1980, Schocken Books.

From *Friend of My Youth*, by Alice Munro. Used by permission of the Canadian Publishers, McClelland & Stewart, Toronto, Ontario.

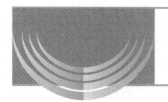

INDEX

"This book is bound
"Repkover™ " to lay
flat open".

PRINTED IN CANADA

To the owner of this book

We hope that you have enjoyed *A Canadian Writer's Workbook,* and we would like to know as much about your experiences with this text as you would care to offer. Only through your comments and those of others can we learn how to make this a better text for future readers.

School _____ Your instructor's name _____

Course _____ Was the text required? _____ Recommended? _____

1. What did you like the most about *A Canadian Writer's Workbook?*

_____

_____

_____

2. How useful was this text for your course?

_____

_____

_____

3. Do you have any recommendations for ways to improve the next edition of this text?

_____

_____

_____

4. In the space below or in a separate letter, please write any other comments you have about the book. (For example, please feel free to comment on reading level, writing style, terminology, design features, and learning aids.)

_____

_____

_____

_____

Optional

Your name _____ Date _____

May Nelson Canada quote you, either in promotion for *A Canadian Writer's Workbook* or in future publishing ventures?

Yes _____ No _____

Thanks!